TH
MUGHAL EMPIRE

THE FORMATION OF THE MUGHAL EMPIRE

Douglas E. Streusand

OXFORD
UNIVERSITY PRESS

OXFORD
UNIVERSITY PRESS

YMCA Library Building, Jai Singh Road, New Delhi 110001

Oxford University Press is a department of the University of Oxford. It furthers the University's objective of excellence in research, scholarship, and education by publishing worldwide in

Oxford New York
Athens Auckland Bangkok Bogota Buenos Aires Cape Town
Chennai Dar es Salaam Delhi Florence Hong Kong Istanbul
Karachi Kolkata Kuala Lumpur Madrid Melbourne Mexico City Mumbai
Nairobi Paris Sao Paolo Shanghai Singapore Taipei Tokyo Toronto Warsaw

with associated companies in

Berlin Ibadan

Oxford is a registered trade mark of Oxford University Press
in the UK and in certain other countries

Published in India
By Oxford University Press, New Delhi

First published 1989
Oxford India Paperbacks 1999
Second impression 2001

ISBN 0 19 564788 2

Printed in India at Sai Printo Pack Pvt. Ltd., New Delhi 110020
and published by Manzar Khan, Oxford University Press
YMCA Library Building, Jai Singh Road, New Delhi 110001

To
Esther, Deborah and Rachel

Contents

Acknowledgements

This book, and the Ph.D. dissertation from which it is derived, would never have been completed without the support of my parents and my wife. My parents have offered constant emotional support, have financed the computer system which has made writing the dissertation possible, and proofread the entire dissertation in two different forms. My wife has supported me for nine difficult years, and, as a result, accepted a way of life she would not otherwise have chosen. I lack words to express my gratitude and love. She also devoted herself to proofreading in spite of the demands of her own profession and children. Our daughters, though they have inevitably viewed my dissertation as a competitor, have, because of their joyful and tractable personalities, made my progress far easier than it might have been.

The body of the work contains my acknowledgements to scholarly works and sources of information. I wish to add my personal thanks to the members of my dissertation committee, John E. Woods, Bernard S. Cohn, and Halil Inalcik, to William H. McNeill, Ronald Inden, Susanne H. Rudolph and Lloyd Rudolph, who might have been on the committee, and, in alphabetical order, Richard Chambers, Robert Dankoff, Walter Kaegi, Heshmat Moayyad, C. M. Naim, and John R. Perry, of the University of Chicago, R. Stephen Humphreys of the University of Wisconsin, Bruce Lawrence and J. F. Richards of Duke University, Richard Eaton, Leslie Flemming, Jerrold Green, and Michael Mahar of the University of Arizona, William Royce formerly of the University of Arizona, Joel Gereboff and Richard C. Martin of Arizona State University, and Peter Hardy of the School of Oriental and African Studies, University of London. William C. Green of Boston University checked the transliterations from Russian.

I am grateful to the American Institute of Indian Studies for a Junior Fellowship in 1982–83. In India, Pratip Mehendiratha and L. S. Suri of the Institute, K. A. Nizami, Iqtidar Husain Siddiqui, Tariq Ahmed and family, Liaqat Moini, and Iqbal Ghani Khan of Aligarh Muslim University, A. Q. Rafiqi of Kashmir University, Ahsan Raza Khan of Himachal Pradesh University, and Rochelle Kessler, Joseph Arlinghaus, Terry Dunn, Mohd. ʻAbd al-Salam and Mohd. ʻAbd al-Kalam provided friendship, moral support and assistance.

I made revisions for publication while a Public Affairs Fellow at the Hoover Institution on War, Revolution and Peace. I am grateful to W. Glenn Campbell, Director of the Hoover Institution and Thomas H. Henriksen, Associate Director responsible for the Public Affairs fellowship programme, for the opportunity to work in the unique setting of the Institution.

Of the many friends who have provided moral support and other kindnesses along the way, I must mention Keith and Deborah Weissman, Linda T. Darling, Kathleen Hatch, Russ Kempiners, Chuck and Peggy Faroe, Boyd Johnson, and Philip Remler in Chicago, Chris and Carol Dubrowski, and Jay Skardon in Arizona, and Jocelyn Morron, Michael and Claudia Lewis, William C. Green, Igor Lukes, and John Zucker elsewhere. My mother-in-law, now Polly Redifer, allowed me to use her home when I could not work at mine. Carol Dubrowski actually made the completion of the dissertation possible by joyfully providing child care without charge.

Keith Weissman, Richard Eaton, and John Zucker helped me cope with the last moment difficulties of dissertating at a distance.

CHAPTER 1
Introduction

When Jalāl al-Dīn Muḥammad Akbar took the throne at Kalanaur on 14 February, 1556 (2 Rabīʿ II 963) he had only a tenuous hold on the Punjab and the Delhi-Agra area. Twenty-six years later he dominated northern India. He not only subjugated the Indo-Gangetic plain, Malwa, Rajasthan, Gujarat and Bengal but also established a new type of regime. This work analyses the nature and development of the Mughal polity.

I began research in Mughal history with the intention of studying elite immigration from Safavī Iran to Mughal India. My research revealed a series of problems in existing Mughal historiography. Considerations external to the subject determined overall interpretations of Mughal history. Historians studied political events, the development of governmental institutions, and military history in separate compartments. Analyses of the patterns of political behaviour did not fit the descriptions of events in the sources. Perhaps most importantly, new contributions to the interpretation of Mughal history remained outside the standard views of the subject. I have attempted to remedy these shortcomings by presenting a coherent account of the development of the political patterns and institutions which we call Mughal. These patterns and institutions developed during the first half of Akbar's reign; Bābur and Humāyūn brought the Tīmūrid dynasty to India but did not develop distinctively Mughal institutions, practices, and political and cultural styles. I have concentrated on the period from 1556 (963) to 1582 (990) for this reason, using later examples to illuminate specific points. The Mughal government and polity did not ossify in 1582 (990), but the fundamental arrangement remained unchanged for almost a century, well into Awrangzīb's reign. The key to understanding the Mughal polity thus lies in the first half of Akbar's reign.

1.1 Themes and Historiography

Modern writers have approached the Mughals from two perspectives. They have sought either to find historical support for contemporary opinions or historical explanations of and solutions for immediate dilemmas, or to place the Mughal empire in a general classification in world history or political sociology.

1.1.1 PRESENT-MINDED INTERPRETATION: THE NATIONAL KINGSHIP HYPOTHESIS

Though he did not write on Akbar's reign specifically, Sir Jadunath Sarkar typifies the present-minded approach.[1] His *History of Aurangzib* includes a chapter entitled 'Aurangzib and Indian Nationality,' with the last section called 'The Significance of Aurangzib's Reign: how an Indian nationality can be formed.'[2] Sarkar represents one of three present-minded approaches to Mughal history, the Hindu communalist approach. For him and most Hindu historians, and for most British historians, Akbar's principle of political toleration was the foundation of the empire and Awrangzib's abandonment of toleration brought the empire down. A. L. Srivastava's biography of Akbar represents this perspective in the study of Akbar's reign.[3] Muslim historians who

[1] The term present-minded is derived from J. H. Hexter, 'The Historian and His Day', in *Reappraisals in History* (New York: Harper & Row, 1961), pp. 1–13. Hexter attributes the expression to R. L. Schuyler.

[2] Sir Jadunath Sarkar, *History of Aurangzib*. 2nd ed., 5 vols. as 4 (Calcutta: n.p., 1952: reprint ed., Bombay: Orient Longman, 1974), 5:362–78. For an appreciation of Sarkar, see J. F. Richards, *Mughal Administration in Golconda* (Oxford: Clarendon Press, 1975), p. vii.

[3] A. L. Srívastava, *Akbar the Great*, 2nd ed., 3 vols. (Agra: Shiva Lal Agarwala, 1972). Other works in this tradition are idem., *The Mughul Empire*, 8th ed. (Agra: Shiva Lal Agarwala, 1977; S. R. Sharma, *The Religious Policy of the Mughal Emperors*, 3rd ed. (New York: Asia, 1972); S. Roy, 'Akbar', in R. C. Majumdar, gen. ed., *The History and Culture of the Indian People*, 11 vols. (Bombay: Bharatiya Vidya Bhavan, 1951–74), 7: 104–74. For a similar perspective in general works on Indian history, see

value Islam over Indian unity turn this interpretation on its head, condemning Akbar's policy on religious grounds, whatever its political effects. The most astute among them, I. H. Qureshi, considers Akbar's political success temporary and superficial.[4]

Other historians who support a secular Indian state emphasize economic factors in Mughal history, minimizing the importance of sectarian considerations. Not surprisingly, most are Muslims with Marxist affiliations who live in the Indian Union. This group includes the best known contemporary Mughal historians, Satish Chandra, Irfan Habib, and M. Athar Ali.[5] They write primarily on Mughal decline. The one writer in this classification who has concentrated on Akbar's reign, Iqtidar Alam Khan, actually follows the Hindu communalist perspective, seeing Akbar's escape from 'the fetters of a pro-Islamic policy' as the vital ingredient of his success.[6] S. A. A. Rizvi, a Shīʿī Muslim of secular orientation, shares the positive Hindu view of Akbar because he identifies 'orthodox', meaning Sunnī and Sharʿī, Islam as narrow, communalist and negative.[7] Iqtidar Alam, as he is known, and Rizvi have made the most important contributions to the study of Akbar's reign, perhaps because of their unusual positions in the present-minded constellation. They go beyond describing events

K. M. Pannikar, *A Survey of Indian History*, 4th. ed. (New York: Asia, 1964), pp. 156–9; Stanley Wolpert, *A New History of India* (New York: Oxford University Press, 1977), pp. 126–34.

[4] Ishtiaq Husain Qureshi, *The Muslim Community of the Indo-Pakistan Subcontinent*, 2nd ed. (Karachi: Ma'ref, 1971), pp. 181–9. More typical Muslim works are S. M. Ikram, *Muslim Civilization in India*, ed. Ainslie T. Embree (New York: Columbia University Press, 1964); Aziz Ahmad, *Studies in Islamic Culture in the Indian Environment* (Oxford: Clarendon Press, 1964), esp. pp. 73–101, 167–218.

[5] Satish Chandra, *Parties and Politics at the Mughal Court, 1707–1740*, 3rd. ed. (New Delhi: People's Publishing House, 1979); Irfan Habib, *The Agrarian System of Mughal India* (Bombay: Asia, 1963); M. Athar Ali, *Mughal Nobility under Aurangzeb* (Bombay: Asia, 1968).

[6] Iqtidar Alam Khan, 'The Nobility under Akbar and the Development of His Religious Policy', *Journal of the Royal Asiatic Society* (1968), p. 35.

[7] Saiyid Athar Abbas Rizvi, *Religious and Intellectual History of the Muslims in Akbar's Reign* (New Delhi: Munshiram Manoharlal, 1975),pp. 339–73. For his views of the varieties of Islam, see idem., *Muslim Revivalist Movements in Northern India* (Agra: Agra University, 1965), pp. 202–331, 418–27, and *A History of Sufism in India*, 2 vols. (New Delhi: Munshiram Manoharlal, 1978–83), 2:197, 463–9.

in accord with their beliefs to discuss concrete political developments. All of the writers cited above have added significantly to our knowledge and understanding of the Mughals. The members of the three groups differ considerably among themselves.[8] In all cases, however, their present-mindedness forces them to express their conclusions in accord with their politico-sectarian perspective and to ignore some aspects of the political developments of Akbar's time.[9]

A second form of present-mindedness involves the classification of the Mughals as imperialists, predecessors of the British who deserve moral condemnation. Opponents of the Mughals thus become the predecessors of the resistance to British rule. A. K. Majumdar writes of Rānā Pratap:

> The *Maharana* loses battles, but never gives up the principle for which he stands—independence, and he regains for posterity the soul of India. The great Shivaji will be proud to claim him as his ancestor, and the revolutionary pursuit movement in Bengal in the twentieth century will draw inspiration from his untiring fight against foreign domination.[10]

This view is indefensible. The British did inherit the Mughal idea of an empire uniting the subcontinent, but the Mughal polity resembled those of earlier principalities in the subcontinent more than it did the British. Though Shivajī and Mohandas Karamchand Gandhi both

[8] For an example of their disagreements, S. R. Sharma whom I classify as a Hindu communalist, has been labelled an apologist for Awrangzīb. See Sharma, *Religious*, p. vii.

[9] Marshall G. S. Hodgson, *The Venture of Islam*, 3 vols. (Chicago: University of Chicago Press, 1974), 3:61, inspired this approach to Mughal historiography. J. S. Grewal, *Muslim Rule in India* (London: Oxford University Press, 1970) and idem., *Medieval India: History and Historians* (Amritsar: Guru Nanak University, 1975) trace the development of British views of Mughal history. See also Bernard S. Cohn, 'African Models and Indian Histories', in *Realm and Region*, ed. Richard G. Fox (Durham, N. C.: Duke University Comparative Studies on Southern Asia Monograph and Occasional Paper Series, no. 14, 1977), pp. 90–113.

[10] A. K. Majumdar, 'Hindu Resistance to Muslim Domination: 1. Mewar', in *History and Culture*, ed. Majumdar, 7:327. Other chapters of this work are entitled 'Muslim Resistance to Mughal Imperialism.' For other examples of this attitude, see Visheshwar Sarup Bhargava, *Marwar and the Mughal Emperors* (New Delhi: Munshiram Manoharlal, 1966); Gopi Nath Sharma, *Mewar and the Mughal Emperors*, with a foreword by A. L. Srivastava (Agra: Shiva Lal Agarwala, 1954).

used the term *swaraj*, they meant entirely different things by it. Modern nationalists drew inspiration from Rānā Pratap and Shivajī, but did not do so on the basis of valid historical analysis.

Although they are only partially aware of it, the present-minded historians propound a causal thesis to explain the development of the Mughal empire, a national kingship hypothesis. It holds that Akbar established a stable, lasting polity, by including Rajputs and other Hindus, Indian Muslims, and Afghans, as well as Muslims of Iranian and central Asian descent in his governing elite. He made both Muslims and Hindus full participants in the Mughal empire and thus created a 'national', as opposed to sectarian, kingdom. To describe the Mughal empire as national is anachronistic; there was no mass involvement or attachment to a geographic or ethnic rather than a dynastic ideal. As Michael Pearson and Peter Hardy have stated, the Mughal empire consisted of the mansabdars; their loyalty to the emperor made the empire real.[11] The concrete form of hypothesis must thus state that Akbar won the loyalty of the great majority of the political elite of north India, Muslim and Hindu, for himself and his dynasty, and thus erected his empire upon an enduring foundation. The single most insightful essay on Mughal politics, Satish Chandra's introduction to his *Parties and Politics at the Mughal Court*, states the hypothesis in these terms.[12]

Verification of this hypothesis requires a close analysis of the development of Akbar's relationship with the existing political elites in Hindustan. The historians who support this hypothesis emphasize in particular the importance of Akbar's religious attitudes in the foundation of his polity. A. L. Srivastava puts this argument clearly:

> [Akbar's] next logical step was to establish his claim to be an impartial ruler of all his people, Muslims as well as non-Muslims. This implied establishment of a common citizenship on the basis of complete toleration to non-Muslims and their association on equal terms with Muslims. Such a policy was sure to bring him into clash [*sic*]

[11] Peter Hardy, *The Muslims of British India* (Cambridge: Cambridge University Press, 1972), pp. 12–15; M. N. Pearson, 'Shivaji and the Decline of the Mughal Empire', *Journal of Asian Studies* 35 (1976): 223–4.

[12] Chandra, *Politics*, pp. xvii–lv, esp. p. xxxi.

> with orthodox *Sunni Ulema* and the Muslim nobility who had enjoyed a privileged position in the State. The two classes combined and raised the standard of rebellion. But Akbar with the support of the Rajputs and Persians and the tacit acquiescence of the bulk of the *Sunni* population emerged triumphant from the contest. The episode convinced him that the right course for him was to disregard the narrow basis of Islamic [*sic*] theory of kingship and to build up a new one based on the essential equality and welfare of diverse creeds and communities in the empire.[13]

Eliminating Srivastava's anachronistic rhetoric—neither citizenship nor the feelings of the overall Muslim population influenced the development of the empire—he argues that Akbar established himself as the impartial ruler of both Muslims and Hindus, thus provoking 'orthodox' Sunnī Muslims to revolt against him. He defeated the rebels with the assistance of the Iranians—Shī'ī Muslims—and Rajputs, and established a new form of kingship emphasizing the equality of all faiths. Historians of Muslim orientation add that Akbar's initiatives involved the suppression of 'orthodox' Islam.[14]

This hypothesis makes the change in the nature of the Mughal ruling class the focus of political change. Iqtidar Alam Khan gives the most concrete description of that transformation. He argues that between 1560 (968) and 1575 (984), the inclusion of Rajputs and Indo-Muslims in the Mughal system and an increase in the number of Persians in high posts caused 'the gradual fading away of the Turani complexion of the nobility as well as the erosion of the Chaghtai traditions and customs of state organization.'[15] He perceives a movement from a Mongol 'tribal' political theory to a Turkish absolutism. His view fits the national kingship hypothesis because he contends that the Chaghatays opposed Akbar at least partially on religious grounds.[16] He comes close to the heart of the matter, but his contention rests on a series of misunderstandings. The lack of a sophisticated view of ethnicity, as opposed to

[13] Srivastava, *Mughal*, p. 178.

[14] Qureshi, *Akbar*, pp. 134–171.

[15] Iqtidar Alam Khan, *The Political Biography of a Mughal Noble, Mu'nim Khan Khan-i Khanan, 1497–1575* (New Delhi: Orient Longman, 1973), p. xvi.

[16] Ibid., pp. xi–xiii; idem., 'Nobility.'

race with a biological basis, permits the idea of genetically embedded theories of sovereignty to take root. Specifically, Iqtidar Alam assumes that the Turkish words *turah* and *yasa* always refer to fundamental law or code, which reflects the political theory of the legislator, i.e. Chingiz Khān. The dictionaries of Doerfer and Clauson, to which he probably has no access, make clear that both terms may refer to either a written fundamental law or to customary law or usage.[17] References to the *turah* and *yāsā* of Chingiz Khān do indicate continuing Mongol influence, but the Chaghatay *turah* or *yasa* probably referred to the usages of the Chaghatay (read Tīmūrid) polity, in which tribal leaders had considerable power.[18] Iqtidar Alam uses Niẓām al-Mulk Tūsī as a representative of Turkish absolutism. Although he was a servant of Turkish masters, the great Saljūq *wazīr* propounded an Iranian theory of kingship and government, to which he sought to make his masters conform. His ideas are in no way Turkish.[19]

In spite of this confusion, Iqtidar Alam makes an important argument. He describes the losers in the political transformation of Akbar's reign not as 'orthodox' Muslims, but as Chaghatays. This term originally referred to the leaders of nomadic groups who had a central position

[17] Gerhard Doerfer, *Turkische und Mongolische Elemente im Neupersichen*, 4 vols., Akaḍemie der Wissenschaften und der Literatur Veroffentlichungen der Orientalischen Kommision, vols. 16, 19–21 (Wiesbaden: Franz Steiner Verlag, 1963–75), 1:264–7, 4:71–82; Sir Gerard Clauson, *An Etymological Dictionary of Pre-Thirteenth Century Turkish* (Oxford: Clarendon Press, 1972), pp. 531–2. Clauson states that *turah*, as *toru*, is originally Turkish, but may have come into modern Turkish dialects through Mongol; Doerfer includes it in his volume of Mongol words. The two lexicographers disagree on the origin of *yasa*; Doerfer classifies it as Turkish but Clauson does not include it and describes the apparently related verb *yāsā* . . . (p. 974) as a Mongol loan word. Neither of them gives battle formation for *turah*, which Doerfer gives for *yāsā* as well as *yasal*, but I suspect it may have had that meaning.

[18] On the later Tīmūrid polity, see H. R. Roemer, 'The Successors of Timur', *Cambridge History of Iran, Volume 6: The Timurid and Safavid Periods*, ed. Peter Jackson and Lawrence Lockhart (Cambridge: Cambridge University Press, 1986), pp. 98–146.

[19] Abū'Ali Hasan Ṭūsī Niẓām al-Mulk, *Siyāsat-nāmah* or *Siyar al-Muluk*, ed. H. Darke (Tehran: B.T.N.K., 1962), trans H. Darke (London: Routledge & Kegan Paul, 1978). Iqtidar Alam does not mention the Ottomans in this context, but the flawed popular image of the Ottomans and the pernicious habit of referring to the Ottoman empire as Turkey may have affected his view of Turkish absolutism.

and considerable autonomy in the Tīmūrid polity in central Asia.[20] Chaghatay officers continued to dominate the transplanted Tīmūrid polity under Humāyūn and Akbar until its nature changed. Even though Iqtidar Alam's conception of the nature of the change is unacceptable, his emphasis on the clash between the political expectations of the Chaghatays and Akbar's imperial programme is extremely astute.

J. F. Richards takes the national kingship hypothesis outside of the present-minded context and equips it with the vocabulary of modern social science. He writes:

> Akbar's political achievement was far more difficult than the simple balancing of ethnic and factional interests with the elite. He and his advisors successfully shaped a new individual and group identity: that of the imperial *mansabdar* or *amir*, i.e. a military commander and imperial administrator.[21]

Elsewhere, he states that Akbar 'could succeed only by transforming the values of high-status warrior-aristocrats of diverse origins.' These warriors and war-leaders had to derive their status and motivation from their participation in empire, rather than their descent, sectarian affiliation, or personal accomplishments, to become '"slave" warrior administrators' rather than '"free" warrior chiefs.'[22] Richards thus directs attention to changes in the political identities, beliefs and expectations of the men who became Mughal mansabdars. His views provide the point of departure for this investigation.

1.1.2 GENERAL INTERPRETATIONS: BUREAUCRACY AND THE GUNPOWDER EMPIRE HYPOTHESIS

Sociologists and world historians classify the Mughal empire as an example of Oriental despotism or bureaucratic empire. Karl A. Wittfogel presents despotism as a forerunner of modern totalitarianism. Without delving at length into his conception of hydraulic society, its political correlates, and the controversy concerning it, he describes these societies

[20] On the meaning of the word Chaghatay, see Roemer, 'Successors', p. 130.

[21] J. F. Richards, 'The Formation of Imperial Authority under Akbar and Jahangir', in *Kingship and Authority in South Asia*, ed. idem., South Asian Studies University of Wisconsin-Madison (Madison: University of Wisconsin Press, 1978), p. 253.

[22] Ibid., p. 254.

as 'dominated by a bureaucratically despotic state.'[23] S. N. Eisenstadt employs centralized bureaucracy as the defining characteristic of a general category of societies, which he calls 'centralized historical bureaucratic empires,' and places between patrimonial societies, feudal societies, and city-states on one side and modern societies on the other in the scale of political development. He would classify Akbar with the founders of centralized polities, who seek 'to establish a more centralized, unified polity [so as to] monopolize political decisions and [set] political goals.' Eisenstadt sees members of existing political elites whose interests tie them to the *status quo* as the main opponents of these centralizing rulers.[24]

Wittfogel and Eisenstadt both stress the presence of a powerful, centralized bureaucracy as the vital characteristic of historical empires. Stephen Blake argues convincingly that an anachronistic assumption that the Mughal empire embodied in less developed form the characteristics of the British Raj has caused a great exaggeration of the power of the Mughal bureaucracy. This error affects the core of interpretive works on Mughal history, many of which date back a number of decades, as well as general studies. Sir Jadunath Sarkar states the assumed connection between the Mughal government and the Raj clearly:

> the real working of . . . [Mughal administration] . . . can be best understood only by men who combine a knowledge of Persian historical manuscripts with experience in the administration of the . . . provinces once subject to Mughal rule,—i.e. by scholarly members of the Indian Civil Service in Upper India.[25]

Blake derives a conception of patrimonial-bureaucratic empires from Max Weber and contends that the Mughal regime fits this category better than that of bureaucratic despotism.[26]

[23] Karl August Wittfogel, *Oriental Despotism* (New Haven: Yale University Press, 1957; reprint ed. with new foreword, New York: Random House Vintage, 1981), pp. 5–6.

[24] S. N. Eisenstadt, *The Political System of Empires*, with a new foreword by the author (New York: Free Press, 1969), pp. 10–12.

[25] Sir Jadunath Sarkar, *Mughal Administration*, 3rd. ed. (1935; reprint ed., Bombay: Orient Longman, 1972), p. 1.

[26] Stephen P. Blake, 'The Patrimonial-Bureaucratic empire of the Mughals', *Journal of Asian Studies* 39 (1979), pp. 77–94.

Weber's model of the patrimonial state describes the regime as an extension of the household of the ruler, whose authority is an expansion of that of the father in a patriarchal family. The army of the patrimonial state consists of the ruler's household troops; its administration is that of his establishment. When such a polity grew too large for the institutions of the household to produce an adequate army and administration, extrapatrimonial officials and soldiers—the soldiers of the ruler's major subordinates—developed. The new officials were not bureaucrats in the modern sense because they served at the ruler's favour and did not obtain their positions solely on the basis of technical qualifications. The dilution of the personal ties to the ruler which made the polity coherent forced the patrimonial-bureaucratic leaders to develop new strategies to develop and maintain the loyalty of their subordinates.[27]

Blake shows the similarity between the Mughal empire and this model through a close and acute analysis of the *Āyīn-i Akbarī*. He demonstrates conclusively that of the ideal types suggested for the Mughal empire the patrimonial-bureaucratic empire is the most applicable, and that historians should give special attention to the ruler's household and what he calls the control mechanisms, the means of keeping the officers loyal. He does not deal with the perceptions of the officers in question or the symbolic aspect of the relationship.[28]

World historians Marshall G. S. Hodgson and William H. McNeill, accepting the idea of bureaucratic dominance, assert that the diffusion of firearms, especially siege artillery, explains the increase in central power which brought the Mughal empire into being. One may describe their view as the gunpowder empires hypothesis. The historical literature on the Mughal army unfortunately fails to deal with this issue. It describes Mughal armies without describing the political significance of Mughal warfare.[29] For this reason, the evaluation of this hypothesis must begin with the views of general historians.

[27] Ibid., pp. 78–80.

[28] Ibid., pp. 80–92.

[29] The standard works are Paul Horn, *Das Heer-und Kriegswesen der Grossmoghuls* (Leiden: E. J. Brill, 1894); William Irvine, *The Army of the Indian Moughuls* (London: n.p.: 1903; reprint ed., New Delhi: Eurasia, 1962); Abdul Aziz, *The Mansabdari System and the Mughul Army* (London: n.p., 1945; reprint ed., New Delhi: Idarah-i Adabiyat-i Delli, 1972); Raj Kumar Phul, *Armies of the Great Mughals* (New Delhi: Oriental Publishers and Distributors, 1978). R. C. Smail, *Crusading*

The renowned Russian orientalist V. V. Bartol'd first asserted that the Mughal, Ottoman, and Safavī empires exceeded their predecessors' in size, centralization, and duration because of the development and diffusion of firearms.[30] Hodgson makes this hypothesis the basis of his treatment of these three empires; he calls the sixth book of his *The Venture of Islam* 'Gunpowder Empires.' McNeill uses the term in his world military history, *The Pursuit of Power*. Hodgson states that the innovations which produced the gunpowder empires began about 1450 (854), when the western Europeans and the Ottomans developed artillery as a decisive weapon, first in sieges and then on the battlefield. Infantry armed with handguns became a vital force in Europe, but in the Islamic world, siege and field artillery caused major political changes. 'The . . . expensiveness of artillery and the . . . untenability of stone fortresses gave an increased advantage over local military garrisons to a well-organized central power which could afford artillery—not always a decisive advantage to be sure,' he writes. Finally, he argues, the use of firearms began a cycle of continuous military innovation which strengthened rulers with the resources needed to support it.[31]

McNeill sees the major Asian empires of the sixteenth century as the products of a halt at a specific point in the cycle of innovation. Firearms, especially siege artillery, gave the central governments which could afford them significant advantages. As a result, they came to rule larger and more centralized empires. Mobility of artillery became the limiting factor on the growth of these empires. McNeill contends that the Mughal 'imperial consolidation remained precarious' because the Mughals could rely less on water transportation than the Ottomans or Muscovites. But after the central governments gained the

---

Warfare (Cambridge: Cambridge University Press, 1956), shows what a study of military organization can accomplish.

[30] Vasilii Vladimirovitch Bartol'd, *Sochineniia* (Collected Works), ed. A. M. Belenitskii, vol. 6: *Raboti po istorii islama i arabskovo khalifata* (Moscow: Izdatel 'stvo nauka glavnaya redak siya, 1966), pp. 199–204; trans. Shahib Suhrawardy as *Mussulman Culture* (Calcutta: University of Calcutta, 1934; reprint ed., Philadelphia: Porcupine, 1977), pp. 99–102. I have not actually consulted Bartol'd's works in Russian but refer to the Russian edition because it is definitive and contains additional useful remarks by the editor.

[31] Marshall G. S. Hodgson, *The Venture of Islam*, 3 vols. (Chicago: University of Chicago Press, 1974), 3:17–18.

advantage of siege artillery, they did not support further development of either artillery or fortification. Any technical change would have threatened their position.[32]

The invasion of Italy in 1494/900 by Charles VIII of France furnishes the paradigm for the effect of the new guns. They nullified existing fortifications. A small fort surrendered as soon as the French emplaced guns against it; a larger citadel which had recently survived a seven year siege fell after eight hours of bombardment. Christopher Duffy compares the tactical surprise to the appearance of blitzkrieg in the Second World War. The French used gunpowder mines when topography prevented them from emplacing guns against specific forts. But the offensive advantage did not last. Within twenty years of the invasion the defenders of forts had used improvised ramparts inside existing walls and countermines to stop the new techniques of siegecraft. Forts with shorter, thicker walls and ground plans suitable for the defensive use of guns became too strong to attack.[33] In western Europe, then, the appearance of effective siege artillery temporarily made stone fortifications useless against organized attack, but a technical riposte reversed the situation within a few decades. McNeill contends that the new guns produced the same advantage for the offense in Asia, but did not provoke the same response.

Not all historians agree with Hodgson and McNeill. Duffy, the most prolific current writer on siege warfare, concedes that there was no technical improvement in fortification in Mughal times, so that Indian forts resembled medieval European castles. But he contends that artillery did not form the most important element of Mughal siegecraft. Like the Europeans in the sixteenth century, the Mughals began their siege with thorough investment of the fort, erected lines of circumvallation, and approached the fort with trenches and mines. 'Where the Mughals... fell short,' he writes, 'was in their inability to finish off the siege by making a breach.' Artillery 'did singularly little to abridge the sieges.' Duffy considers both indigenous guns and gunners and those imported

[32] William H. McNeill, *The Pursuit of Power* (Chicago: University of Chicago Press, 1982), pp. 95–8.

[33] Christopher Duffy, *Siege Warfare* (London: Routledge, Kegan Paul, 1979) pp. 9–13; McNeill, *Pursuit*, pp.87–90, explains the improvements in the manufacture of guns and their results.

from Europe inferior to men and munitions in Europe.[34] Irfan Habib doubts that firearms explain Mughal success because:

> Artillery was not the decisive arm of their army and they were never able to employ it successfully against really strong forts. Their real strength lay in cavalry and it was in battle in the open field, in rapid movements, that they remained invincible until . . . the Marathas found a decisive answer in scattered and decentralized warfare.[35]

The gunpowder empires hypothesis thus contends that, in addition to permitting the Mughals to conquer their empire, firearms fundamentally altered the relationship between imperial centre and provincial periphery. The new arrangement prevented continuing innovation in military technology comparable to what occurred in the West because it favoured the central government which alone had the resources to innovate. If the hypothesis is correct, then the first years of Akbar's reign should show a nullification of existing forts forcing potentates in the provinces to surrender much of their power and autonomy. It directs attention to the relationship between the imperial centre and provincial governors, whether the governors owed their positions entirely to the emperor or had local roots. It also suggests that an understanding of the role of fortresses must be a part of any general explanation of Mughal politics. The criticisms of Habib and Duffy suggest that Mughal artillery did not make existing forts untenable and that Mughal superiority on the battlefield outweighed their capability in siege warfare. The pattern of military activity then, should reveal whether Hodgson and McNeill or their critics are correct.

1.1.3 THEMES AND STRUCTURE

Wittfogel and Eisenstadt discuss the Mughal empire in the context of their general social theories. Though they pay far more attention to its individual characteristics than the sociologists, Hodgson and McNeill

[34] Duffy, *Siege*, pp. 227–30. Duffy suffers from ethnocentrism—when writing on European matters he routinely calls Protestants heretics—and uses only old secondary works on the Mughals: (Irvine, *Army* and Sir Richard Burn, ed., *Cambridge History of India Volume 4: the Mughul Period* (Cambridge: Cambridge University Press, 1937.), but his expertise and judgement command respect.

[35] Irfan Habib, *Agrarian System of Mughal India* (New York: Asia, 1963), p. 317.

also deal with the Mughal empire primarily as part of the category of gunpowder empires. Blake, a Mughal specialist, likewise defines his task as finding the appropriate ideal type, though he seeks to use the classification to improve our understanding of the Mughals. The Indian historians view the Mughal empire alone, but deal with it from contemporary perspectives. I seek to improve upon the present-minded and general perspectives. I am writing history, not political sociology; my purpose is to understand the Mughal empire as a unique entity, not to classify it. But historians must categorize polities in order to teach about them and compare them. The conclusion presents a new categorization, or rather capsule description, of the Mughal empire, to facilitate comprehension of its significance in Indian history and in world history. That description rests on an effort to understand the Mughal empire on its own terms, rather than in accord with an external perspective.

The first half of Akbar's reign saw the development of a new set of administrative institutions and practices, a new conception of kingship and the constitution of government and society, a new military system, and new norms of political behaviour.

To facilitate comprehension of the political change which constituted the formation of the Mughal empire, one may isolate four elements of the transformation. The separation of these components is heuristic, not comparable to any distinctions of which the actors were aware. They are: the increasing centralization of power, the growing acceptance of Akbar's position as imperial sovereign and of the Mughal constitution, the change in the sovereign cult of the empire, and the development of the mansabdari system and the class of mansabdars.

In using the word constitution, I refer to Ronald Inden's concept of cultural/symbolic constitution rather than to a written fundamental law or set of unwritten assumptions comparable to one. Inden conceives of constitutions as including a broad set of beliefs and assumptions about the nature of sovereignty, the structure and function of government, normative social structure, cosmology and the relationship of government and society to it, rituals, and notions of proper and improper behaviour. Inden's conception resembles Eric Voegelin's description of 'cosmological empires', in which the political and social order represent the order of the universe.[36] The reconstruction of the Mughal constitution depends on information on Mughal court rituals, texts describing Mughal government, especially the *Āyīn-ī Akbarī* of Abū al-Fażl, the descriptions of events in chronicles and the interpretation of Mughal architecture.[37]

The concept of sovereign cult facilitates reframing questions about Akbar's religious policy and its meaning. Most pre-modern monarchs upheld a specific religious doctrine and institution as a justification for their status, in addition to claiming a divine mandate to rule. The Byzantine emperor was the champion of Orthodox Christianity; the Maurya and Gupta emperors supported Buddhism. The Mughals' contemporaries in the Islamic world, the Ottomans and Safavīs, supported Sunnī and Shī'ī Islam. The established doctrine and institution which received the official support of the monarch and provided justification for his position was the sovereign cult. With this concept in mind, the question about Akbar's policy becomes: what was Akbar's sovereign cult and how did his choice affect the development of his empire?[38]

Because of the need to re-establish the historiography of Akbar's

[36] Eric Voegelin, *The New Science of Politics* (Chicago: University of Chicago Press, 1952; reprint ed., 1987), pp. 52–9.

[37] Unfortunately, Inden's published works do not fully explain his views. His 'Ritual, Authority and Cyclic Time in Hindu Kingship', in J. F. Richards, ed., *Kingship and Authority in South Asia*, South Asian Studies, University of Wisconsin-Madison 3 (Madison: University of Wisconsin Press, 1978), pp. 28–73, and an unpublished paper, 'Cultural-Symbolic Constitutions in Ancient India', 1978, plus two years of work with him, have communicated his ideas to me. Broader literature relevant to this point includes Michael Polanyi, *The Tacit Dimension* (Garden City, New York: Doubleday, 1966); Sir Lewis Namier, *England in the Age of the American Revolution*, 2nd. ed. (London: Macmillan, 1961), J. G. A. Pocock, *Politics, Language and Time* (New York: Atheneum, 1973); Marshall Sahlins, *Culture and Practical Reason* (Chicago: University of Chicago Press, 1976); idem., *The Use and Abuse of Biology* (Ann Arbor: University of Michigan Press, 1976); Karl R. Popper, *The Poverty of Historicism* (Boston: Beacon, 1957). Bernard S. Cohn, 'Representing Authority in Victorian India', in *The Invention of Tradition*, ed. E. J. Hobsbawm and Terence Ranger (Cambridge: Cambridge University Press, 1983), pp. 165–209, applies this type of analysis to Victorian India.

[38] Ronald Inden suggested the concept of sovereign cult, but not the term.

reign on a new basis, the temptation to ignore the issues which have preoccupied previous writers exists. But Akbar's religious programme had great political importance; to ignore it would make the study of his regime incomplete. Keeping several distinctions in mind, however, can prevent repeating mistakes. In writing political history, not hagiography or heresiography, Akbar's personal religious sentiments, and those of Shaykh Aḥmad Sirhindī for that matter, are irrelevant except as they affected the political order of the empire. The events of the sixteenth (tenth) century determined neither the cause nor the outcome of the twentieth (fourteenth) century struggle for independence and for or against partition. Images of a timeless, essential, Hindu India, damaged or polluted by outside influences, or of Sunnī, Shar'ī Islam as the only true or orthodox Islam against which all Muslims should be evaluated impede rather than facilitate understanding Mughal history.[39]

The concept of political compromise illuminates the formation of the Mughal empire. The regime—the continuing pattern of political dynamics—survived because it satisfied both the ruler and the members of the political elite. It represented a compromise in two senses, one between the ideals represented in the rituals and texts which propounded the constitution and economic and military realities, and the other between the desires and expectations of the ruler and those of the mansabdars. The Mughal polity was thus the product of the Akbarī political compromise. My subject is the nature and development of that compromise.

The body of the work consists of five chapters. The first reviews the political and institutional precedents for the Mughal empire and the political situation in Hindustan at the beginning of Akbar's career. The second chapter evaluates the gunpowder empires hypothesis and discusses the pattern and mechanism of the expansion of the empire and their effects on its politics. The remaining three chapters discuss political developments from 1556 (963) to 1574 (982), the mature Akbarī constitution and programme, and the response to that programme which produced the compromise.

[39] On the development and significance of Western views of India, see Ronald Inden, 'Orientalist Constructions of India', *Modern Asian Studies* 20 (1986), pp. 401–46.

1.2 Sources

This section has two parts, a general discussion of the sources for Mughal history and the ways in which they can and cannot be used and a specific comment on the sources for Akbar's reign. This work rests on the study of the Persian chronicles and dictionaries of political biography, with additional information from travellers' accounts and from occasional letters and other documents. The original contribution comes in interpretation, not in the collection or presentation of new facts, so using all possible sources was neither necessary nor possible. Although the collections of documents available in the various archives of Rajasthan, in the Andhra Pradesh archives, and in such collections as the Inayat Jang now in the National Archives of India deserve more attention that they have received so far, the surviving documents are too fragmentary and scattered for a new Mughal historiography to arise from them.[40] The collections cover the Deccan and Rajasthan, not the heart of the Mughal empire. Turning to narrative sources in other languages, even historians with the necessary linguistic abilities rarely cite the sources in Sanskrit, Hindi and other Indian languages. Only for Maratha history do non-Persian narrative sources provide a framework.[41]

The chronicles are original but formal sources, i.e. they are the work of contemporary observers, and frequently participants in the events they describe, but were intended and prepared for future consumption.

[40] Richards, *Golconda*, pp. 317–22 discusses some of the Mughal document collections; this work is the most significant one to rely to any great extent on Mughal documents. Mohd. Ziauddin Ahmed Shakeb, ed. *Mughal Archives: A Descriptive Catalogue of the documents pertaining to the reign of Shah Jahan 1: Durbar papers and a miscellany of singular documents* (Hyderabad: State Archives, Government of Andhra Pradesh, 1977), gives a good idea of the documents available. R. A. Alavi, *Studies in the Medieval Deccan* (New Delhi: Idarah-i Adabiyyat-i Delli, 1977) contains research based to some degree on these documents.

[41] E. G. Srivastava, *Akbar*, 1:501–3, lists fourteen different texts in Sanskrit, Hindi, and Rajasthani, but rarely cites them. For a general discussion of non-Persian sources, see idem., 'The Sources', R. C. Majumdar, gen. ed., *The History and Culture of the Indian People*, 11 vols. (Bombay: Bharatiya Vidya Bhavan, 1951–74), vol. 7 *The Mughul Empire*, pp. 15–17. Govind Sakharam Sardesai, *New History of the Marathas*, rev. ed., 3 vols. (Bombay: Phoenix, 1957) depends almost entirely on texts in Marathi.

Their authors did not, however, intend them to provide information for later historians seeking to understand the Mughal empire; they were not preparing answers for our questions. The official chronicles formed a part of the symbolic package of Mughal kingship. Abū al-Fażl's *Akbar-nāmah*, which presents Akbar as the culmination of human history, goes far beyond other Mughal chronicles as a presentation of sovereignty, but differs in degree rather than nature. By official chronicles, I refer to works produced under imperial sponsorship, with access to official documents. Men wrote chronicles without official sanction to fill what they perceived as gaps in existing records and for other purposes. As Azra Alavi astutely explains, Khwājah Kāmgār Ḥusaynī asserts that he wrote the *Ma'āsir-i Jahāngīrī* to fill the gap in the history of Jahāngīr's reign created by the premature end of the *Tūzuk-i Jahāngīrī*, but also sought to defend the reputation of his family, especially his great-uncle Abdullah Khān Firūz-i Jang.[42]

These chronicles have their drawbacks, but show clearly what contemporaries considered important. Close analysis of their language brings to light the social, political, and philosophical assumptions which structured the Mughal polity. More concretely, the chronicles of Shah Jahan's reign concentrate on three things: military activity, the ruler's activities, especially travel and the exchange of gifts with the mansabdars, and changes in mansab rank and official appointments. We therefore know that contemporaries considered these activities central, and worth remembering. The events described in the chronicles were outputs, and the system which produced them does not appear completely and explicitly in the texts. The chronicles and biographical dictionaries do, however, provide the material necessary to reconstruct it.

Travellers' accounts provide useful raw data and different perspectives on the Mughal polity and society. Even such astute observers as François Bernier and Sir Thomas Roe did not fully understand what they saw and

[42] Azrá Alavi, Introduction to *Ma'asir-i-Jahāngīrī*, by Khwajah Kamgar Husaini (Bombay: Asia, 1978), pp. 5–10. For general accounts of the Persian sources, see Srivastava, 'Sources', pp. 1–15. See also K. A. Nizami, *On History and Historians in Medieval India* (New Delhi: Munshiram Manoharlal, 1983), pp. 1–52, 141–60, 224–44; Rizvi, *Intellectual* (New Delhi: Munshiram Manoharlal, 1975), pp. 233–300; Harbans Mukhia, *Historians of Historiography during the Reign of Akbar* (New Delhi: Vikas, 1976).

experienced; they were outsiders, with access to common knowledge—rumour and gossip—and not to inside information. Travellers' accounts can only supplement the Mughal sources; they cannot provide a research framework.[43]

Three chronicles dominate the literature of Akbar's reign: the *Akbar-nāmah*, the *Muntakhab al-Tawārīkh* of 'Abd al-Qādir Bada'ūnī and the *Ṭabaqat-i Akbarī* of Niẓām al-Dīn Aḥmad Bakhshī. The *Akbar-nāmah* presents not only Akbar's reign but the whole of human history as portrayed in the mature Akbarī political programme. It contains the most facts about the reign, but must also be read with the greatest care, and not only because of the complexity and difficulty of Abū al-Fażl's Persian style. All official histories were written to persuade, but the *Akbar-nāmah* is a masterpiece of historiographical propaganda. The entire presentation serves to glorify, justify, and explain the status of Akbar in accord with his view of himself. As K. A. Nizami and Iqtdar Alam Khan, from their very different perspectives, have shown, this fact makes the *Akbar-nāmah* difficult to use.[44] Akbar did not begin his reign with a complete political agenda which he gradually revealed and actualized, but groped, improvised, and evolved. Because this study concentrates on the period of groping, improvisation, and evolution, Abū al-Fażl's assertions frequently receive critical scrutiny.[45]

Bada'ūnī's *Muntakhab al-Tawārīkh* is the antithesis of the *Akbar-nāmah*. Written in secret without official sponsorship, it gives the views of an intellectual and official who perceived himself and his colleagues of similar views as disenfranchised by a regime of which he had had high hopes. Though jealous and bitter, it supplements Abū al-Fażl's account, filling vital gaps. Bada'ūnī's complete independence from fear or the desire for favour gave him a unique and valuable perspective. Except when he was personally involved, however, he adds interpretation, not information. His facts frequently come from the *Ṭabaqat-i Akbarī*.[46] Compared to the other two chronicles, the *Ṭabaqat* is a

[43] François Bernier, *Travels in the Mughal Empire*, 2nd ed., trans. Archibald Constable, Rev. Vincent A. Smith (London: Oxford University Press, 1934; reprint ed., New Delhi: Oriental Books Reprint, 1983); Sir Thomas Roe, *The Embassy of Sir Thomas Roe to India*, ed. Sir William Foster (London: Humphrey Milford, 1926).

[44] Nizami, *Historians*, pp. 141–60, 224–44; Iqtidar Alam Khan, 'Nobility', pp. 29–36

[45] Nizami, *Historians*, pp. 141–60; see also Mukhia, *Historiography*, pp. 41–89.

[46] Nizami, *Historians*, pp. 240–2; Mukhia, *Historiography*, pp. 89–132.

mundane recounting of events. As *bakhshī* of Gujarat, and later *mīr bakhshī*, Niẓām al-Dīn Aḥmad had an intimate knowledge of the workings of Mughal government and was an eyewitness of many important events.[47] The text, however, gives just the opposite feeling. Even when he describes his own participation in events, he does so in an impersonal manner, without mentioning his own feelings or giving a sense of immediacy.[48] In addition, the *Ṭabaqat-i Akbarī* is much briefer than the other two works.

For the early part of Akbar's reign, two other chronicles are vital: the *Tarīkh-i Akbarī*, generally known as the *Tarīkh-i Qandahārī*, of Hajjī Muḥammad 'Arif Qandahārī, and the *Taẕkira-yi Humāyūn wa Akbar* of Bayāzīd Bayāt. Both of these men served in the establishments of high officers. Qandahārī was the *mīr-i sāmān* (chief of the household) of Bayrām Khān, Akbar's regent, and later served under Muẓaffar Khān Turbatī, one of the leading administrators. Bayāzīd Bayāt served in the household of Mun'im Khān, who became chief officer with the title Khān-i Khānān after the death of Bayrām Khān. He dictated his memoirs in his old age, in accord with an imperial order for the collection of recollections of Humāyūn—an early instance of oral history. These works contain crucial information from the personal experience of their authors, but even for the early periods the major chronicles are more valuable.[49]

In addition to these standard sources, I have consulted the hitherto uncited *Ṭabaqat-i Tīmūri* of Muḥammad Barārī Ummī ibn Muḥammad Jamshīd ibn Jabbārī Khān ibn Majnūn Khān Qāqshāl. Though composed in the reign of Shāh Jahān, this brief history of the Tīmūrid dynasty represents a different historiographical tradition from the other works and gives insight into the attitudes of Akbar's officers not available in the other sources.[50]

[47] *Bakhshīs* were the officials responsible for the administration of the *mansabdari* system, on the central and provincial level. See Ishtiaq Husain Qureshi, *The Administration of the Mughal Empire* (Patna: N.V. Publications, n.d.), pp. 77–9; Ibn Hasan, *Central Structure*, pp. 210–33; Saran, *Provincial Government*, pp. 182–3.

[48] E.g. T.A., 2:370–1.

[49] Nizami, *Historians*, pp. 230–2, 238–9; Mukhia, *Historiography*, pp. 155–60.

[50] Muhammad Barārī Ummī ibn Muḥammad Jamshīd ibn Jabbārī Khān ibn Majnūn Khān Qāqshāl, *Tabaqat-i Tīmūri*, Ousely ms. 311 (filmed by Oxford University Press, 1982).

1.3 Terminology and Technicalities

The members of the dynasty which we call the Mughals knew themselves as Tīmūrids and were not Mongols, the meaning of Mughal in Persian. Marshall G. S. Hodgson, in his quest to purify scholarly terminology, refers to the Mughals as the Indo-Tīmūrids.[51] Though desirable, his usage has not become standard; I call them Mughals in accord with standard usage. I use the term Mughal in several ways, which I shall delineate in order to avoid ambiguity. As an ethnic term, I use it as in the Mughal texts, to refer to the Turkish speaking pastoral nomads of central Asia and greater Iran. Otherwise, the Mughals means the members of the Mughal dynasty and the officials who shared their political agenda, to the dynasty in an institutional sense. In some cases, the meaning of the term becomes more general, as in Mughal India or the Mughal period. I use imperial as a synonym for Mughal and in no other way.

I use India for the entire subcontinent and the Indian Union for modern India in the political sense. As in the Mughal texts, Hindustan refers to the Indo-Gangetic plain and its immediate environs, not including the Deccan, Kashmir, or Afghanistan.

I do not employ the term orthodox for any variety of Islam because no authoritative mechanism exists in Islam to determine orthodoxy or heterodoxy. Especially in the subcontinent, perceiving Sunnī, Sharʿī Islam as the only valid Islam distorts the situation.

I use the English terms emperor, king, monarch, sovereign, and ruler, with associated adjectives, interchangeably to refer to the Mughal ruler, rather than using transliterated Persian epithets. The usage of the individual epithets deserves some attention, however. The Mughals used the term *sulṭān*, which normally designated a sovereign, for princes, e.g. Sulṭān Salim, the future Jahāngīr, so my usage of prince is a translation of *sulṭān* or *shāhzādah* (king's son). The most common term for the emperor is *pādishāh* or *bādshāh*, but compound expressions such as *haẓrat-i khāqānī* are frequently used.

In accord with the standard usage in Islamic studies, I have employed full transliteration for Persian, Turkish, and Urdu words, using the system of the *International Journal of Middle East Studies*. I have used

[51]Hodgson, *Venture*, 3:62n.

w rather than *v* for *vav* in accord with Indian pronunciation, except for terms of primarily Iranian provenance, e.g. Safavī. I have not transliterated words which have become standard in English, such as alim and ulama, and the following terms which appear very frequently: *mansabdar*, *jāgīr*, *amīr* and *umarā*, with related words. Mansab meant an official post in the Mughal government, with a numerical rank.[52] A mansabdar was the holder of such a post. The mansabdari system was the institution of an official hierarchy with numerical rank. A jāgīr was a concession of the land revenue for a certain area to an official as his salary; a jagirdar was the holder of such a concession. An amīr was a mansabdar with a rank of one thousand or above; umarā is the Arabic broken plural of amīr. I have arbitrarily used *beg* to transliterate the Turkish cognate of amīr. I have transliterated Mongol words in their Persianized forms and used standard transliterations without diacritical marks for Sanskrit words and for the names of Rajput dynasties. In quotations and the titles of published texts in footnotes and the bibliography I have preserved the original forms. I have spelled place names in accord with standard usage and without diacritical marks. I have also given both Gregorian and *hijrī* (in brackets) dates, as is common practice in Islamic studies.

I have used abbreviations, listed following the bibliography entries, for the Persian chronicles cited most frequently. When there is a published translation for a Persian text, I cite both together, with the volume number, if different, and page number of the translation separated from the next entry by a slash (/). When quoting a translated work, I have used the published translation, noting changes where necessary. I accept responsibility for the translations I have used.

[52] As I shall describe in the text, the mansabdari system developed over time in the first half of Akbar's reign. For convenience, I have used the term mansab for a post in Akbar's government before the definitive establishment of the system.

CHAPTER 2
In the Beginning

Akbar created the Mughal empire from two sets of components, what he found in Hindustan and what he, or rather his father, had brought with him from central Asia. He synthesized these two legacies to produce a distinctly Mughal polity and culture. The fusion involved individuals, institutions, patterns of behaviour, and literary and artistic styles. Understanding the Mughal synthesis requires examining its components as Akbar found them. The political precedents and circumstances are discussed under two headings, Islamic and Indian.

2.1 Islamic Precedents

Islamic refers not to Islam as a religion, but to Islamic civilization. The political characteristics of pastoral nomad confederations, for example, have nothing to do with the teaching of the Prophet Muḥammad.[1] Most students of political thought in Islamic civilization have ignored this distinction. Emphasizing it, however, raises the question of what aspects of Islamic civilization are related to Islam.

2.1.1 GENERAL PATTERNS

Most discussions of Islamic political thought concentrate on the concept of caliphate in the Sharīʿah and on the political ideas of Muslim philoso-

[1] On this distinction, see Marshal G. S. Hodgson, *The Venture of Islam*, 3 vols. (Chicago: University of Chicago Press, 1974), 1:57–60.

phers.[2] From this perspective, political practice in the Islamic world fell far short of Islamic norms, and the ideas which affected actual political functioning represented deviations from Islam as a result of outside influence and counsels of expediency. This tradition of scholarship involves a fundamental misunderstanding.

Central features of the theories of kingship current in the Islamic world from Umayyad times to the present came from non-Islamic sources, but major Muslim thinkers like Abū Ḥāmid Muḥammad al-Ghazālī perceived no conflict between these ideas and Islam. The Iranian tradition of kingship, the major external influence on Islamic kingship, had definite normative content. While most historians perceive a conflict between that tradition and Islam, many Muslims believed in a fusion of the two.[3]

Because of al-Ghazālī's central position in Islamic civilization, the interpretation of his work provides the best example. So respected in his time and fundamental in determining the future course of Islamic thought that he was considered the *mujaddid* (renewer) of Islam for his century, Ghazālī dealt with political issues in a series of Arabic works on Islamic law and a single Persian mirror for princes, the *Naṣīhat al-*

[2] E.g. E. I. J. Rosenthal, *Political Thought in Medieval Islam* (New York: Cambridge University Press, 1958); A. K. S. Lambton, 'Islamic Political Thought', in *The Legacy of Islam*, ed. Joseph Schacht and C. E. Bosworth, 2nd ed. (Oxford: Clarendon Press, 1974), pp. 404–24; idem., 'Quis Custodiet Custodes: Some Reflections of the Persian Theory of Government', *Studia Islamica* 5, 6 (1956): 125–48; idem., 'Justice in the Medieval Persian Theory of Kingship', *Studia Islamica* 17 (1962): 91–119, both reprinted in idem, *Theory and Practice in Medieval Persian Government* (London: Variorum, 1980); idem., *State and Government in Medieval Islam*, London Oriental Series, vol. 36 (Oxford: Oxford University Press, 1981); Daniel Pipes, *In the Path of God: Islam and Political Power* (New York: Basic Books, 1983), pp. 57–63.

[3] My view of Islamic kingship follows that of my teacher John Woods, as he presented it in a course on kingship and society which he taught with Ronald Inden and Michael Dalby. On kingship in general, see A. M. Hocart, *Kings and Councillors*, ed. with an Introduction by Rodney Needham, and a Foreword by E. E. Evans-Pritchard (Chicago: University of Chicago Press, 1970); idem., *Kingship* (London: Oxford University Press, 1927; reprint ed., 1969); F. W. Buckler, 'The Oriental Despot', *Anglican Theological Review* 10 (1927–8): 238–49, reprinted in *Legitimacy and Symbols: The South Asian Writings of F. W. Buckler*, ed. M. N. Pearson, Michigan Papers on South and Southeast Asia no. 26 (Ann Arbor: Center for South and Southeast Asian Studies, the University of Michigan, 1985) pp. 176–87.

Mulūk. The Arabic works address the issue of the possibility of legitimate government in the disordered time after the loss of effective power by the 'Abbāsid caliphate. Simplifying radically, Ghazālī presents a justification, under the Sharī'ah, for government by a *sulṭān*, with no more than the recognition from the caliph.[4] Lambton, the only writer to address this text directly except the English translator F. R. C. Bagley, separates the *Naṣīhat* from the rest of Ghazālī's political work. In the more recent of her two analyses, she writes: 'in spite of his attempt to create an amalgam of Islamic and pre-Islamic ideas, he... by his emphasis on the innate power of the ruler and his unaccountability except to God, helped to perpetuate the fundamental disharmony between the ideal of Islam and the ideal of pre-Islamic Persia.'[5] Ghazālī's frequent references to ideas and exemplars of pre-Islamic Iranian kingship clash with Lambton's belief that 'All political theories in Islam start from the assumption that Islamic government existed by virtue of a divine contract based on the Sharī'ah.'[6] The situation which Ghazālī describes involves no contract and hence cannot be Islamic.

In his time, however, Ghazālī came closer than any other individual to representing Islam. The content of the *Naṣīhat* does not contradict his Arabic works but complements it. His writings from a religio-legal perspective demonstrate the legitimacy of the sultanate from a Shar'ī perspective. The *Naṣīhat* explains what the *sulṭān* should do. Ghazālī contends that both religion—the Sharī'ah (Islamic law)—and kingship come from God. He does not find this position, or the Iranian doctrine and lore that he draws upon, contradictory to Islam. His chapter on the qualities required of kings begins with the contention that the Qur'ān itself holds that kingship comes from God and that religious men should recognize this fact. He asserts that the justice of the kings of pre-Islamic Iran permitted their dynasty to survive. He intermixes examples from the careers of Muhammad, earlier prophets, Muslim caliphs, Sasanian *pādishāhs* and, occasionally, later Muslim rulers, without distinction.

[4] Leonard Binder, 'Al-Ghazali's Theory of Islamic Government', *Muslim World* 45 (1955), pp. 229–41; A. K. S. Lambton, *State and Government*, pp. 106–17, 126–9; H. Laoust, *La Politique de Gazali*, Bibliotheque d'Etudes Islamiques, Tome 1 (Paris: T. Guethner, 1970).

[5] Ibid, p. 126.

[6] Lambton, 'Islamic Political Thought', p. 404.

His discussions of the Sasanians leaves no doubt that he considered them exemplary rulers but for their lack of Islam, which was not available in their time. He does not find fault with them for their Magian beliefs, but asserts that kingship without Islam disappeared with the advent of Islam.[7]

Ghazālī thus synthesized Shar'ī and Iranian ideas in a single doctrine, expressed in different works. Later developments added new tiles to the mosaic of ideas of kingship in the Islamic world.

By the sixteenth (tenth) century, the doctrines of kingship in most of the Islamic world involved a synthesis of pre-Islamic Arabian, Muslim, Iranian, and Turko-Mongol elements. Different dynasties had different versions. The doctrine of the central Asian Tīmūrids formed the specific precedent for the Mughals. Like other such doctrines in the medieval Islamic world, it had two elements, conformation to Islamic standards and a divine mandate to rule. In the treatise on ethics known as the *Akhlāq-i Jalālī*, Jalāl al-Dīn Dawānī expresses the standard Islamic theory of government after the destruction of the 'Abbāsid caliphate. Describing the Āqquyūnlū ruler Uzun Ḥasan, Dawānī argues that his rule was legitimate because his military victories demonstrated divine support, he ruled justly, and he supported the enforcement of the Sharī'ah. The preservation of the Sharī'ah made Uzun Ḥasan a caliph.[8] Support for the Sharī'ah became the principal Islamic criterion for legitimate rule in the post-caliphal period.

Dawānī's reference to justice does not mean only the punishment of the guilty and protection of the innocent. It refers to an aspect of the Iranian theory of kingship, the circle of justice. The circle represents

[7] Abū Ḥāmid Muḥammad ibn Muḥammad Ghazālī Ṭūsī, *Naṣīhat al-Mulūk*, ed. Jalāl al-Dīn Humā 'ī (Tehran: Silsilah-yi Intishārat-i Anjuman-i Millī), 1972 (1351) [solar], pp. 81–101, 198–219; trans. F. R. C. Bagley as *Ghazali's Book of Counsel for Kings* (London: Oxford University Press, 1964), pp. xxxviii–lvi, eg. pp. 45–56, 119–33.

[8] Jalāl al-Dīn Muḥammad ibn As'ad Dawānī, *Lavāmi'al-Ishrāq fī Makārim al-Akhlāq* (Lahore: Nawal Kishore 1866–7), pp. 3, 9, 235–6; John E. Woods, *The Aqquyunlu: Clan, Confederation, Empire* (Chicago: Bibliotheca Islamica, 1976), pp. 115–17. See also Sir Hamilton Gibb, 'Some Considerations on the Sunni Theory of the Caliphate', in *Studies on the Civilization of Islam*, ed. Stanford J. Shaw and William R. Polk (Boston: Beacon, 1962), pp. 144–8. I have not seen the translation of the *Akhlāqi Jalāli, Practical Philosophy of the Muhammadan People*, trans. W. F. Thomas (London: Oriental Translation Fund, 1839).

the interaction of the four elements of society: the peasants, the imperial treasury (which represents the bureaucracy), the army and the king. The peasants pay taxes into the treasury, which supports the army, which defends and extends the king's power. The king completes the circle by giving justice to the peasants, i.e. making taxation fair and protecting them from oppression.[9] When society operates in accord with this ideal, it brings divine approval to the king, revealed by favourable weather and harvests, victory in battle, and, eventually, admission to paradise. Justice thus symbolized the proper order and functioning of the cosmos as well as the kingdom. Eric Voegelin uses the expression 'cosmological empire' for this type of political doctrine. He writes, 'Rulership becomes the task of securing the order of society in harmony with the cosmic order....' In this view, rebellion or opposition creates cosmic disorder, not a mere political dispute.[10]

Enforcement of the Sharī'ah involved specific restrictions on non-Muslims. The distinction between *kāfirs* (unbelievers) and *ahl al-kitāb* (people of the book) disappeared in practice. Bernard Lewis describes the situation effectively:

> The Qur'an recognizes Judaism, Christianity, and a rather problematic third party, the religion of the Sabians, as earlier, incomplete and imperfect forms of Islam itself, and therefore containing a genuine if distorted divine revelation. The inclusion of the not very precisely defined Sabians made it possible by legal interpretation to extend the kind of tolerance accorded to Jews and Christians much more widely, first to Zoroastrians in Persia, then to Hindus in India and other groups elsewhere. Communities professing recognized religions were allowed the tolerance of the Islamic state. They were allowed to practise their religions, subject to certain conditions, and to enjoy a level of communal autonomy.[11]

[9] The most convenient references on the circle of justice are Lambton, 'Justice', pp. 96–101, idem., 'Quis', pp. 135–6.

[10] Eric Voegelin, *The New Science of Politics* (Chicago: University of Chicago Press, 1952), p. 54. Voegelin explains the idea of cosmological empires on pp. 52–9, drawing on the Achaemenid inscriptions at Bisitun (spelled Behistun in his source) and the Mongol orders of submission.

[11] Bernard Lewis, *The Jews of Islam* (Princeton: Princeton University Press, 1984), p. 20.

The conditions to which Lewis refers made the dominant status of Islam unmistakeable. The payment of the *jizyah* was the most important of these requirements. *Ahl al-kitāb* became *dhimmī* (protected people, transliterated *żimmī* from Persian) when they agreed to pay the *jizyah*.

The justification for the *jizyah* comes in the famous verse of the Qur'ān: 'Fight those who believe not in God and the Last Day and do not forbid what God and His Messenger have forbidden—such men as practise not the religion of truth, being out of those who have been given the Book—until they pay the tribute out of hand and have been humbled.'[12] *Jizyah* is translated tribute. Whatever it meant at the time of the revelation of the Qur'ān, Muslims came to interpret the verse to mean that *dhimmīs* should signify their humiliation and submission to Muslim rule by paying a capitation tax, rather than a tax on land. Requiring only non-Muslims to pay a capitation tax appeared humiliating because the Byzantine and Sasanian ruling classes had exempted themselves from capitation and required all other groups to pay it. The tax structure thus defined Muslims as the ruling class.[13] Treatment of Hindus as *dhimmīs* even though they worshipped idols began with the Arab conquest of Sind in 711(92).[14] During the Delhi Sultanate, the *jizyah* was sometimes collected as a land tax or political tribute from non-Muslims, retaining the implication of submission. Fīrūz Shāh Tughluq apparently attempted to establish collection of the *jizyah* in accord with the Sharī'ah; I have no information on the *jizyah* in India from his time to that of Akbar.[15] But even if it was not collected as an

[12] Qur'ān, IX, 29, translated in A. J. Arberry, *The Koran Interpreted*, 2 vols. as 1 (New York: Macmillan, 1974), 1:210. Other translations, e.g. Abdullah Yusuf 'Ali, *The Holy Qur'an* (Washington, D.C.: Islamic Center, 1978), p. 447 and Mohammed Marmaduke Pickthall, *The Meaning of the Glorious Koran* (New York: New American Library, n.d.), pp. 146–7, do not differ significantly in content. These three translations were originally published in 1955, 1934, and 1930.

[13] Hodgson, *Venture*, 1:242; Andre M. Andreades, 'Public Finances: Currency, Public Expenditure, Budget, Public Revenue', in *Byzantium*, ed. Norman H. Baynes and H. St. L. B. Moss, (Oxford: Clarendon Press, 1948), p. 82; Arthur Christensen, *L'Iran Sous Les Sassanides* (Copenhagen: Ejner Munksgaard, 1944), pp. 98–105; Daniel C. Dennett, *Conversion and the Poll Tax in Early Islam* (Cambridge: Harvard University Press, 1950), pp. 14–16.

[14] S. M. Ikram, *Muslim Civilization in India*, ed. Ainslie T. Embree (New York: Columbia University Press, 1964), pp. 11–12.

[15] *Encyclopedia of Islam*, 2nd ed., s.v. *Djizyah*, iii. India, by Peter Hardy.

individual tax, the *jizyah* served the same fundamental purpose. It separated the non-Muslims who paid it, directly or indirectly, from the Muslims who did not, and demonstrated their subordinate status. In other words, it created a basic social division, between Muslims and *dhimmīs*.

Although he wrote almost a century later, Dawānī's doctrine fits Tīmūr's actions. The great conqueror posed as a champion of the Sharī'ah; he justified his invasion of India on that basis.[16] The most famous of the Tīmūrid chronicles, the *Ẓafar-Nāmah* of Sharaf al-Dīn 'Alī Yazdī, portrays him in that light.[17] But Tīmūr's motivation came from the Turko-Mongol tradition. It supplied his claim to a divine mandate to rule. Tīmūr believed himself the heir to Chingiz Khān and sought to reconstruct the Mongol empire not as it had been but as it should have been. The Chingiz Khānid theory of kingship held that God had designated Chingiz Khān the sole legitimate ruler of the world, and that he had transmitted sovereignty to his descendants. *The Secret History of the Mongols*, the most important source on Chingiz Khān's early career, depicts him as the descendant of a wolf, which had been born at the express command of Heaven. His ancestor in the eighth generation, Buzūnjār, was one of the three sons of Ālan-Qū'-ā, a Mongol woman who conceived her children by a ray of light or golden man whom Heaven had emanated. *The Secret History* mentions several instances of divine intervention in Chingiz Khān's early career. Because Chingiz Khān and then his family claimed a monopoly on legitimate sovereignty, their opponents appear as rebels against the cosmic order, not as ordinary enemies.[18]

[16] See Tīmūr's *fath-namah* on the conquest of Delhi to his son Pir Muḥammad of Shiraz, in 'Abd al-Ḥusayn Navā'ī, ed. *Asnad u Maktūbāt-i Tarīkhī-yi Īrān az Tīmur tā Shāh Ismā'īl* (Tehran: B.T.N.K., 1962 (1341)), pp. 69–70.

[17] Mawlana Sharaf al-Dīn 'Alī Yazdī, *Zafar-nāmah*, ed. Muḥammad Abbāsi, Tehran: Amīr-i Kabīr, 1957–8 (1366). Yazdi wrote for Tīmūr's son and effective successor, Shah Rukh, and his work reflects his master's beliefs.

[18] *The Secret History of the Mongols*, trans. Francis Cleaves (Cambridge: Harvard University Press, 1982), pp. 1, 3–5, 25–6, 36-7, 47–8, 91. Eric Voegelin, 'The Mongol Orders of Submission to the European Powers', *Byzantion* 15 (1940–1): 378–413, is the fundamental work on Mongol political ideas; Igor de Rachelwiltz, 'Some Remarks on the Ideological Foundations of Chingiz Khan's Empire', *Papers in Far Eastern History* 7 (1973): 20–36 is also useful. Voegelin integrates his analysis of Mongol doctrine

Tīmūr claimed Ālan-Qū'ā and her celestial paramour as common ancestors with Chingiz Khān and projected himself as the recreator and guardian of the divinely commanded empire. He did not claim sovereignty in his own name, but acted as the agent of a puppet pretender to the throne of a renewed and reunited Mongol empire. His treatment of conquered cities reflects the view of his opponents as rebels.[19] Though he presented himself as the executive agent for the Chingiz Khānid mandate to rule, this status involved a form of sovereignty which was transmitted to his descendants, who ruled in their own names.[20]

The transmission of sovereignty to the ruler's descendants (plural) forms a common feature of the empires founded by pastoral nomads, known to historians as collective sovereignty. In brief, the doctrine of collective sovereignty holds that each male descendant of the original conqueror carried what one may call a sovereign gene, a claim to participate in the world empire. As a possessor of the sovereign gene, he was entitled to an appanage, a part of the empire to rule in his own name. The founders of the nomadic empires made the original distribution of appanages to their children. After their deaths, either family councils (known as *quriltay* in Mongol) or warfare determined the distribution of appanages and succession to the paramount throne. Continuing struggles over succession and distribution led to the fragmentation of these empires into small, struggling principalities. The major dynasties which fit this pattern include the Saljūqs, the Ayyūbids, the Chingiz-Khānid Mongols, the Tīmūrids, and the Āqquyūnlū.[21]

---

into his broader view of politics in *New Science*, pp. 52–9. I use Heaven to translate the term Tanri, the Turko-Mongol term for an omnipotent but impersonal heaven or sky, similar to the Chinese concept of *t'ien*. Rene Giraud, *L'Empire des Turcs Celestes* (Paris: Adrien-Maisonneuve, 1960), p. 15 and passim, translates the term as Dieu-Ciel. For the history and variations of the term, see Sir Gerald Clauson, *An Etymological Dictionary of Pre-Thirteenth Century Turkish* (Oxford: Clarendon Press, 1972), p. 523–4; Doerfer, *Elemente*, 2:577–85. Charles O. Hucker, *China's Imperial Past* (Stanford: Stanford University Press, 1975), p. 55, is my source on the Chinese concept.

[19] Jean Aubin, 'Comment Tamerlan Prenait les Villes', *Studia Islamica* 19 (1963): 83–122.

[20] This discussion of Tīmūr's ideas is based on the comments of John Woods, who is working on a major biography of Timūr.

[21] On collective sovereignty and the appanage system in general, see Martin B. Dickson, 'Uzbek Dynastic Theory in the Sixteenth Century', *Proceedings of the 25th International Congress of Orientalists*, 4 vols. (Moscow: 1963), 3:208–16; Woods,

In addition to the doctrine of kingship, the traditions of the Tīmūrid polity formed an important precedent for the Mughals. They determined the political expectations of the Chaghatay officers. The Tīmūrid polity was one of a series of pastrol nomad confederations in the Islamic world; in other words much or most of its military power resided in nomad tribes. For this reason, the chiefs of these tribes formed a major, and frequently the dominant, element of the political elite of these polities. This situation fitted the appanage system well. The provinces of the empire which were the appanages of princes were frequently also the territories controlled by specific tribes in the confederation. The chiefs of the tribes frequently acted as the guardians of the princes who governed these provinces, and, when the ruler of a dynasty was weak, manipulated them for their own purposes. To counterbalance the power of the tribal chiefs, the rulers of the confederations relied upon their own war-bands, or central armies. These groups consisted of 'free individuals recruited from nomadic and seminomadic groups, trained and paid by the Sultan, but not constituted in clan contingents.'[22] The members of the war-band formed the second element of the political elite. Members of the sedentary population, normally Iranians, filled official posts concerned with finance, administration, and religious matters.[23]

Aqquyunlu, pp. 12–16. On the Saljūqs, see C. E. Bosworth, 'The Political and Dynastic History of the Iranian World (AD 1000–1217)', in *The Cambridge History of Iran 5: the Saljuq and Mongol Periods*, ed. J. A. Boyle (Cambridge: Cambridge University Press, 1968), pp. 1–184. On the Ayyūbids, see R. Stephen Humphreys, *From Saladin to the Mongols: the Ayyubids of Damascus, 1193–1260* (Albany: State University of New York Press, 1977). The most convenient reference on the Mongols and Tīmūrids is Rene Grousset, *The Empire of the Steppes*, trans. Naomi Walford (New Brunswick, NJ.: Rutgers University Press, 1970), pp. 189–465; see also Vasilii Vladimirovich Bartol'd, *Sochineniya* (Collected Works) ed. A. M. Belenitskii, vol. 2 pt. II: *Raboti po otd'el'nim probl'mam istorii Srednei Azii Ulugh Be i yego vrem'ya* (Moscow: Izdatelstvo nauka glavnaya redak siya, 1966), pp. 23–196, trans. by V. Minorsky and T. Minorsky as V. V. Barthold, *Four Studies on the History of Central Asia*, vol. 2: *Ulugh Beg*, (Leiden: E. J. Brill, 1958) and H. R. Roemer, 'Timur in Iran', and 'The Successors of Timur', in *Cambridge History of Iran, Volume 6: The Timurid and Safavid Periods*, ed. Peter Jackson and Lawrence Lockhart (Cambridge: Cambridge University Press, 1986), pp. 42–146. On the Āqquyūnlū, see Woods, *Aqquyunlu*.

[22] Woods, *Aqquyunlu*, p. 8.

[23] Ibid., pp. 7–12; Roemer, 'Successors', pp. 127–32.

The Iranian bureaucrats carried, and attempted to put into effect, the Iranian tradition of centralized imperial administration, which looked back to the pre-Islamic Sasanian empire. The *Siyāsat-nāmah* of Niẓām al-Mulk Ṭūsī, expresses this tradition.[24] It emphasizes direct imperial control of the army and of the financial administration in the provinces. These desiderata differed radically from the political realities of pastoral confederations, but fitted the desires of the rulers, who sought to increase their power and decrease their dependence on the tribal chieftains. Bureaucrats who believed in this political tradition frequently joined the members of the war-band in supporting the ruler against the tribal elite.[25] Though frustrated by the political realities of the medieval Islamic world, the centralizing tradition remained alive and influential nonetheless, and affected Ottoman, Ṣafavī, and Mughal political goals, practices, and institutions.[26]

Most medieval Islamic states recruited their armies either from pastoral tribes or by military slavery. Military slavery involved the recruitment of large numbers of men in early adolescence, training them as professional soldiers, and employing them, after manumission, as professional soldiers and eventually as military and political officers. The system produced close ties between the slaves and their masters and thus offered greater central control. The war-band resembled a slave army in miniature; principalities which relied on slave armies also used tribal levies from peripheral areas. One may thus describe tribal and slave

[24] Abū 'Alī Ḥasan Ṭūsī, Nizām al-Mulk, *Siyāsat-nāmah* or *Siyar al-Muluk*, ed. H. Darke (Tehran: B.T.N.K., 1962), trans. H. Darke (London: Routledge & Kegan Paul, 1978).

[25] E.g. Woods, *Aqquyunlu*, pp. 156–7.

[26] For the influence of this tradition on the Ottomans, See Halil Inalcik, *The Ottoman Empire: the Classical Age, 1300–1600*, trans. Norman Itzkowitz and Colin Imber (London: Weidenfeld & Nicholson, 1973), pp. 65–9; idem, 'Land Problems in Turkish History', *Muslim World* 45 (1958): 221–24; *Encyclopedia of Islam*, 2nd ed., s.v. 'Kanun: Financial and Public Administration', and 'Kanunname', by Halil Inalcik. Joel Shinder, 'Early Ottoman Administration in the Wilderness: Some Limits on Comparison', *International Journal of Middle East Studies* 9 (1978): 497–517, is an interesting counterpoint to this position. On the Safavīs, see H. R. Roemer, 'The Safavid Period', in Jackson and Lockhart, eds., *Cambridge Iran 6*, pp. 262–6, 268–70; Roger Savory, 'The Safavid Administrative System', ibid., pp. 367–72. These accounts do not refer explicitly to the influence of the tradition of imperial administration, but the content of Shah 'Abbas's political programme leaves little doubt of such influence.

military organizations as the ends of a continuum, with various principalities filling different places in the range.[27]

The Turko-Mongol institution of *nawkarī*, by which the Chingiz-Khānids recruited their war-bands, resembles military slavery. It deserves independent notice because it approximates the status of mansabdar more closely than any other precedent. Although it came to mean a servant in both Persian and Ottoman Turkish, *nawkar* originally referred to a specific type of dependant of a Mongol chieftain. The term literally means companion; the standard translation of it is antrustion, the name for the free followers of the chiefs of the Franks in the Merovingian period. In Mongol society, the *nawkar* gave up his original tribal status, identifying himself only with the leader he served. Though not military slaves in the strict sense of the term in the Islamic world, the *nawkar* shared some important characteristics with the *mamlūk*. Both received a new identity from their master and owed enormous loyalty to him.[28] The *nawkar* formed the sovereign's personal guard.[29]

Both the pastoral confederation and the military slave based polities were what Marshal Hodgson calls military patronage states. The doctrine of the military patronage state involved 'the conception of the whole state as a single military force,' with all economic and cultural resources at its disposal. A fundamental distinction separated the members of the army/government and the subjects who supported it.[30] In the Ottoman empire, state servants, whatever their specialty, were known as *askerī* (military), as opposed to the *ra 'iyyah* (flock), who paid taxes.[31]

Andre Wink presents a radically different view of the Islamic back-

[27] On military slavery, see Daniel Pipes, *Slave Soldiers and Islam* (New Haven: Yale University Press, 1981), pp. 1–102.

[28] B. Vladimirtsov, *Le Regime Social des Mongols*, preface by Rene Grousset, trans. Michel Carsow (Paris: Adrien-Maisonneuve, 1948), pp. 110–23. Gerhard Doerfer, *Turkische und Mongolische Elemente im Neupersichen*, 4 vols., Akademie der Wissenschaften und der Literatur Veroffentlichungen der Orientalischen Kommision, vols. 16, 19–21 (Wiesbaden: Franz Steiner Verlag, 1963–1975), 1:521–6, discusses the usage of the word in Persian.

[29] Vladimirtsov, *Regime*, pp. 110–23.

[30] Hodgson, *Venture*, 2:404–10.

[31] Inalcik, *Classical*, pp. 65–9.

ground for Mughal expansion in the subcontinent in his recent book, *Land and Sovereignty in India*. He emphasizes the concept of *fitnah*. His view requires detailed examination. The Arabic word *fitnah* originally meant test or temptation, and came to refer to the temptation to flaunt divine law and revolt against the order of Muslim society, hence revolt in general.[32] Wink argues, however, that revolt or disorder is a 'singularly inadequate translation' of *fitnah*.[33] Following Ibn Khaldun, as interpreted by M. M. Rabi, he asserts that *fitnah*, the political breakup of the unitary *ummah*—the Muslim community—is 'an indispensable constituent of Muslim monarchy.'[34] Through *fitnah*, 'political sovereignty', natural politics, developed.[35] In this view, *fitnah* means no more than forging alliances, creating a sovereignty 'characterized by dispersal through shifting combinations with local powerholders.'[36]

Muslims condemned *fitnah* because they viewed natural politics as a deviation, juxtaposed against a 'transcendent conception of universal dominion.'[37] Wink, unaware of the change in the significance of the term *khalīfat* described by Dawānī, sees the Mughal use of the term *khalīfat* as evidence of continuity in the idea of universal sovereignty from classical Islamic times. He sees *fitnah* as the idiom of Muslim politics, especially of conquest, in spite of that condemnation.[38]

Wink's analysis has two steps, the argument that *fitnah* as described by Ibn Khaldūn formed the basic mechanism of politics in the Islamic world, and the contention that the historians of the Mughal and Maratha periods referred to this political mechanism when they used the term. The first step is acute and interesting; the second, false. Wink gives no evidence that either pre-Mughal or Mughal chroniclers perceived the political tactics of men whom they considered legitimate, but not actual,

[32] *Encyclopedia of Islam*, 2nd ed., s.v. 'Fitnah', by L. Gardet; Bernard Lewis, *The Political Language of Islam* (Chicago: University of Chicago Press, 1988), pp. 96–7.

[33] Andre Wink, *Land and Sovereignty in India: Agrarian Society and Politics under the Eighteenth-Century Maratha Svarajya* (Cambridge: Cambridge University Press, 1986), p. 26.

[34] Ibid., p. 23; Muhammad Mahmoud Rabi', *The Political Theory of Ibn Khaldun* (Leiden: E.J. Brill, 1967), pp. 100–36.

[35] Ibid., p. 24.

[36] Ibid., pp. 26–8.

[37] Ibid., pp. 29–30.

[38] Ibid., pp. 29–33.

universal rulers as *fitnah*. If a given tactic or activity assisted the expansion or ordering of the legitimate realm, it could not be *fitnah*. The standard translation of *fitnah* as rebellion or disorder is thus correct. One must bear in mind, however, that one man's *fitnah* was another man's legitimate action. Wink's valuable contribution comes in realizing that, for a disengaged historian or sociologist like Ibn Khaldūn, designating what the chronicles call *fitnah* as rebellion confuses rather than explains events. His reassessment of *fitnah* thus forms another method of 'getting behind the sordid record', as Bernard S. Cohn has referred to the imperative of interpreting the eighteenth (twelfth) century.[39]

2.1.2 ISLAMIC PRECEDENTS IN THE SUBCONTINENT

In order to understand what Akbar achieved, one must realize where the Delhi Sulṭāns failed. The conventional division of the Sultanate into the period of the Slave Kings and then a sequence of dynasties—the Khaljīs, Tughluqs, Sayyids, and Ludīs—obscures the failure of any of the Delhi Sulṭāns to establish a lasting political idea. Political idea means the combination of a doctrine of kingship and related world view, political, administrative and military structures, and economic, social, and geographic bases, which makes the ruler and central government the focus of loyalty and of expectations of success.[40] None of the dynasties lasted as anything more than figureheads for more than three generations; most survived for only two. Individuals like 'Ala' al-Dīn Khaljī and Ghazī Malik Tughluq generated considerable loyalty, but could not pass it on to their heirs. The survival of the Mughal polity for a century and a half and of the Mughal dynasty for three centuries shows what the Mughals achieved and the Delhi Sulṭāns did not.[41]

Of the Delhi Sulṭāns, Muḥammad ibn Tughluq and Shīr Shāh Sūr

[39] Bernard S. Cohn, 'Political Systems in Eighteenth Century India,' *Journal of the American Oriental Society* 82 (1962): 312.

[40] My definition of political idea is adapted from Hodgson, *Venture*, 2:12.

[41] In addition to the standard account in Romila Thapar, *A History of India, Volume 1* (Harmondsworth: Penguin, 1966), Yusuf Husain, *Indo-Muslim Polity: Turko-Afghan Period* (Simla: Indian Institute of Advanced Study, 1971) is a convenient and insightful summary of the history of the Delhi Sultanate. On the Afghan dynasties, see Iqtidar Husain Siddiqui, *Some Aspects of Afghan Despotism in India* (Aligarh: Three Men Publication, 1969).

deserve special attention. Muḥammad ibn Tughluq may have been as mad as his popular reputation makes out, but he made an effort to establish a new political idea. He sought new legitimacy by requesting a diploma of office from the 'Abbāsid shadow-caliph in Cairo, the only Indian ruler to do so, and, in order to overcome the opposition of some of the ulama to several of his policies he claimed to be a *mujtahid*. His famous effort to transfer the entire population of Delhi to a new capital at Dawlatabad was another aspect of his attempt to recast the polity of the Delhi Sultanate. One may depict Muḥammad ibn Tughluq as an unsuccessful predecessor of Akbar.[42] Shīr Shāh Sūr, who expelled Humāyūn from India and established his rule over most of Hindustan, did not establish a new political idea during his six years as sulṭān. His administrative practices influenced Akbar and he did appoint a number of Hindus to high office.[43]

2.1.3 BĀBUR AND HUMĀYŪN

Akbar's grandfather and father made several changes in the Tīmūrid doctrine of kingship which they inherited. Bābur took the title *pādishāh* as ruler of Kabul in 1507 (913); earlier Tīmūrids had used the title *mirzā*. He probably made the change in order to indicate his status as the pre-eminent Tīmūrid and to place his sovereignty on the same level as that of his rivals, Shāh Ismā'īl Ṣafavī and Shaybanī Khān Uzbeg.[44]

During Humāyūn's brief second reign in Delhi, he introduced a new model of administration and social structure, which suggests that he intended major changes in the doctrine of kingship. He divided the imperial servants into three groups, the men of *dawlat* (fortune, i.e.

[42] On Muḥammad ibn Tughluq, see Huṣain, *Indo-Muslim*, pp. 146–59; Mohammad Habib, 'Muhammad ibn Tughluk', in *Collected Works of Mohammad Habib*, ed. K. A. Nizami, vol. 2: *Politics and Society in the Medieval Period* (New Delhi: People's Publishing House, 1981), pp. 279–85.

[43] On Shīr Shāh, see Iqtidar Husain Siddiqui, *History of Sher Shah Sur* (Aligarh: P. C. Dwadash Shreni, 1971).

[44] Zahīr al-Dīn Muḥammad Bābur Pādishāh Ghazī, *Bābur-Nāma*, facsimile ed. Annette Susannah Beveridge. Gibb Memorial Series no. 1. (London: E. J. W. Gibb Memorial Trust, 1905; reprint ed. 1971), trans Annette Susannah Beveridge, 2 vols. (London: By the Author, 1921; reprint ed., 2 vols. as 1: New Delhi: Oriental Books Reprint, 1979), f. 215/1:344.

the good fortune of the ruler and thence his government, the modern Persian word for state), including the other members of the Tīmūrid family, military and administrative officers, and soldiers; the men of *sa'ādat* (good fortune, happiness, success), the philosophers, ulama, and Sufis; and the men of *murād* (desire), architects, artists, merchants, and singers.[45] The classification of other Tīmūrids with imperial servants marks the abandonment of the concept of the appanage state and modification of the doctrine of collective sovereignty. Being a Tīmūrid no longer made a prince a co-sovereign, entitled to an autonomous domain. He became a servant of the current ruler and his potential successor. Each Tīmūrid male carried the sovereign gene, but only one exercised it. Humāyūn spent most of his career dealing with consequences of collective sovereignty, i.e. securing his position against his brothers Mirzā Kāmrān, Mirzā 'Askarī and Mirzā Hindal. They failed to support him against Shīr Shāh.[46] Humāyūn most likely sought to modify the doctrine of collective sovereignty in response to this ordeal. His idea is an important, but hitherto unnoticed, precedent for Akbar's programme.

2.2 Indian Precedents

In describing non-Islamic precedents as Indian, I do not wish to imply that Islam is alien to, and has no legitimate place in, the subcontinent. The term Indian refers to the culture which the Muslims encountered in the subcontinent. Though there had been Muslims in the subcontinent for some eight centuries, there was no synthesis of the Islamic and Indian doctrines of kingship before Akbar's time. In the subcontinent and the Indian religious tradition, kings acted as the chief worshippers of the head deity which they recognized.[47] In Vedic times, royal status hinged on the performance of the horse sacrifice (*asvamedha*).[48] Buddhist

[45] A.N. 7–60/642–7.

[46] Iqtidar Alam Khan, *Mirza Kamran* (New York: Asia, 1964), is the most insightful account of Humāyūn's wars with his brothers.

[47] I use the term Indian religious tradition to cover Vedic religion, Buddhism, Jainism, and Hinduism, on the model of Abrahamic religion for Judaism, Christianity and Islam.

[48] My knowledge of Indian kingship comes from Ronald Inden. The references to other authors in this section are for the convenience of the reader. The most convenient summary of pre-Mughal Indian history is Thapar, *India*. She discusses the horse sacrifice on p. 54.

dynasties like the Mauryas used the erection of *stupas* (repositories for relics of the Buddha), as statements of sovereignty.[49] Buddhist rulers also supported monasteries. Several dynasties used both Vedic and Buddhist symbols. Hindu kings, before and during the Muslim penetration of the subcontinent, occupied a complex position. They appeared as both transcendent but ascetic worshippers, with passive rather than active authority, and divine warriors and administrators, active in every sphere of royal concern.[50] Texts on kingship describe the king as the husband of the earth or country and the people as their offspring. The king is also a partial descendant (as opposed to a full incarnation) of Vishnu (at least in Vaishnavite dynasties) and simultaneously a descendant of the sun or moon. He serves as an *axis mundi* and a microcosmic representation of the universe, subsuming in his nature portions of the deities who guard the eight points of the compass.[51] His realm forms a replica of the universe. The capital, and within it the king's palace and audience hall, form a microcosm within the microcosm, with the king's throne at its centre.[52]

The king's nature guarantees the safety and prosperity of his subjects by controlling all the elements of his kingdom, including political rivals. He does so with gifts and punishments and through participation in rituals. Hindu kings acted as sacrificers, presenting burnt offerings to the gods, and participated in *puja*, 'attend[ing] to the bodily needs of a deity placed in an enlivened image or emblem. . . .'[53]

The ritual for the installation of a Hindu king reflects the complexity of the doctrine of kingship. The *rajyabhiseka* (royal bath) has two parts. The first involves the transformation of the king into a micro-

[49] On *stupas*, see Benjamin Rowland, *The Art and Architecture of India*, rev. J. C. Harle (Harmondsworth: Penguin, 1977), pp. 77–9.

[50] Ronald Inden, 'Ritual, Authority and Cyclic Time in Hindu Kingship', in *Kingship and Authority in South Asia*, ed. J. F. Richards, South Asian Studies, University of Wisconsin Madison, no. 3 (Madison, Wi: University of Wisconsin, Madison South Asian Studies), pp. 28–73. The previous two sentences paraphrase part of p. 29. The idea of the kingdom as microcosm corresponds to Voegelin's concept of the cosmological empire; *New Science*, pp. 54–9.

[51] On the concept of *axis mundi*, see Mircea Eliade, *The Sacred and the Profane*, trans. Willard R. Trask (New York: Harcourt, Brace & World, 1959), pp. 33–7.

[52] Inden, 'Ritual', pp. 29–35.

[53] Ibid., p. 36.

cosmic Cosmic man, embodying all the elements of the kingdom and all the sources of royal power. It expresses the passive aspect of Hindu kingship. In the second part, the king becomes active, performing ritual worship and taking the throne in his hall of audience. He distributes gifts to Brahmins, appoints and dismisses officials, and makes a triumphal procession around the capital. The procession represents the king's annual conquest of the four quarters (*digvijaya*), a military procession around the perimeter of the kingdom. In theory, all potential enemies submit to the king at his approach because of his majesty and obvious power, pay tribute and are confirmed in their positions. If they do not, the king attacks them. Because the king alternates between passivity (during the rainy season) and activity, the *rajyabhiseka* represents the pattern of his year. It is performed at the king's accession and annually on the anniversary thereof.[54]

This doctrine of kingship affected the pattern of politics in the subcontinent. Hindu kings sought to gain the submission of their rivals, whom they accepted as subordinate chiefs and headmen, rather than to establish direct rule and collect taxes from the peasants themselves. Conquest thus meant something different in the subcontinent from elsewhere. Hindu kingdoms, even the most powerful like the Chola and Rashtrakuta empires, had a less coherent structure than their contemporaries in the Islamic world.[55] Burton Stein adapts Aidan Southall's concept of the segmentary state to discuss the empires of medieval India. He writes of:

> the pyramidally segmented type of state, so-called because the smallest unit of political organization—a section of a peasant village—was linked to ever more comprehensive units of political organization of an ascending order (e.g. village, locality, supralocality, and kingdom) for various purposes, but each unit stood in opposition to other similar units . . . for other purposes.[56]

[54] Ibid., pp. 35–59. On the *digvijaya*, see Richard Lannoy, *The Speaking Tree* (London: Oxford University Press, 1971), p. 321.

[55] For these dynasties, see K. A. Nilakantha Shastri, *The Cholas* (Madras: 1955); Anant Sashiv Altekar, *Rashtrakutas and their Times* (Poona: Oriental Book Agency, 1967), esp. pp. 26–7.

[56] Burton Stein, *Peasant State and Society in Medieval South India* (Delhi: Oxford University Press, 1980), pp. 264–5. Southall propounds the concept of segmentary

Stein emphasizes two characteristics of the segmentary state, pyramidal segmentation and the division between ritual and political sovereignty. The centre had a monopoly of ritual sovereignty, but not of actual political control. The ritual monarch was the actual ruler at the centre, but his power decreased as the distance from the centre increased. His ritual subordinates exercised power in distant segments. Stein argues that:

> overarching *political* control may not be very important at all. . . . In a segmentary state, while political control is appropriately distributed among many throughout the system, ritual supremacy is legitimately conceded to a single centre.[57]

Though he restricts his comments to south India, Stein's model merits broader application.[58]

2.3 Hindustan before the Akbarī Transformation

When Akbar took his father's throne, he confronted a series of regional polities and smaller fragments. No dynasty had unified Hindustan for some two centuries. Shīr Shāh Sūr had died in 1545 (952), only six years after he first claimed sovereignty. His successor Islām Shāh reigned for nine disorderly years. After Islām Shāh died, three members of the Sūr dynasty, ʿAdil Shāh, Sikandar Shāh, and Aḥmad Shāh contested the throne. Humāyūn had defeated Sikandar Shāh and driven him into the hills of the Punjab, but the other contenders were as yet undefeated. Further afield, Bāz Bahādur, the son of a Sūrī governor, ruled Malwa; an independent dynasty ruled the important commercial province of Gujarat; and the Afghan Kararānī dynasty ruled the great province of Bengal. The Sisodia Rānās of Mewar were pre-eminent in Rajasthan, but other dynasties, most importantly the Kachwahas of Amber, the Rathors of Marwar and Bikanir, and the Hadas of Bundi, also governed autonomous principalities. Other Rajput dynasties, like the Bhaghellas

state in his *Alur Society: A Study in Process and Types of Domination* (Cambridge, England: W. Heffer and Sons, 1956), which I have not seen.

[57] Ibid., p. 269.

[58] This description of Indian precedents with no mention of caste may strike some readers as strange. I refer them to Ronald Inden, 'Orientalist Constructions of India', *Modern Asian Studies* 20 (1986): 401–46.

of Pannah, existed outside of Rajasthan. Akbar thus confronted a variety of Hindu and Muslim dynasties, each with its own set of officers.

These dynasties formed only the tip of the political iceberg with which Akbar collided. He also confronted the armed peasantry of Hindustan.

2.3.1 THE ARMED PEASANTRY

Discussing the armed peasantry and its significance at this point creates a logical difficulty. The Mughal chronicles reveal the existence of a surplus of military manpower; the Dutch historian/ethnomusicologist Dirk Kolff has described the existence of the armed peasantry which created it.[59] Most of the Kolff's evidence for the existence of the armed peasantry comes from Akbar's reign or later. Such a phenomenon could not, however, spring into existence in a few years or even a few decades. The evidence for Akbar's time and after thus applies to the beginning of his reign.

Abū al-Fażl asserts that the Mughal empire supported 342,696 cavalry and 4,039,097 infantry. His access to official records and the exactness of his figures for each province and district suggest that he did not deliberately exaggerate.[60] This figure must have included roughly ten per cent of the male population.[61] Earlier historians who have discussed the issue have not understood the significance of these figures.[62] Rather than a society of peaceful peasants who wished only to be left alone, north India was a society armed cap-à-pie, an enormous reservoir of military manpower. The English traveller Peter Mundy

[59] Dirk Herbert Arnold Kolff, 'An Armed Peasantry and Its Allies: Rajput Tradition and State Formation, 1450–1850' (Ph.D. dissertation, Rijksuniversiteit te Leiden, 1983).

[60] A.A., 2:1–283/141–367. On the interpretation and different manuscript versions of this section, see Irfan Habib, *The Agrarian System of Mughal India* (Bombay: Asia, 1963), pp. 163–7.

[61] Kolff, 'Armed', pp. 13–14. Kolff unaccountably gives no source for his total population, but Colin McEvedy and Richard Jones, *Atlas of World Population History* (Harmondsworth: Penguin, 1978), pp. 182–5, estimates the population of the entire subcontinent at 100,000,000 in 1500 and 145,000,000 for 1650. Assuming an even sex ratio, Kolff's estimate is reasonable.

[62] Irfan Habib, *The Agrarian System of Mughal India* (Bomaby: Asia, 1963), pp. 163–9; Paramata Saran, *The Provincial Government of the Mughals*, 2nd ed. (New York: Asia, 1973), pp. 240–8.

hired more than twenty soldiers at a time for his journeys between Agra, Surat, and Patna in 1632–3 (1042); one of the convoys in which he travelled had a total of four hundred and forty guards.[63] The records of the Dutch East India Company disclose that in 1637 (1048) the company hired thirty-seven soldiers, armed with bows or muskets, to protect a convoy of twenty-two wagons. In 1644 (1054), it hired one hundred and ninety guards to guard a convoy carrying Rs 300,000.[64] The casual hiring of these guards shows that soldiers could be hired readily and that they were needed to protect convoys from brigands—i.e. other soldiers who were unemployed.

The ease of hiring soldiers made the assembly of armies of several thousand men simple. When Sulṭān Khusraw fled from Jahāngīr's court and sought to take Lahore, he was able to gather ten thousand men within a few days, though he could not take Lahore. After Murtażā Khān Shaykh Farīd Bukharī defeated that army outside Lahore, the prince held a council of war. Ḥasan Beg Badakhshī, his chief advisor, argued that he should head for Kabul, since Ḥasan Beg's personal treasury was in Rohtas, on the way. With that treasure in his possession, Khusraw could once again raise an army in a short time. This argument determined his decision.[65] These events revealed that the number of men willing and able to serve as soldiers exceeded the ability of either the Mughal government or of alternative employers to keep them all on retainer.

The alternative employers were the zamindars. Irfan Habib has shown that Abū al-Fażl's lists of troop strengths for each province and district indicate the military followers of the local zamindars. His interpretation rests convincingly on the format of the tables in the manuscripts of the

[63] Peter Mundy, *The Travels of Peter Mundy in Europe and Asia*, ed. R. C. Temple, 5 vols. (London: Hakluyt Society, 1914–24), 2:256–7, 261, 294–6.

[64] A.R.A., The Hague, Coll. Geleynssen, no. 102, Geleynssen to C. Jansen Silvius, Agra 25. ix.1637; A.R.A., The Hague, 1157f. 408v., C. Weijlandt to A. Van Diemen, Surat 5. vii.1644; A.R.A., The Hague Coll. Geleynssen no. 113, 'Notitie der naamen van 77 pijons . . .' and 'Notitie der naamen van 65 pijons . . .,' cited by Kolff, *Armed*, pp. 14–15.

[65] Mu'tamad Khan, *Iqbalnamah-yi Jahangiri*, Ed. Maulavi 'Abd al-Hayy and Maulavi Ahmad 'Ali Sahun (Calcutta: Asiatic Society of Bengal, 1865), pp. 9–14; T.J., 30–41/1:52–65; Baini Prasad, *History of Jahangir* 5th ed. (Allahabad: Indian Press, 1973), pp. 129–34.

Āyīn-i Akbarī. All zamindars had military retainers; some had artillery, elephants, and small forts (*qal 'achah*). The zamindars normally employed a nucleus of retainers from their own caste, which the Mughal sources refer to as an *ulus*, supplemented with peasants. Habib shows his belief in peasant pacifism by saying that the peasants were 'impressed' by the zamindars, rather than choosing to serve.[66] But Kolff, who has studied peasant culture closely, gives a different view: 'the roots of the martial tradition [of the peasant soldiers] were in the villages and towns of Hindustan . . . military sports were very much part of the daily life of the village.'[67] He concludes that 'the peasant masses of north India . . . were professionally skilled in the use of all sorts of weapons.'[68] The peasants were all infantrymen; they fought with sword and spear or with firearms. Only a few social groups used the bow.[69]

Zamindars, with their private armies, existed throughout Hindustan. Their power and position varied enormously. Some were a little less powerful than the potentates of Rajasthan; others were peasants who collected, as much through habit as by force, a cut of what their neighbours produced. Almost all of the literature on the zamindars refers to Mughal times. But they formed a part of the political universe of Hindustan in the beginning of Akbar's reign. They controlled a significant proportion of the military power of Hindustan, though their power was generally limited to the immediate locality. Kolff's investigations of the relationships of the Purbiya Rajputs of north-eastern Malwa with the Khiljī sulṭāns of Malwa, the Sulṭāns of Gujarat and then with Shīr Shāh show that these chieftains had alternately cooperated with and opposed Muslim rulers.[70] The zamindars thus formed a vital part of the political structure which Akbar faced.[71]

[66] Habib, *Agrarian*, pp. 165–7.

[67] Kolff, 'Armed', p. 34.

[68] Ibid., p. 36. The discussion of these issues is on pp. 34–6.

[69] Ibid., p. 34.

[70] Ibid., pp. 80–117. Kolff intends this chapter as much to elucidate the changes in the concept of Rajput during the sixteenth century as to reveal the relationships of Rajput zamindars outside of Rajasthan with Muslim rulers.

[71] On zamindars under the Mughals in general, see Habib, *Agrarian*, pp. 136–89; S. Nurul Hasan, 'Zamindars under the Mughals', in *Land Control and Social Structure in Indian History*, ed. Robert Eric Freykenberg (Madison: University of Wisconsin Press, 1969), pp. 17–28; Ahsan Raza Khan, *Chieftains in the Mughal Empire* (Simla: Indian Institute of Advanced Study, 1977).

2.3.2 THE COMPONENTS OF THE MUGHAL RULING CLASS

This background reveals that the groups which formed the Mughal ruling class had different political expectations and agendas as well as ethnic and religious characteristics. The Mughal polity had to satisfy these varied expectations. Individuals and groups who could not accept the status of mansabdar could not become or remain part of the Mughal system for long. This winnowing out of the discontented was a basic part of the political transformation.

The officers who had accompanied Humāyūn to Hindustan and became Akbar's subordinates came from three different backgrounds. Most were Chaghatays, who expected the status of amīrs in a pastoral nomad confederation, meaning a central position in the ruling class and considerable autonomy in the provinces. There were also sedentary bureaucrats, seeking to put the Iranian tradition of centralized, bureaucratic government into practice. Lastly, there were Turkmen, Turkish speaking pastoral nomads from the Ṣafavī empire. Bayrām Khān, Humāyūn's chief subordinate and Akbar's guardian and then regent, was a Turkmen, specifically a member of the Bahārlū clan of the Qarāquyūnlū family, which had once ruled a confederation in Western Iran.[72] The Turkmen tribes of eastern Anatolia and western Iran had formed the Qarāquyūnlū, Āqquyūnlū, and Qizilbāsh (i.e. Ṣafavī) confederations, but Bayrām Khān and his relatives had not been tribal chieftains under Bābur and Humāyūn and probably had no tradition of status within the Tīmūrid polity.[73]

This typology differs from the normal division of the officers who supported Humāyūn into Turks or Chaghatays and Persians.[74] The difference exists because the ethnicity does not explain the political characteristics of the men involved. Bureaucrats from Tabriz and

[72] On the Qarāquyūnlū dynasty, see H. R. Roemer, 'The Turkmen Dynasties', in Jackson and Lockhart, *Cambridge Iran 6*, pp. 147–74. On Bayrām Khān specifically, see *Encyclopedia of Islam*, 2nd ed., s.v. Bairam Khan, by A. S. Basmee Ansari.

[73] Bayrām Khān's grandfather Yar Beg and father Sayf 'Ali Beg had served under Bābur (for Yar Beg, see B.N., 55b/91, 121/189, 308b/546) and Bayrām Khān was a close companion and then amīr of Humāyūn. See Z.K., 1:11–20; M.U., 1:371–84/368–78.

[74] As in Iqtidar Alam Khan, 'The Nobility under Akbar and the Development of His Religious Policy', *Journal of the Royal Asiatic Society* (1968), pp. 29–31.

from Andijan carried the same political tradition, even if their native languages were different.

In addition to the Chaghatays, bureaucrats and Turkmen who entered Hindustan with Humāyūn, a steady flow of immigrants from the Ṣafavī empire and the Uzbeg principalities came to Hindustan. Most were Iranian bureaucrats. Their linguistic and technical skills made them desirable recruits for Mughal service, the greater wealth of Hindustan and thus of its rulers was a substantial lure, and the unsettled political conditions of the Ṣafavī empire before the reign of Shāh 'Abbās I made emigration desirable.[75]

Turning to the groups which the Mughals encountered in Hindustan, they included the Hindu clerical castes, Rajputs, Indo-Muslim notables, and Afghans. The members of the Hindu clerical castes, like the Kayasths and Khattris, had the same political self-perceptions and expectations as the Muslim bureaucrats. Persianized in everything but religion, they participated in the same tradition of centralized administration as their Iranian counterparts.[76]

Discussing the Rajputs poses a series of difficulties. Dirk Kolff re-defines the concept of Rajput, which suggests that scholarship which does not embody his insights is no longer valid. The realization that the Rajputs formed an open status group, not a caste, does not, however, invalidate studies of the Rajput ethos and self-perception based on Rajasthani sources. Norman Ziegler has presented a dramatic new view of the relationship between the Rajputs and the Mughals, though his views have not become current among Mughal historians. Drawing on Rajput oral literature, he asserts that the Rajputs perceived Muslim

[75] Afzal Husain, 'Growth of Irani Element in Akbar's Nobility', *Proceedings of the Indian Historical Congress* 36 (1975): 166–79, gives a basic account of the immigration from Iran during Akbar's reign.

[76] For the attitudes of the members of these castes, see J. F. Richards, 'Norms of Comportment among Imperial Mughal Officers', in *Moral Conduct and Authority: the Place of Adab in South Asian Islam*, ed. Barbara Daly Metcalf (Berkeley: University of California Press, 1984), pp. 271–6; Karen Isaksen Leonard, *Social History of an Indian Caste* (Berkeley: University of California Press, 1979), pp. 12–15; Pandit Raghuvara Mitthulal Shashtri, 'A Comprehensive Study of the Origin and Status of Kayasth', *Man in India* 2 (1931): 116–89; P. V. Kane, 'The Kayastha', *New Indian Antiquary*, 1 (1929): 739–43; Yusuf Husain, 'Les Kayasthas, ou "scribes" caste hindoue iranisee, et la culture musalmane dans Inde', *Revue d'etudes Islamiques* 1 (1927): 455–8.

rulers to be of the same caste (*jati*) as themselves, but different in power and status. They saw themselves not as kings, but as kings' sons, the literal meaning of Rajput, who had lost the sovereign mastery of true Ksatriya kings. Muslim rulers sometimes filled the sovereign slot in the Rajput view of the social order, even before Akbar. The Rajput ethos required seeking attainment through service to one's master; the Muslims had become the masters. Rather than requiring hostility, the Rajput world view actually encouraged participation in Muslim polities.[77] As Kolff's account of the vicissitudes of the Purbiya Rajputs in the Khiljī and Sūrī polities shows, Muslim attitudes did not permit the Rajputs a secure position. Specifically, the ulama repeatedly forced Muslim rulers to break with Purbiya war-lords who kept Muslim women as concubines. This difficulty prevented the Rajputs from attaining a permanent and secure position under a Muslim ruler. It did not, however, prevent frequent cooperation and alliance.[78] The presence of Rajput chieftains and warriors thus did not imply implacable opposition to Muslim rule.

The category of Indo-Muslim notables covered a great variety of men. It included Muslim zamindars with considerable military power, ulama, and members of important Sufi families. Some were as strong as all but the greatest Rajputs. Others had only wealth, prestige and influence. The categories overlapped. The ancestors of Shaykh Farīd Bukharī, who received the title Murtażā Khān and was highly influential under Akbar and Jahāngīr, had lived on charitable land grants on the basis of their status as *sayyids*.[79] His great-great grandfather, Shaykh 'Abd al-Ghaffār Dihlawī, however, instructed his descendants to leave their grants and serve as soldiers.[80] The famous *sayyids* of Bārah, who were zamindars in what became the *sarkar* of Saharanpur under the Mughals and is now the Muzaffarnagar district of Uttar Pradesh, had made the transition to the status of amīr under the Sūrs.[81] These rural

[77] Norman Ziegler, 'Action, Power and Service in Rajasthani Culture: A Social History of the Rajputs of Middle Period Rajasthan', Ph.D. Dissertation, University of Chicago, 1972, pp. 73–5, 133–5, 137–43, 156, 167–74.

[78] Kolff, 'Armed', pp. 80–117.

[79] Descendants of the prophet.

[80] M.U., 2:633–41/521–27.

[81] M.T., 2:18/11. This does not contradict Abū al-Fażl's statement that Sayyid Maḥmūd was a subordinate of Bayrām Khān, A., N., 2:33/54. For comments on the sayyids of Bārah in general, see A.A., 1:424–32.

notables with Islamic credentials served under Afghan masters; we lack specific information on their perception of those masters and their own role under them. The urban notables—ulama and Sufi shaykhs—retained loyalty to the idea of Afghan rule until well into Akbar's reign.[82] Military defeat produced rapid defections of Indo-Muslim officers from Afghan rulers. Officers presumably had more to lose than did their relatives who lived on revenue grants. As peripheral members of the Afghan regimes, they presumably lacked the fixed political expectations of the groups named above. Many had territorial roots, however, and they did not identify themselves with the imperial regime as the bureaucrats did. The few Afghan officers who entered Mughal service in the first half of Akbar's reign did not differ significantly in background or expectations from the Indo-Muslims.[83]

The study of political behaviour in Hindustan before and after the Mughal period offers another way to identify the desires and objectives of the political elite. Because of the continuous constraint of an effective central power, the actions of mansabdars during the Mughal period may not reveal their desires and objectives. The predecessors and successors of the mansabdars, in the fifteenth and early sixteenth (ninth and tenth) centuries and then in the eighteenth (twelfth) century, faced fewer constraints. The broad similarity in the political patterns of these two disordered periods suggests continuity in the ambitions of the political contestants.

In his brief but seminal article on eighteenth (twelfth) century politics in the Varanasi area, Bernard S. Cohn describes four levels of political activity: the imperial, the secondary, the regional and the local. The impotent Mughals occupied the imperial level, for only they participated in politics throughout the subcontinent. Dynasties like the Nizams of Hyderabad, which developed from imperial governorships, occupied the secondary level, seeking to dominate 'major historical, cultural or linguistic regions'. Regional actors—the Rajahs of Varanasi in the case study—received their status from imperial or secondary actors and sought control of smaller areas within the secondary regions. Local actors, who were members of established lineages, adventurers, tax

[82] Iqtidar Husain Siddiqui, *Mughal Relations with the Indian Ruling Elite* (New Delhi: Munshiram Manoharlal, 1983), pp. 67–8, 101–4.

[83] M. Athar Ali, *The Apparatus of Empire: Awards of Ranks, Offices, and Titles to the Mughal Nobility, 1574–1658* (Delhi: Oxford University Press, 1985), pp. 1–11.

collectors with political aspirations, or indigenous chiefs, derived their authority from secondary and regional actors and had direct control over the local peasants, merchants, and artisans, from whom they collected revenue.[84] On each level, the actors sought increased freedom of action and greater security. They tried to reduce the importance of lower level actors and to decrease their own dependence on higher level actors.[85]

Stewart Gordon describes one regional polity, the principality of Bhopal. Its founder, Dūst Muḥammad Khān, established his power by subordinating a series of Rajput zamindars in eastern Malwa, first as a Mughal officer and then on his own account, beginning in 1709 (1121). In 1723 (1135), Niẓām al-Mulk, who later founded the principality of Hyderabad, defeated Dūst Muḥammad Khān and forced him to accept a Mughal mansab, pay *pīshkash*, and surrender his strongest fort. When Dūst Muḥammad Khān died in 1728 (1140), Niẓam al-Mulk, now acting as the ruler of Hyderabad, determined which of his sons succeeded him. Dūst Muḥammad Khān tried to make himself an autonomous regional ruler, but Niẓām al-Mulk forced him to accept a dependent position, within the Mughal empire and then within the principality of Hyderabad.[86]

The applications of Cohn's categories reveal a series of secondary and regional polities in the century and a half before Akbar's reign. Vijaynagar, the Bahmani Sultanate in the Deccan and the Sultanate of Bengal became independent of Delhi even before the death of Muḥammad ibn Tughluk in 1351 (752). Independent dynasties appeared in Gujarat, Malwa, and Jaunpur before Tīmūr's invasion of Hindustan in 1398 (801). These provincial dynasties occupied the secondary level of politics. Smaller principalities, like those of Samana, Bayana, and Kalpi, occupied the regional level. The Sayyid and Ludī dynasties which ruled Delhi from 1398 (801) to 1526 (932) did not differ from their contemporaries in other provinces except for the prestige of ruling Delhi.[87]

[84] Cohn, 'Political Systems', pp. 312–14.

[85] Ibid., pp. 313–20. Muzaffar Alam, *The Crisis of Empire in Mughal North India: Awadh and the Punjab, 1707–48* (Delhi: Oxford University Press, 1986), pp. 20–133 discusses the development of Awadh as an autonomous province.

[86] Stewart Gordon, 'Legitimacy and Loyalty in Some Successor States in the Eighteenth Century', in *Kingship*, ed. Richards, pp. 286–92.

[87] This analysis is my own. The best summary is Husain, *Indo-Muslim*, pp. 168–86.

This brief summary suggests that, whatever their differences, political contenders—for that is what imperial officers were or would have been in periods of central weakness—sought a secure geographic and political position. This desire clashed directly with the idea of officers as extensions of a bureaucratic regime, without individual power. The Mughal political compromise had to bridge this gap.

2.3.3 GEOGRAPHY

Geographic circumstances affected the development of the Mughal polity. There was no fixed territorial element to either Islamic or Indian doctrines of kingship beyond that of centre and periphery. For nearly four hundred years, Delhi had been the centre of Muslim life in Hindustan. Sulṭān Sikandar Ludī's construction of a new capital in Agra in 1505 (910) did not alter this perception.[88] Delhi remained the chief Muslim city of Hindustan. Bābur refers to it as the capital (*bā-yi takht*) of Hindustan and possession of it indicated sovereignty during the struggle of Humāyūn and Mirzā Kāmrān in India.[89] No dominant dynasty had ruled from Delhi for almost two centuries, but the reputation of the city remained intact. It was still the cultural and social centre of Muslim life in Hindustan.

From another perspective, the Indo-Gangetic plain formed the centre of Hindustan. It was the great agricultural region for growing grain and rice, and the only part of the subcontinent with navigable rivers. The lack of geographic obstacles other than the rivers made political boundaries fluid. Autonomous dynasties normally ruled Bengal in the east and Sind in the west. Beyond these extremes, the central government of the plain generally ruled where the land was flat and cultivated. The hills north of the plains and the areas which remained forested were less amenable to distant authority. Since they produced little agricultural

[88] Sir Wolseley Haig, 'The Lodi Dynasty', in *The Cambridge History of India Volume 3: Turks and Afghans*, ed. Sir Wolseley Haig (Cambridge: Cambridge University Press, 1928; reprint ed., New Delhi: S. Chand, 1958), p. 242. Unfortunately, Iqtidar Husain Siddiqui, *Some Aspects of Afghan Despotism in India* (Aligarh: Three Men Press, 1969) does not address this issue.

[89] *Bābur-nāma*, f. 261v/463; Gulbadan Begum, *Humāyūn-nāmāh*, facsimile ed. Annette Susannah Beveridge, trans. as *The History of Humayun* by Annette Susannah Beveridge (London: Royal Asiatic Society, 1902; reprint ed., New Delhi: Oriental Books Reprint, 1983), p. 20/117, 42/137.

revenue, they were also of less value. The Indo-Gangetic plain itself was the venue for super-regional polities in northern India. The rough terrain surrounding it produced lasting local polities, predominantly Rajput. The geographic setting thus determined the political pattern which the Mughals encountered.

2.4 Conclusions

The precedents which Akbar inherited and circumstances which he confronted determined the pattern of conflict in his region. Transplanting the Mughal polity to Hindustan brought the basic conflict between tribal amīrs and bureaucrats, which is a more accurate way of describing the conflict between Turk and Tājīk, to the subcontinent. The Rajputs and Indo-Muslims with specific geographic ties opposed the agenda of imperial centralization as the Chaghatays did, but not to the same degree. The resistance of the ulama to the inclusion of Rajputs in a Muslim regime had been a persistent element of politics before the return of the Tīmūrids and was thus another problem which Akbar had to face.

CHAPTER 3
The Process of Expansion

The expansion and political transformation of the Mughal empire proceeded together. Separation of the two processes has only heuristic validity, but the complexity of the overlapping developments makes dividing them useful. The discussion of expansion has three parts: an analysis of the nature and limitations of Mughal military superiority and its political consequences, comments on the nature of the Mughal regime in the provinces, and a review of Mughal expansion from 1556 (963) to 1582 (990). It includes evaluation of the gunpowder empires hypothesis.

3.1 Mughal Military Superiority and Its Significance

The overall pattern of military activity reveals as much about the military environment as accounts of specific battles and sieges. A European parallel shows how. During the Hundred Years War, the English repeatedly showed their ability to defeat the French in field battles. For this reason, few battles occurred. The English advantage in the field did not end the war because their victories merely permitted them to conduct long and difficult sieges. The defenders of towns had great advantages over besiegers and the French concentrated on defending their cities because they had no alternative.[1]

[1] Sir Charles Oman, *The Art of War in the Middle Ages*, 2 vols. (Boston: Houghton Mifflin, n.d.; reprint ed., New York: Burt Franklin, 1959), 1:52, 2:148, 196.

3.1.1 AKBAR'S BATTLES

A similar paucity of battles marks Mughal history. Only three famous encounters pitted Mughal rulers with all their strength against enemies of the dynasty. The two victories at Panipat, Bābur over Ibrāhīm Ludī in 1526 (932) and Bayrām Khān over Hīmū in 1556 (964) and Bābur's defeat of Rānā Sangā at Khanwa in 1527 (933) established Mughal supremacy in the field. Shīr Shāh's victories over Humāyūn at Chausa and Bilgram demonstrate that his stratagems permitted him to evade Mughal superiority, not that he overcame it. None of the encounters on Humāyūn's return amounted to a major engagement because of the division of his opponents. The two remaining battles of Akbar's time which have received considerable attention, Tukaroi in 1575 (982) and Haldighati in 1576 (984), were provincial rather than imperial encounters. Akbar was present on neither field. The Mughals had shown superiority in battle; that reality remained the dominant military fact in the subcontinent well into the eighteenth century.

Mughal superiority in the field rested on firearms, but only partly so. At the first battle of Panipat and at Khanwa, Bābur used the same tactics as the Ottomans used against the Ṣafavīs at Chaldiran in 1514 (920) and against the Hungarians at Mohacs in 1526 (932), and that the Ṣafavīs used against the Uzbegs at Jām in 1528 (935).[2] He had an Ottoman gunner, Ustād 'Alī Qulī, in charge of his deployment. Ustād 'Alī Qulī arranged a row of carts, joined by ropes of rawhide, across the Mughal centre. The artillery and infantry sheltered behind this barrier. This technique was known in Turkish as *ṭābūr jangī*. At Panipat, the guns in the centre and the mounted archers on the wings, who attacked the flanks of the Afghan army, delivered heavy blows to Ibrāhīm Ludī's force. Khanwa followed much the same pattern.[3]

[2] On Chaldiran and Moḥacs, see V. J. Parry, 'The Reigns of Bayazid II and Selim I, 1481–1520', and 'The Reign of Sulayman the Magnificent, 1520–66', *A History of the Ottoman Empire to 1730*, ed. M. A. Cook (Cambridge: Cambridge University Press, 1976), pp. 70, 81–2. On Jām, see H. R. Roemer, 'The Safavid Period', in *The Cambridge History of Iran, Volume 6: the Timurid and Safavid Periods*, ed. Peter Jackson and Lawrence Lockhart (Cambridge: Cambridge University Press, 1986), p. 236; Martin B. Dickson, 'Shah Tahmasb and the Uzbeks' (Ph.D. dissertation, Princeton University, 1958), pp. 127–39.

[3] The basic account is of course Bābur's own, Ẓahir al-Dīn Muḥammad Bābur

The second Panipat did not conform. Before the main engagement began, the Mughal advance guard captured Hīmū's artillery. On the field itself, Hīmū relied on an elephant charge to defeat the Mughals by shock action. The Mughals did not employ a *ṭābūr jangī* and apparently had no guns. They withdrew before the weight of the elephants but used their capabilities as mounted archers to attack them on the flanks and spray them with arrows. The Mughal centre retreated behind a ravine which the elephants could not cross and relied upon archery as well. The Afghan forces and their Hindu commander fought hard, and made the outcome uncertain for some time, but to assert that the Mughals triumphed only because Hīmū was wounded and captured is an exaggeration.[4]

The combination of artillery and mounted archers gave the Mughals superiority in battle. The role of archers deserves special attention. Even in the seventeenth century, expert mounted archers provided more firepower than infantrymen with matchlocks or firelocks. Bernier writes in his account of Samugarh: 'It cannot be denied that the cavalry of this country manoeuvre with much ease and discharge their arrows with astonishing quickness; a horseman shooting six times before a musketeer can fire twice.'[5] Writing of the Ottoman bow, which was similar to the Mughal weapon, John Francis Guilmartin writes that 'the Turkish bow of the sixteenth century was capable of delivering a higher volume of accurate and effective fire at longer ranges than any competing weapon.' The smoothbore musket had an accurate range of

---

Pādishāh Ghazī, *Bābur-Nāma*, facsimile ed. Annette Susannah Beveridge. Gibb Memorial Series no. 1. (London: E. J. W. Gibb Memorial Trust, 1905; reprint ed. 1971), trans. Annette Susannah Beveridge, 2 vols. (London: By the Author, 1921; reprint ed., 2 vols. as 1: New Delhi: Oriental Books Reprint, 1979), ff. 264–267r, 318r–324r/ pp. 468–75, 563–74. Secondary accounts include Paul Horn, *Das Heer-und Kriegswesen der Grossmoghuls* (Leiden: E. J. Brill, 1894), pp. 71–6, and Raj Kumar Phul, *Armies of the Great Mughals* (New Delhi: Oriental Publishers and Distributors, 1978), pp. 271–7 (Panipat only).

[4] A.N., 2:35–41/58–65; M.T., 2:14–17/7–9; T.A., 2:131–2; A. L. Srivastava, *Akbar the Great*, 2nd. ed., 3 vols. (Agra: Shiva Lal Agarwala, 1972 *Akbar*, 1:24–6); Sir Jadunath Sarkar, *Military History of India* (Bombay: Orient Longman, 1960), pp. 65–9.

[5] François Bernier, *Travels in the Mughal Empire*, trans. Archibald Constable, rev. Vincent Smith (London: Oxford University Press, 1934; reprint ed., New Delhi: Oriental Books Reprint, 1983), p. 48.

less than one hundred yards, even in the nineteenth century; the best estimate for the bow, in the hands of an expert, suggests twenty-five per cent accuracy against a man on horseback at 280 yards on a calm day. Both weapons could penetrate armour at a hundred yards, but the musket's effective range of five hundred yards against unprotected targets slightly exceeded that of the bow. Guilmartin's estimate of six aimed shots per minute for a fresh, trained archer resembles Bernier's. In addition to the advantage of their bows as missile weapons, mounted archers had greater strategic and tactical mobility than any infantry and could deliver a decisive charge with sword and spear. Armies of mounted archers had only one great disadvantage: only an expert could be an effective archer on horseback.[6] The Turk and Mongol nomads of central Asia learned to ride and use the bow in early childhood; the mounted archers of the Ottoman and Mughal armies were professional soldiers who learned the trade from their male relatives.[7] Like the Ottoman *sipāhī* army, the Mughal army of mounted archers was a fixed asset, not easily replaced, but it would have been even more difficult for one of the Mughal's rivals in the subcontinent to raise a substantial force of mounted archers from scratch.[8] In the subcontinent, war horses were as rare as mounted archers.

In his *War Horse and Elephant*, Simon Digby attributes the military superiority of the Delhi sultanate to an effective monopoly on reliable supplies of war horses and elephants. In the Indo-Gangetic plain, the Deccan and south India, climatic and other conditions made it impossible to raise horses comparable to steeds imported from Iran,

[6] John Francis Guilmartin, Jr., *Gunpowder and Galleys*, Cambridge Studies in Early Modern History (Cambridge: Cambridge University Press, 1974), pp. 146–56; see also Thomas Esper, 'The Replacement of the Longbow by Firearms in the English Army', *Technology and Culture* 61 (1965): 382–93.

[7] On the Ottoman *sipāhīs*, see Klaus Rohrborn, *Untersuchung zur Osmanischedn Verwaltungsgeschichte*, Studien zur Sprache, Geschichte, und Kultur des Islamichen Orients n.s. 5 (Berlin: Walter de Gruyter, 1973), pp. 29–34; Halil Inalcik, *The Ottoman Empire: the Classical Age*, trans. Norman Itzkowitz and Colin Imber (London: Weidenfeld and Nicholson, 1973), p. 114. On the Mughal forces, see R. A. Alavi, 'New Light on Mughal Cavalry', *Medieval India: A Miscellany* 2 (1972): 70–99, reprinted in his *Studies in the History of the Medieval Deccan* (New Delhi: Idarah-i Adabiyat Delli, 1977).

[8] On the Ottoman army, see Guilmartin, *Gunpowder*, pp. 251–2, 272–3.

central Asia, or Arabia, or to horses from the northeast and northwest of the subcontinent.[9] Once established in Gujarat and Bengal, the Mughals controlled the local war horse sources and the land routes and the most important ports for the horse trade. Their opponents in the subcontinent lacked access to the horses, as well as to the troopers, necessary to create an army of mounted archers capable of challenging the Mughals in the field.

The Mughal reliance on battlefield artillery and mounted archers transformed the tactical system of Indian warfare. Digby contends that under the Delhi sulṭāns elephants, not horses, formed the core of the army. The size of the empire reflected the size of the elephant stable.[10] The situation changed radically in Akbar's time. His forces defeated major opponents who relied on elephant charges.[11] Akbar did use large numbers of elephants in some early campaigns. The last expedition against Khān-i Zamān 'Alī Qulī Khān in 1567 (974) included some 2000 war elephants, which were useful in fording the Ganges and in battle. Elephants led the storming of Chitor in 1568 (975) and served prominently on both sides at Haldighati. Abū al-Fażl describes the imperial elephant stable at length.[12] Jahāngīr reportedly maintained twelve thousand elephants. But elephants became less important in battle. In the war among Shāh Jahān's sons they served primarily as command vehicles, not shock weapons. The sources do not give an unambiguous explanation, but Horn, Irvine and Phul agree that elephants became less valuable and more vulnerable as the number of firearms increased.[13] Mughal mounted archers, though not a new development, contributed to this major change. John Francis Guilmartin contends that the proliferation of cast-iron cannon ended the domination of a system of naval warfare based on galleys in the Mediterranean

[9] Simon Digby, *War Horse and Elephant in the Delhi Sultanate* (Oxford: Oxford Monographs, 1971), pp. 23–54.

[10] Ibid., pp. 50–82.

[11] In addition to the second Panipat, Mu'nim Khān Khān-i Khānān's victory over Dā'ūd Kararāni at Tukaroi involved the defeat of an elephant charge. A.N., 3:122–6/174–9; T.A. 2:305–7; M.T., 2:194–6/196–8.

[12] A.A., 1:127–39/123–39, 685.

[13] Horn, *Heer*, pp. 51–4; William Irvine, *The Army of the Indian Moghuls* (London, 1903; reprint ed., New Delhi: Eurasia, 1962), p. 177; Phul, *Armies*, pp. 64–6.

in the sixteenth (tenth) century.[14] The Mughal combination of artillery and mounted archers ended the elephant-based system of warfare in India.

The Mughals established military superiority in the field early in Akbar's reign. They came to assume their ability to win battles; most of their opponents also assumed the probability of losing them. Before besieging Chitor in 1567 (975), Akbar sought to lure Rānā Udai Singh of Mewar into battle. He entered Mewar with only a small force, hoping the Rānā would leave the mountains and attack him so that the Mughals could win an easy victory in battle. Udai Singh did not take the bait, but prepared Chitor to face a siege.[15] Akbar thus assumed that he could defeat a larger enemy army; Udai Singh assumed that he could not defeat a smaller Mughal force. Dā'ūd Khān Kararānī and Udai Singh's son Rānā Pratap did not make similar calculations, but, to judge from the results, should have.

The battle of Tukaroi resembles the second Panipat in that the Afghans relied on an elephant charge. They broke the Mughal centre, actually drove Mun'im Khān from the field, and plundered his camp. The Mughal wings held, however, and the centre rallied and engaged the Afghans with arrows. Eventually, Dā'ūd Khān's army broke and fled.[16] The narrow margin of victory at the second Panipat and at Tukaroi does not call into question the change in dominant military system; it merely shows that the Mughals needed the combination of artillery and mounted archers to win easy victories.

Haldighati falls in a different category. It involved not a major Mughal army but a small detachment under Kunwar Mān Singh, who had not yet succeeded to the throne of Amber. The engagement meant nothing. Because Rānā Pratap survived, the Mughal victory did not end Sisodia resistance to the Mughals. Had Rānā Pratap defeated Mān Singh, a

[14] Guilmartin, *Gunpowder*, p. 175, 263.

[15] A.N., 3:314/464. Abū al-Fazl is explicit: *bijunūd-i ma 'navī iktifā' namūdah pīshtar nazhat farmūd ki shayād rānā kamī-yi 'asākir iqbal shanīdah az shi 'āb-i jibal bīrūn āyad wa kār-i u bi' āsānī sāktah*.

[16] M.T., 2:194–96/196–98; A.N., 3:122–26/174–79; T.A., 2:305–7; T.H.W.A., p. 342-4; Sarkar, *Military*, pp. 70–4; Iqtidar Alam Khan, *The Political Biography of a Mughal Noble: Mun'im Khan Khan-i Khanan, 1497–1575* (New Delhi: Orient Longman, 1973), pp. 142–3.

larger Mughal punitive expedition would have driven him back into the hills or defeated him far more thoroughly than his fellow Rajput did. Pratap commanded some three thousand Rajput and Afghan horsemen, supported by a few Bhil archers.[17] Mān Singh had some four thousand troopers from his own principality, a thousand other Rajputs, and five thousand Muslim troops. The Muslims were mostly Indo-Muslims commanded by the *sayyids* of Bārah, but included some Mughals as well. Both sides had some elephants, neither had artillery, but the imperial force included some musketeers. The battle itself pitted the shock of a Sisodia cavalry and elephant charge, against imperial forces employing a combination of fire and shock. Both sides fought hard, but the Mughal archers and gunners turned the tide, killing the elephant drivers controlling the heart of the Sisodia advance. The outcome of the battle reinforced the image of Mughal superiority.[18]

The victories of Akbar's reign confirmed the Mughal dominance of the battlefield which Bābur had established. He succeeded in sieges as well, but with greater difficulty and at greater cost.

3.1.2 AKBAR'S SIEGES

The Mughals established their ability to take major fortresses with the conquests of Chitor, Ranthambor and Kalinjar in 1568–9 (976–7).

Akbar's victory at Chitor was the first Mughal success against a major fortress and the only instance of conquest of a major fortress by storm in Mughal history. A fortified city rather than a citadel, Chitor was the capital of Mewar, the Sisodia Rajput principality which Rānā Sangā had ruled. Akbar probably hoped that a victory over the current Rānā,

[17] None of the sources discloses how the Afghan amīr Hakīm Khān Sūr came to fight under Rānā Pratap. Presumably he was a member of the Sūr ruling family.

[18] G. N. Sharma, *Mewar and the Mughal Emperors* (Agra: Shiva Lal Agarwala, 1954), pp. 97–107 and Srivastava, *Akbar*, 1:188–97, are convenient secondary accounts of Halidghati, but suffer from a Rajput bias. James Tod, *Annals and Antiquities of Rajasthan*, 2 vols., with a foreword by Douglas Sladen (London: George Routledge and Sons, 1914; reprint ed. New Delhi: M. N. Publishers, 1978), 1:268–70 gives a confused account from the Rajput bardic tradition; he states for example that Salim was present at the battle. The references in the Mughal sources are A.N., 3:173–6/244–7; T.A., 2:323; T.M., 2:230–4/236–41. Bada'ūnī participated in the battle. Sarkar, *Military*, pp. 75–83 gives a useful account.

Udai Singh, would lead to the submission of all the Rajput principalities. Although it had twice fallen to Muslim armies, Chitor was reputedly the greatest fortress of Hindustan. It stands on a ridge three miles long, twelve hundred yards wide, and four hundred feet above the surrounding plain. The sides of the ridge are quite steep; the walls of the fortress follow its perimeter. Sixteenth century siege artillery had an optimum range of sixty yards so guns could not be used against the walls unless they were emplaced on the slope.[19] The main entrance way zigzags up the hillside through seven gates.[20]

Akbar began operations against Chitor in the autumn of 1567 (975), with the appointment of Āṣaf Khān Harawī as jagirdar of Bayana, the nearest Mughal territory to Chitor, with instructions to prepare for the arrival of the imperial army.[21] The Mughals occupied two small forts, Suisupur, 150 miles northeast of Chitor, and Mandalgarh, 40 miles northeast of Chitor.[22] As mentioned above, Akbar advanced with a small force in the hope of enticing Udai Singh into battle, but the Rānā, knowing that the Mughals were short of siege equipment (*asbāb-i qal'ah-gīrī*), prepared Chitor for a siege instead. He left a garrison of 5000 Rajputs with enough provisions for several years and destroyed crops in the surrounding areas before withdrawing into the hills himself. Akbar established a camp outside Chitor on 20 October 1567 (14 Rabī' II 975). The siege began with the construction of lines of circumvallation. The imperial surveyors mapped the area and the *bakhshīs* established sites for siegeworks surrounding the ridge. It took a month to complete the investment.[23] Meanwhile, Akbar sent Āṣaf

[19]Guilmartin, *Gunpowder*, p. 164.

[20]For descriptions of Chitor, see Sharma, *Mewar*, pp. 70–71; T.A., 2:216; M.U., 1:83/40; Tod, *Annals*, 2:604–13. I visited Chitor as an American Institute of Indian Studies Fellow in 1983.

[21]T.A., 2:214–15. On Āṣaf Khān, see M.U., 1:77–83/36–40.

[22]T.A., 2:215; A.N., 2:302–3/443–4.

[23]A.N., 2:314/465. I translate *murchal* as lines of circumvallation, or field fortifications, not a battery. The point is important because the Mughals did not surround Chitor with guns. I chose my translation after consulting F. Steingass, *A Comprehensive Persian-English Dictionary* (London: Routledge, 1892; reprint ed., New Delhi: Oriental Books Reprint, 1973); Irvine, *Army*, p. 271; Horn, *Heer*, p. 103, 121; Duffy, *Siege*, p. 229; and Gerhard Doerfer, *Turkische und Mongolische Elemente im Neupersichen*, 4 vols., Akademie der Wissenschaften under der Literatur Veroffentlichungen der Orientalischen Kommision, vols. 17, Akademie der Wissenschaften under der

Khān to take Rampur, sixty miles southeast of Chitor, and Ḥusayn Qulī Khān (later Khān-i Jahān) in pursuit of the Rānā, who had fled towards Udaipur and Kumbhalmir. Ḥusayn Qulī Khān took Udaipur, defeated the Sisodia forces wherever he encountered them, and took much booty, but failed to capture Udai Singh.[24]

After the completion of the siegeworks, the Mughal forces began attacks on the walls. Abū al-Fażl states that the Mughals tried to storm the fort because of their high spirits, even though it was impossible to succeed, but A. L. Srivastava contends that Akbar had real hopes for their efforts.[25] I believe that Akbar probably knew he could not take Chitor by *coup de main* but had every incentive to try anyway, in the hope of avoiding a long siege.[26] The extemporaneous attacks had no effect and suffered heavy casualties from the archers and musketeers on the walls. Akbar then ordered the excavation of two mines and a *sābāṭ* (approach trench). To avoid the delay of sending for heavy siege guns from Delhi or Agra, he also ordered the casting of a twenty-five pounder gun in the camp.[27] When the garrison heard of the casting of a gun, they realized they could not hold the fort and opened negotiations. They sent one Sandā Silāhdār and later a Muslim officer named Ṣāḥib Khān, to the imperial camp and offered to submit to Akbar and

---

Literatur Veroffentlichungen der Orientalischen Kommision, vols. 16, 19–21 (Wiesbaden: Franz Steiner Verlag, 1963–1975), 1:229–32.

[24] A.N., 2:314–15/465; T.A., 2:216. On Ḥusayn Qulī Khān see M.U., 1:645–53/645–49.

[25] A.N., 2:315–466; Srivastava, *Akbar*, 1:107.

[26] Though a work of fiction, C. S. Forester, *Commodore Hornblower* (Boston: Little, Brown, 1942), pp. 275–6, gives an excellent example of this type of reasoning.

[27] A.N., 2:315–6/466–7; T.A., 2:216–17. For the weight conversion, see Irfan Habib, *The Agrarian System of Mughal India* (Bombay: Asia, 1963), pp. 366–7. I translate Abū al-Fażl's *dīg* as gun, not mortar, in opposition to Beveridge, Horn (*Heer*, p. 29), and Steingass, *Comprehensive*. *Dīg* originally meant pot, suggesting a high trajectory, large-bore weapon, but that does not make sense in context. Bābur mentions the casting of a *dīg* for use against a fort which was later used effectively against Rānā Sangā at Khanua and the Bengali army at Gogra. Mortars were not battlefield weapons in the sixteenth century and a single mortar, firing shot, would not have been a serious threat to the garrison of a large fort like Chitor. Also, a mortar would not have required an approach trench to fire at Chitor; a low trajectory gun would have. *Dīg* must have meant a low trajectory gun for breaching walls, not a mortar for shooting over them. *Dīg* may have meant a gun cast on site.

pay *pīshkash*. Several of Akbar's officers wished to accept the offer and end the exigencies of the siege, but Akbar disagreed and demanded the submission of the Rānā. The negotiations failed.[28]

After the negotiations failed, the fighting became more intense. Nearly two hundred men were killed every day in the construction of the *sābāṭ* alone. The description of the *sābāṭ* in the sources is confusing. It was either a trench or a covered passage above ground. G. N. Sharma argues that it must have been the latter because the nature of the soil made digging a trench impossible, but if the Mughals could mine they could trench.[29] The *sābāṭ* probably was a trench, with the excavated soil forming walls above ground level. It began beyond gun or bow range of the fortress, was wide enough for ten men to ride abreast, and deep enough to protect a man on an elephant. To sustain the morale of the sappers Akbar distributed large amounts of cash to them. But the miners reached the walls of Chitor first. They placed two large charges under the wall, one of roughly three tons, one of two tons. The miners exploded the charges on 17 December 1567 (15 Jumādā II 975), fifty-eight days after the siege had commenced and about four weeks after the completion of the lines of circumvallation. Both fuses were lit at the same time, but were of different lengths. The first charge destroyed a tower on the walls and made a large breach. Mughal troops charged into it and were immolated in the second explosion; they suffered two hundred casualties and the garrison forty. A third mine failed to make a breach.[30]

These failures encouraged the garrison, but Abū al-Fażl reports that Akbar had understood that a long siege was inevitable and counted on the *sābāṭ* to produce a lasting breach. The famous Rājah Tūdar Mal and

[28] A.N., 2:316–17. T.A. mentions neither the casting of the gun nor the negotiations, but states that the purpose of the *sābāt* was to bring artillery within range of the wall: *bidavar-i qal 'ah rasānīdah dīvar-i qal 'ah bizarb-i tūp mīyandāzand wa jawānān-i mardānah azan rakhnah dar qal 'ah midarāyand*. Regarding the attitude of the Mughal officers, Abū al-Faẓl writes, *buzargān urdu-yi mu 'alā az taraddud-i da' mī bitang amadah dar bar khāstan azīn mahalakah kūshish namūdand*.

[29] Sharma, *Mewar*, pp. 72–3.

[30] A.N., 2:316–18/467/9; T.A., 2:216–18. Beveridge's translation of *burj* as bastion rather than tower is anachronistic.

Qāsim Khān Mīr-i Bahr supervised its construction.[31] On 28 February 1568 (29 Sha'bān 975), the Mughals made a breach at the *sābāṭ*. Jaymal, the Rajput officer whom Udai Singh had left in charge of Chitor, came forward to direct the defence of the breach and attempts to repair it. Akbar, who had previously acted as a sharpshooter, identified Jaymal as an important officer by his cuirass and shot and killed him. Jaymal's death destroyed the garrison's morale.[32] Within an hour, the besiegers observed fires in several places inside the fort. Rājah Bhagwan Dās identified them as the flames of *jawhar*, the ritual burning by the Rajput warriors of their families to save them from dishonour in defeat.[33] Although the garrison had actually withdrawn from the breach, Akbar ordered an assault for the next day. The Mughals used three hundred elephants in the charge; the Sisodia defenders sought and found death in battle. The eight thousand members of the garrison perished; Akbar also ordered the execution or imprisonment of some thirty thousand peasants who had allegedly participated actively in the defence. Abū al-Fażl reports that the Mughals took very few casualties and only a few Rajput musketeers escaped.[34]

The Mughal conquest of Ranthambor came less than a year after Chitor; 130 miles southwest of Agra and 75 miles southeast of modern Jaipur, it was closer to the Mughal centre of power but less important than Chitor as a fortress and political focus. Unlike Chitor, Ranthambor is located in rough terrain, with a hill called Ran overlooking the fort. Surjan Hādā, the ruler of the Rajput principality of Bundi, held the fort in the capacity of a subordinate of the Rānā.[35] Ranthambor was thus effectively the capital of a principality, an obstacle to operations

[31] On Rājah Tūdar Mal, see M.U., 2:123–9; 951–7; on Qāsim Khān, M.U., 3:62–66/ 2:511–14.

[32] A.N., 2:318–20/T.A., 2:318. Tod, *Annals* 1:261–2, does not concede that it was Akbar who killed Jaymal.

[33] For traditional comments on *jawhar*, see Tod, *Annals*, 1:215–49. For a modern analysis, see Kolff, 'Armed', pp. 7–8, 112–17, 204.

[34] A.N., 2:320–4/472–6; T.A., 2-218–19. Bada'ūnī's account of the siege, M.T., 2:102–5/105–7, does not add to Abū al-Fażl and Nizām al-Dīn. For recent secondary accounts, see Srivastava, *Akbar*, 1:104–10; Ishtiaq Husain Qureshi, *Akbar* (Karachi: Ma'aref, 1978), pp. 71–3.

[35] Tod, *Annals*, 2:381–2.

against Mewar, and a prestigious fortress. Akbar sent an expedition under Ashraf Khān against Ranthambor in April 1568 (Shawwāl 974), but recalled it because Ibrāhīm Ḥusayn Mirzā and Muḥammad Ḥusayn Mirzā renewed their revolt.[36]

Akbar led a second expedition himself, leaving Agra on 21 December 1568 (2 Rajab 976) and reaching Ranthambor on 10 February 1569 (23 Sha'bān 976). Surjan prepared to defend the fort. As at Chitor, the siege began with a survey of the ground, the preparation of lines of circumvallation and the complete investment of the fortress. Heavy fighting began with the completion of the investment. In March (Ramażān), Akbar decided that the fort could not be taken without the construction of a *sābāṭ*, so Qāsim Khān and Rājah Tūdar Mal were again put in charge of construction. Apparently the *sābāṭ* permitted the Mughal forces to bring fifteen heavy guns to the top of the hill. Called *ẓarb-zan*, the weapons fired balls weighing three hundred pounds. They required four hundred oxen each to pull them, and seven hundred labourers worked on emplacing them. Presumably the guns were brought from Delhi or Agra because there is no mention of casting them below Ranthambor. Once the Mughals had the guns in place, they swiftly breached the walls and damaged building inside them.[37]

After the guns had opened a breach, Surjan opened negotiations, sending his sons to submit to Akbar. They obtained an audience through the intervention of Rājah Bhagwan Dās and his son Mān Singh, performed the *sijdah*, received robes of honour and were sent back to their father.[38] When his sons returned, Surjan requested that a high officer be sent to reassure him and conduct him to court. Akbar sent Ḥusayn Qulī Khān, who brought him to Akbar on 22 March 1569 (4 Shawwāl 976). Akbar agreed to his request to remain in the fort

[36] A.N., 2:329–30/484; T.A. 2:221–2. I discuss the rebel Mirzās in the next chapter. On Ashraf Khān, see M.U., 1:73–5/301–2.

[37] A.N., 2:333–5, 336–7/489–91, 493–4; T.A., 2:224; M.T., 2:107/110–11. David James, *Islamic Art: An Introduction* (London: Hamlyn, 1974), p. 11, reproduces a miniature from an *Akbar-nāmah* in the Victoria and Albert Museum showing the emplacement of guns against Ranthambor.

[38] The Mughal chronicles do not mention Bhagwan Dās and his son as intermediaries. Bada'ūnī (M.T., 2:107/111) states only that the intercessors were zamindars. Tod (*Annals*, 2:382) names Bhagwan Dās and Mān Singh; I am following him. The mention of *sijdah* may be an anachronism.

three days before joining Akbar's entourage. Surjan left his sons as hostages and carried out his part of the agreement.[39] Tod gives details of the agreement between Surjan and Akbar and of Surjan's career in Mughal service. The treaty made the Hādās, as rulers of Bundi, subordinates of the Mughals but immune from the *jizyah*, which had not yet been eliminated, and from *dāgh* and gave them certain other privileges.[40]

Kalinjar represented a less important obstacle, though Shīr Shāh Sūr had died in the course of besieging it. Located in modern Uttar Pradesh, ninety-five miles southwest of Allahabad, it was the possession of Rājah Rām Chand, the ruler of the principality of Bhath or Pannah. He had already submitted to Akbar as the ruler of Pannah, but did not have permission to hold Kalinjar.[41] The fortress is located on a flat hill, eight hundred feet above the surrounding plain; Rām Chand had purchased it in the Sūrī period. When Akbar departed for Ranthambor, he ordered Majnūn Khān Qāqshāl, Shāham Khān Jalayir, and other officers with jāgīrs near Kalinjar to take the fort.[42] When Rām Chand heard of the fall of Chitor and Ranthambor, he decided to submit, surrendered the fort to the imperial forces, and sent the keys and suitable *pīshkash* to Akbar on 11 August 1569 (26 Ṣafar 977). Akbar accepted his submission, and granted him a jāgīr at Arail in Allahabad province in addition to his principality.[43]

The accounts of these three sieges do not support the gunpowder empires hypothesis as Hodgson and McNeill state it. The Mughals could take the strongest forts in Hindustan, but only through difficult and prolonged sieges. Gunpowder, whether propelling balls or exploding in a mine, did permit them to breach the walls of fortresses, but the available weapons hardly nullified Chitor and Ranthambor. The Mughal conquest of Hindustan was not a blitzkrieg. As Habib asserts, Mughal superiority in the field outweighed their ability to take for-

[39] A.N., 2:337–9/494–6; M.T., 1:107–9/111–12; T.A., 2:224. For secondary accounts, see Srivastava, *Akbar*, 1:113–15; Qureshi, *Akbar*, pp. 73–4.

[40] Tod, *Annals*, 2:384–85.

[41] I discuss Rām Chand's submission on pp. 73–4.

[42] On Majnun Khān, see M.U., 3:207–11/38–41. On Shahām Khān, M.U., 2:603–5/728–9.

[43] A.N., 2:340–1/498–9: T.A., 2:225–6; M.T., 2:120/124; Srivastava, *Akbar*, 1:115; Qureshi, *Akbar*, p. 73.

tresses. Once in place, guns could breach the walls of Chitor and Ranthambor, but the surroundings of the fortresses made deploying them difficult and time-consuming. It took so long and maintaining a siege was so difficult, that the defenders had reason to hope that the siege would end before the walls were breached. In most cases, Clausewitz's dictum that 'time which is allowed to pass unused accumulates to the credit of the defender' does not apply in sieges, but it did in the Mughal empire.[44]

As McNeill asserts, the long overland supply line made maintaining sieges difficult. The problem of dragging guns overland prevented Akbar from bringing any to Chitor. The experience there most likely caused him to transport guns, with great difficulty, from Agra to Ranthambor. The Mughal army travelled less than three miles a day on that journey, probably because of the weight of the guns. But the Mughals had to transport food and fodder as well. In the sixteenth century, it was difficult to transport grain—for horses or their riders—in bulk, except by water.[45] Āṣaf Khān's preparations for the passage of the imperial army involved the collection of provisions. Udai Singh scorched the earth around Chitor to make foraging more difficult for Akbar's men; Ḥusayn Qulī Khān plundered the rest of Mewar to deprive the Rānā of agricultural revenue and food for his army and to add to imperial stocks. The tight circumstances of the mansabdars who wished to accept a negotiated settlement at Chitor probably involved shortages of provisions, and, because of the costliness of those provisions, of money. Akbar's force had to take Mandalgarh and Suisupur before attacking Chitor because they would have served as secure bases for Sisodia raids on the Mughal supply lines. The siege would probably have been impossible with such a threat.[46]

[44] Carl von Clausewitz, *On War*, ed. and trans. Michael Howard and Peter Paret (Princeton: Princeton University Press, 1976), p. 357.

[45] On this point, see Fernand Braudel, *The Mediterranean and the Mediterranean World in the Age of Phillip II*, trans. Sian Reynolds, 2 vols. (New York: Harper & Row, 1972–3), 1:276–95; Inalcik, *Classical*, pp. 125–6; M.A. Cook, *Population Pressure in Rural Anatolia* (London: Oxford Univesity Press, 1972), pp. 1–2; Owen Lattimore, *Inner Asian Frontiers of China* (New York: American Geographical Society, 1940), p. 174.

[46] R. C. Smail, *Crusading Warfare* (Cambridge: Cambridge University Press, 1956), pp. 60–2, 204–15, drew my attention to the need to understand the specific function of each fortress in context. Also see Clausewitz, *War*, pp. 393–403.

3.1.3 EVALUATION

The Mughals enjoyed a definite but limited margin of military superiority over their rivals in Hindustan. Bābur and his descendants brought a new military system to the subcontinent. It supplanted the existing elephant-based system and remained dominant until the appearance of infantry armies on the European model in the eighteenth century. The cost of artillery and the difficulty of obtaining mounted archers and appropriate mounts prevented the Muslim and Hindu principalities from developing an army capable of facing the Mughals in the field. After the victories at Tukaroi and Haldighati, the Mughals never encountered an enemy willing to offer battle other than Ṣafavīs in Afghanistan. The difficulties of logistics made the outcome of sieges less certain. From another perspective, offering battle ended the possibility of reaching an accommodation with the Mughals, but negotiation formed a regular part of siegecraft.

The strain of maintaining a siege made obtaining the conditional surrender of a fortress attractive to the Mughals. The swifter the submission of the commandant, the greater the reward he received from them. Fortresses were units of political bargaining power, more valuable intact than surrounded and damaged. In addition, early submission indicated greater willingness to become part of the Mughal regime. Siege operations strengthened the Mughal bargaining position and eroded that of the defender. The combination of carrot and stick, of military operations and political concessions, was the mechanism of Mughal expansion. The limited but distinct Mughal military superiority thus affected the essential characteristics of the polity and political class, which included many individuals who had submitted to the Mughals as a result of a combination of coercion and incentives. The status of mansabdar had to reflect the terms of their submissions.

The Mughals did not permit even men who submitted promptly to retain possession of important forts. Even an apparently loyal officer like Rām Chanḍ could not hold a fort like Kalinjar, far from a hostile frontier. The Mughals maintained a monopoly on major fortresses throughout their empire. As J. F. Richards has mentioned, Akbar constructed a series of fortresses. In addition to the famous Agra for he built fortified cities at Allahabad and Lahore and a fort at Ajmer. He also strengthened existing forts at Rohtas on the Kahan River (a tributary of the Jhelum), Attock on the Indus, and another Rohtas on the Son River in Bihar.[47] The fortresses on the northwest frontier and in the eastern Gangetic plain did guard the frontiers against external enemies. But the final defeat of the Afghans in Bengal and Orissa did not end the usefulness of Allahabad and Rohtas.

Mughal fortresses served as bulwarks against revolt, because the Mughals alone had the ability to take them, except in unusual circumstances. They could not become the bases for disloyal provincial governors because the governors did not control them. The Mughals, like the Ottomans, appointed commandants for major forts who were responsible directly to the emperor.[48] Later Mughal history offers several examples of the role of fortresses in resisting revolts. When Sulṭān Khusraw revolted against his father Jahāngīr in 1606 and fled west from Agra, Dilāvar Khān, governor-designate of Lahore, hastened to the city ahead of him and prepared it for defence. His action made it impossible for Khusraw to take the city.[49] When Khān-i Jahān Ludī ceded the Balaghat to the Niẓām-Shāhīs without imperial orders, Sipāhdār Khān, the commandant at Ahmadnagar, refused Khān-i Jahān's orders to surrender the fort. Neither Khān-i Jahān nor the Niẓām-Shāhī generalissimo Ḥāmid Khān could compel him to do so.[50]

These findings require revision of the gunpowder empires hypothesis. Firearms did form a vital element of Mughal military superiority, but not the only one. Sole possession of a complete array of artillery, infantry

[47] J. F. Richards, 'The Formation of Imperial Authority under Akbar and Jahangir', *Kingship and Authority in South Asia*, ed. idem, South Asian Studies, University of Wisconsin Madison, vol. 3 (Madison, Wi.: University of Wisconsin, 1978), p. 255. I have corrected the locations from Irfan Habib, *Atlas of the Mughal Empire* (New Delhi: Oxford University Press, 1982). Richards's connection of the fortresses to the overall pattern of Akbar's rule is extremely astute, but his views on the functions of fortresses are mechanical.

[48] Irvine, *Army*, pp. 268–9; Phul, *Armies*, pp. 296–7. On the Ottomans, see Inalcik, *Classical*, p. 105; P. M. Holt, *Egypt and the Fertile Crescent* (Ithaca: Cornell University Press, 1966), pp. 38–51.

[49] Khwajah Kamgar Husaini, *Ma'asir-i Jahangīrī*, ed. Azra Alavi (New York: Asia, 1978), p. 80–2; Mu 'tamad Khan, *Iqbal-nāmah-yi Jahāngīrī*, ed. Maulavi 'abd al-Hayy and Maulavi Ahmad 'Ali Sahun (Calcutta: Asiatic Society of Bengal), pp. 9–14; T.J., pp. 30–36/1:59–62; Beni Prasad, *History of Jahangir*, 5th. ed. (Allahabad: Indian Press, 1973), pp. 130–1.

[50] M.J., p. 488; M.U., 2:427–9/873–4; Prasad, *Jahangir*, p. 389.

armed with firearms, and an army of mounted archers, 'the full panoply of military might', gave the Mughals their dominance.[51] One cannot deny the importance of artillery; Abū al-Fażl does not. He writes: 'Guns are wonderful locks for protecting the august edifice of the state, and befitting keys for the doors of conquest. With the exception of the Ottoman empire, there is perhaps no country which in its guns has more means of securing the government than this.'[52] But the ability to breach the walls of stone forts lacked the fundamental importance which Hodgson and McNeill attribute to it. More importantly, the Mughals did not perceive provincial fortresses as potential centres for revolt, but as obstacles to revolt. Without any positive evidence, several hypotheses explain the failure of the Mughals to upgrade existing fortifications as the Europeans did to cope with new siege artillery. The locations of most of the fortresses of Hindustan made the siting of guns against them so difficult that the inadequacy of the forts themselves may have escaped notice. The Mughals may have had no access to the new science of fortifications and little incentive to seek it out.[53] Perhaps most importantly, after the first few decades of Akbar's reign, the Mughals had no reason to expect their fortresses to face a major siege, except in Afghanistan.

Firearms contributed to centralization, the distinguishing characteristic of the gunpowder empires, in a more complex way. Almost all Islamic polities faced the difficulty of combining the administrative centralization which they desired with the financial decentralization which the level of economic development and sophistication required. The incomplete monetarization of economies, the rudimentary level of banking institutions, and the difficulty of transporting large sums of cash made the central collection of revenue and distribution of cash salaries impractical.[54] For this reason, Muslim rulers from the 'Abbāsids

[51] I have borrowed this phrase from Henry Kissinger's definition of a superpower. See his *American Foreign Policy*, expanded ed. (New York: Norton, 1974), p. 55.

[52] A.A., 1:124/119. I have substituted Ottoman Empire for Blochman's Turkey as the translation of Rūmistān.

[53] On the issue of incentive, see Bernard Lewis, *The Muslim Discovery of Europe* (New York: W. W. Norton, 1982). I do not believe that the European fortifications in India reflected sixteenth century improvements.

[54] On these problems, see the works cited in note 46 above, and Inalcik, *Classical*, p. 107; idem., 'Capital Formation in the Ottoman Empire', *Journal of Economic History*

to the Mughals and their contemporaries conceded land revenue from specified areas, and the burden of collecting it to their servants directly as their salaries. Before the sixteenth century, the concessions were most common called *iqtā'*; the Ottomans used the term *tīmār*, the Ṣafavīs *tīyūl*, the Mughals jagir or *tīyūl*. This practice carried the problem of preventing the recipients from making themselves autonomous. Different dynasties dealt with the problem in different ways; no solution was perfect.[55] Because the troops paid from provincial land revenue greatly outnumbered those paid directly from the central treasury, the ruler's position was always tenuous. In confederations of nomadic tribes, the ruler's personal war-band was never strong enough to counterbalance the confederate tribes.[56] The military changes in the sixteenth century greatly strengthened the central government as long as it retained control of the infantry and artillery. Its combined arms could always defeat the mounted archers from the provinces. This fact accounts for the greater coherence of the gunpowder empires as compared with their predecessors.

There remains McNeill's contention that the difficulty of moving siege guns long distances overland made the Mughal 'imperial consolidation' precarious. The situation in the Deccan suggests that overland logistics in general, not transporting guns specifically, hampered the Mughals in imposing their will in the Deccan. But the precariousness of Mughal power has another aspect. The Mughals clearly ruled a less centralized realm than the Ottomans did; the military organization of the two empires reflects that fact. The *tīmār* system made the great majority of private soldiers, paid by revenue concessions in the provinces, direct employees of the central government.[57] In the Mughal empire, the central government employed only the officers of the provincial army, the mansabdars, and had only tenuous connections

29 (1969): 103; *Encyclopedia of Islam*, 2nd. ed., 'Hawala', by Halil Inalcik, and Braudel, *Mediterranean*, 2:483–96.

55 Claude Cahen, 'L'Evolution de L'Iqtā' du XI' au XIII' Siecle', *Annales* 8 (1953): 25–52; Ann K. S. Lambton, 'Reflections on the Iqtā', *Arabic and Islamic Studies in Honor of H. A. R. Gibb*, ed. G. Makdisi (Leiden: E. J. Brill, 1965), pp. 358–76.

56 On the role of the war-band, see John E. Woods, *The Aqquyunlu: Clan, Confederation, Empire* (Chicago: Bibliotheca Islamica, 1976), pp. 7–16.

57 On the *tīmār* system, see Rohrborn, *Untersuchungen*; Inalcik, *Classical*, pp. 104–19.

with most private soldiers.[58] The contrast between Ottoman and Mughal military organization raises fundamental questions about the Mughal polity, which further exploration of the process of expansion should resolve.[59]

3.2 What Victories Meant

During the Hundred Years War, English victories in the field won only the ability to besiege cities. Just what did victories bring the Mughals? For Bābur, Humāyūn, and Akbar, triumphs in the field brought them the ability to occupy the major cities of the western and central Indo-Gangetic plain—Lahore, Delhi, and Agra—and to establish control over the countryside as well. Control meant a modicum of order and the collection of agricultural revenue. A brief discussion of the expansion of the Ottoman empire and of Ottoman methods of rural revenue assessment illuminates the Mughal system.

3.2.1 Comparison with the Ottomans

Halil Inalcik's article on 'Ottoman Methods of Conquest', now more than thirty years old, provides excellent material for comparison and contrast. Inalcik emphasizes the gradual nature of the expansion of the Ottoman empire, except during the reign of Yildirim Bayezid, 1389 (791)–1403 (805), and divides it into two phases, winning suzerainty over neighbouring principalities and establishing direct Ottoman rule, which meant the *taḥrīr-tīmār* system, over these areas. He describes the Ottoman policy as gradual assimilation of newly conquered areas to an Ottoman standard form of administration, modified in accord with local conditions. *Taḥrīr* meant survey, a survey of all the sources of revenue in the newly conquered region and of all the recipients of

[58] I discuss this situation at length in the next two sections. For overviews of the jāgīr system, see Habib, *Agrarian*, pp. 257–98; Athar Ali, *Nobility*, pp. 74–94.

[59] This analysis of the Mughal military environment provides a different explanation for the lack of battles in Mughal history than that of Andre Wink, *Land and Sovereignty in India* (Cambridge: Cambridge University Press, 1986), pp. 26–7. Wink is quite correct, however, in drawing attention to the 'political use of military power', the 'mixture of coercion and conciliation', and 'intervention in and making use of existing local conflicts'.

revenue listed in these regions. These recipients were primarily the holders of *tīmārs*, land revenue assignments which supported a single cavalryman. The Ottomans conducted *taḥrīr* immediately upon the conquest of an area and every several decades thereafter. The first survey had the character of a description of the existing revenue system, transforming it into an Ottoman institution. Later surveys made changes, bringing local practices into conformity with Ottoman standards. By virtue of the *tīmār* system, which one might describe as a soldier in every village, and the extremely detailed records of the revenue surveys, the Ottoman administrative system extended beyond the village level to the individual taxpayer.[60]

3.2.2 THE ARMED PEASANTRY AND THE MUGHAL REGIME IN THE PROVINCES

The military potential of the countryside made a military and fiscal regime comparable to the *taḥrīr-tīmār* system impossible in the Mughal empire. A single cavalryman could not cope with a village of soldiers, not to mention a zamindar who controlled the power of a number of villages. In order to maintain anything like order in the provinces, the Mughal provincial army had to function as a series of standing contingents. The Mughal provincial army thus confronted a series of private zamindar/peasant armies. Both forces depended on agricultural revenue from the same sources.

The most common form of land revenue assessment in the Mughal empire reflected this situation. Procedures and methods varied enormously in time and space, but the most common system was known as *nāsaq* (method, arrangement). *Nāsaq* involved negotiation between the tax assessor/collector [*amīn* in *parganahs* (districts) which paid their revenue to the central treasury, *'āmil* in jagirs] and the local officials and zamindars. The collector made an assessment of the production of the area on the basis of local records and calculated his cash demand in

[60] Halil Inalcik, 'Ottoman Methods of Conquest', *Studia Islamica* 2 (1954), pp. 103–29. See also idem., *Classical*, pp. 107–9; idem., 'The Problem of the Relationship between Byzantine and Ottoman Taxation', *Akten des XL Internationalen Byzantinisten Kongresses 1958* (Munich: C. H. Beck, 1966), pp. 237–42; *Encyclopedia of Islam*, 2nd. ed., s.v. 'Kanun: Financial and Public Administration', and 'Kanunname', both by Halil Inalcik.

accord with local prices.[61] His assessment stood unless the local officials challenged it. If they did, the assessor negotiated with them. Normally, they reached a compromise; if not, the assessor had to collect the revenue by threat or force. The two local officials involved were the *qānūngū* and the *chawdhurī*. Men held these positions by imperial diploma, but the appointment recognized rather than bestowed local status. The *qānūngū* collected and kept records of the cultivated area, crop production, revenue demand, tax rates, and prices in his *parganah*.[62] The revenue records of the central government depended on those of the *qānūngūs*, most of whom were members of Hindu accounting castes. The *chawdhurī* was normally a leading zamindar of the *parganah* and actually collected the revenue of the *parganah* from the other zamindars and paid it to the imperial recipient. His signature on the revenue assessment guaranteed payment.[63]

The imperial representative and the *chawdhurī* thus confronted each other, annually or biennially, to decide which share of the revenue should go to the zamindars and which to the imperial treasury or assignee. The collector had the stronger hand because the Mughals could, if necessary, defeat any zamindar. The Mughals normally received 90 per cent of the land revenue for this reason.[64] But if the collector pushed the *chawdhurī* so far that a military expedition was required, he reduced his profit severely. The *chawdhurī*, on the other hand, risked ruin if his inflexibility forced the imperials to take action against him. For this reason, bargaining normally produced a settlement acceptable to both sides. Zamindar revolts—revenue wars—were nonetheless commonplace in the Mughal empire. H. K. Naqvi finds evidence of 144 such uprisings in Akbar's reign.[65] In some areas, fighting occurred every time the Mughals attempted to collect taxes.[66] Routine administration in such areas required the use of force.

[61] Habib, *Agrarian*, pp. 215–19, 289–93.

[62] Ibid., pp. 288–90.

[63] Ibid., pp. 292–4.

[64] Ibid., pp. 148–54.

[65] H. K. Naqvi, *Urbanization and Urban Centres under the Great Mughals* (Simla: Indian Institute of Advanced Study, 1971), pp. 160–86.

[66] The Mughals had two terms describing such areas, *mawas* and *zur talab*; see Habib, *Agrarian*, p. 331. I do not know the etymology of *mawas*; the two elements of *zur talab* mean force and demand.

The Mughal regime in the provinces thus did not reach the individual peasant, or even many villages. It consisted of the series of relationships between Mughal officials and the zamindars. After the defeat of the regional dynasty, Mughal conquest consisted of the development of these connections, which constituted a revenue settlement (*band u bast*). The settlements consisted of recognition of zamindars, *chawdhurīs*, and *qānūngūs*, determination of the amount of revenue which the conquered area would produce, and assignment of that revenue to Mughal recipients for the first time.[67] This situation explains the unusual fluidity of Mughal expansion. Mughal government had no roots; the elimination of the governor and his army ended Mughal rule in the province. The Mughals had to conquer Malwa and most of Bengal twice for this reason.

3.3 The Course of Expansion in Hindustan

Ignoring minor principalities which owed their prolonged survival to rough terrain, Mughal expansion had three phases: establishment of Mughal dominance in central Hindustan, absorption of secondary principalities north of the Narbada, and the conquest of the Deccan. Although the first Mughal foray in the Deccan took place early in Akbar's reign, the major movement south began well after 1582 (990), so this section deals with only the first two phases. They overlapped, since the Mughals secured their dominance by defeating the last Sūrī claimant in 1561 (968) and invaded Malwa the same year. It would be more accurate to speak of processes rather than phases. The second Panipat ended the immediate danger to Akbar from the Sūrs; he and Bayrām Khān did not face a threat serious enough to require them to take the field during the next five years. This victory cleared the way for the Mughals to take over the relationships with zamindars and urban notables which the Sūrs had, and thus establish a new regime. The submission of Sayyid Maḥmūd Bārah, as a zamindar of the Duab as well as an amīr of Sikandar Sūr, typified this process. Rājah Bihārah Mal Kachwaha, the first Rajput to enter Mughal service, had previously established an alliance with Hajjī Khān, the Sūr governor of Mewat

[67] For examples of the making of a revenue settlement after conquest, see A.N., 2:168–260, 3:65/91, 548–49/830–32.

and Ajmer. He offered Hajjī Khān his daughter in marriage, thus defining himself as the Khān's subordinate ally.[68] Hajjī Khān attacked Narnaul, which was held by Majnūn Khān Qāqshāl. Rājah Bihārah Mal arranged a surrender which permitted Majnūn Khān to rejoin Akbar. Majnūn Khān reported the Rājah's intervention to Akbar, and he was summoned to court and had audience. He and his followers impressed Akbar by their courage in the presence of a rogue elephant. This incident began the Rajput role in the Mughal polity. The establishment of the marriage relationship came later, but represented only a change from alliance with a Sūrī governor to one with the Mughal sovereign.[69]

Both Ziegler and Kolff describe marriage alliances as the concrete form of the political relationships of Rajput chiefs, in Rajasthan and elsewhere. Ziegler states that the offer of a daughter in marriage made the offerer a subordinate ally of the recipient, thus securing his status, and that Rajputs had given their daughters to Muslim rulers before.[70] At this point Akbar had not yet gone beyond his predecessors.

The second phase of expansion involved the absorption of the Rajput principalities of Hindustan, not all of which were in Rajasthan, and the conquest of the Muslim regional kingdoms, Malwa, Gujarat, and the Kararānī Afghan principality which included Bihar, Bengal and Orissa. The conquest of Malwa in 1561 (968) began the process, but I shall discuss the absorption of the Rajput principalities first. The submission of Rājah Bihārah Mal demonstrated that Akbar could develop useful relationships with Rajputs; the Kachwahas also used their influence on him to preserve existing Rajput dynasties.

The first principality, that of Bhath or Pannah, near the ruins of Khajuraho, became part of the empire in 1563 (970). Its ruler, Rājah Rām Chand Bhaghella, had sheltered Ghazī Khān Tannurī, a retainer of Bayrām Khān who had participated in his master's rebellion. Āṣaf Khān Harawī attacked Rām Chand when he refused to surrender Ghazī

[68] Kunwar Refaqat Ali Khan, *The Kachwahas under Akbar and Jahangir* (New Delhi: Kitab Publishing, 1976), p. 7.

[69] A.N., 2:20/36, 45/70, 155–56/240–42; M.U., 2:111–13/409–11.

[70] Norman Ziegler, 'Action, Power, and Service in Rajasthani Culture: A Social History of the Rajputs of Middle Period Rajasthan', Ph.D. Dissertation, University of Chicago, 1972, pp. 137–43, 156.

Khān, and besieged him in his capital. Through the intercession of Rājah Bir Bar and Zayn Khān Kūkah, however, Akbar permitted him to submit and retain his principality. Abū al-Fażl, who mentions only the intercession of famous Rājahs, neither explains the decision nor describes it as a significant precedent, but does mention that Rām Chand was one of the 'famous Rājahs of India' and that his 'forefathers had ruled over the country for generations.' Presumably, the long-standing relationship of dynasty and subjects affected or determined Akbar's acceptance of Rām Chand's submission.[71] In addition, the Bhaghellas had no claim to imperial sovereignty or history of opposition to the Mughals.

In 1563–4 (961), the Mughals absorbed two more principalities: the Gakkhar country, the hills between the Indus and the Beas in the Punjab, and part of Marwar. The Gakkhars were Muslims rather than Rajputs, but the same principle applies. In both cases, members of the ruling dynasty, Kamāl Khān Gakkhar and Rām Singh Rathor, had entered Mughal service and obtained Akbar's assistance in taking their ancestral thrones from an uncle and brother. Kamāl Khān was entirely successful; Rām Singh gained control of most of the principality but his brother Chandar Sen held out against him, and the Mughals.[72] These principalities were remote—i.e. outside the Indo-Gangetic plain—had a long history of autonomy, and their rulers had never claimed imperial sovereignty. They exemplify the Mughal exploitation of local conflicts to extend their sovereignty.[73]

[71] A.N., 2:59/91, 98–99/148, 148/229–30, 182–3/280–3; Srivastava, *Akbar*, 1:68, cites a Sanskrit history of the Bhagellas of Bhatha or Pannah, the *Virabhanudaya Kavyam* of Madhava, ed. K. K. Lele and A. S. Upadhyaya (Lucknow: N.K. Press, 1938), which must be the source of the identity of the intercessors. The town of Panna, as the name appears on the John Bartholemew Travel Map of the Indian Subcontinent, is about twenty miles southwest of Khajuraho. According to Sir Wolseley Haig, 'Akbar, 1556–1573', in Sir Richard Burn, ed., *Cambridge History of India Volume 4: The Mughal Period* (Cambridge: Cambridge University Press, p. 87 n.2), Bhath is the correct transliteration.

[72] A.N., 2:191–4/296–300, 197/305; T.A., 2:159–62, T.Q., pp. 113–14; Tod, *Annals*, 2:21–3; Visheshwar Sarup Bhargava, *Marwar and the Mughal Emperors* (New Delhi: Munshiram Manoharlal, 1966), pp. 44–55. Although Jodhpur is certainly a great fort, Abū al-Fażl's notice of its fall is so brief that the Mughals probably did not have to mount siege operations in order to take it.

[73] Cf. Wink, *Land and Sovereignty*, pp. 26–7. This process is what Wink recognizes as *fitnah*.

This description also fits the small principality of Garha Katanga, the northern part of Gondwanda. Āṣaf Khān's decision to conquer Garha Katanga thus requires explanation. Abū al-Fażl and Bada'ūnī agree upon one. Āṣaf Khān decided to conquer Garha Katanga on his own, after his victory at Pannah brought him into contact with the principality and he learned of its wealth. He did have Akbar's permission, but acted on his own initiative. The texts do not indicate that he ever attempted to negotiate, or that the Rānī Durgawatī, the ruler of Garha Katanga, ever considered submitting. Even if Āṣaf Khān's greed caused the episode, it fits the general pattern of Mughal expansion: resistance to the end meant destruction; submission, even at the last moment, as in the case of Surjan Ray at Ranthambor, meant survival. The heroism of Rānī Durgawatī is beyond doubt; one also cannot doubt that it led only to her death and the extinction of her dynasty and principality.[74]

After the defeat of the Uzbeg rebels, Akbar turned his attention to the reduction of Mewar, the leading Rajput principality. I have already described the siege of Chitor in 1567–68 (975). Although the Sisodias had sought to dominate Hindustan until Bābur's victory at Khanwa in 1527 (933), Akbar clearly sought the submission of the Rānā rather than the conquest of Mewar. What Akbar would have done if Khān-i Jahān, after the completion of the siege of Chitor, had captured Rānā Udai Singh, or Mān Singh, after Haldighati, had taken Rānā Pratap, I can only speculate. He might well have executed the resistant Rānā, and sought to replace him with a malleable member of the family. As already noted, the victory at Chitor facilitated the Mughal acquisitions of Ranthambor and Kalinjar. It also encouraged the remaining rulers of Rajasthan to submit to the Mughals. Chandar Sen, the leader of resistance to the Mughals in Marwar, attended Akbar in Ajmer in 1570 (978). Ray Kalyan Mal of Bikanir came also and offered Akbar his niece in marriage, which proposal Akbar accepted. Rawāl Har Ray of Jaisalmer also offered his daughter, but asked to be excused from attending court. Akbar sent Rājah Bhagwan Dās, the son of Bihārah Mal and father of Mān Singh, to bring Har Ray's daughter to court.[75]

[74] A.N., 2:208–16/323–33, T.A., 2:170–1; M.T., 2:66–7/65–6; Srivastava, *Akbar*, 1:79–84.

[75] A.N., 2:358–9/518–19.

The conquests of Malwa, Gujarat, Bihar and Bengal involved a series of advances and retreats. Adham Khān and Pīr Muḥammad Khān conquered Malwa in 1561 (968). After the recall of Adham Khān to Agra, Pīr Muḥammad Khān led an invasion of Khandesh, where Bāz Bahādur, the ruler of Malwa, had fled. Pīr Muḥammad Khān's defeat and death permitted Bāz Bahādur to regain control of Malwa a year after losing it. Akbar immediately assigned 'Abdullah Khān Uzbeg to reconquer the province with Khwājah Mu'īn al-Dīn Aḥmad Farankhūdī to arrange a revenue settlement. 'Abdullah Khān defeated Bāz Bahādur without difficulty and the Mughals ruled the province from then on.[76] The first campaign against Gujarat began on 4 July 1572 (20 Ṣafar 980). Akbar secured the submission of I'timād Khān Gujirātī, one of the two kingmakers in the province. After the conquest of the capital, Ahmadabad, he assigned the occupied part of the province to Khān-i A'ẓam and the unoccupied southern part, with obligation to conquer it, to I'timād Khān. Reports that I'timād Khān had disloyal intentions caused Akbar to direct the subjugation of the rest of the province, including the vital port of Surat, himself. These operations, opposed mostly by the rebel Mirzās, extended into April 1573 Z̄ū al-Hijjah (980). Akbar left Khān-i A'ẓam as governor and returned to Agra.[77]

As soon as Akbar departed, two Gujirātī officers who had not submitted, Ikhtiyār al-Mulk and Shīr Khān Fulādī, assembled armies and besieged Khān-i A'ẓam in Ahmadabad. This crisis produced one of the most famous episodes of Akbar's career, his forced march to Gujarat. He covered the 450 miles from Agra to Ahmadabad in nine days with a small force. Aided by the inability of Ikhtiyār al-Mulk to believe Akbar was present, the imperial detachment defeated a much larger Gujirātī army. Akbar confirmed Khān-i A'ẓam as governor but assigned Āṣaf Khān Ghiyās al-Dīn 'Ali Qazwīnī and Rājah Tūdar Mal as *dīwān* to make a new revenue settlement and distribution of jāgīrs.[78] In 1577 (985), Muẓaffar Ḥusayn Mirzā, the last of the rebel Mirzās, invaded Gujarat

[76] A.N., 2:166–9/256–61.

[77] A.N., 2:369–72/536–40, 3:4–27/6–36; T.A., 2:235–52; M.T., 2:139–49/143–53; T.Q., pp. 251–74; Srivastava, *Akbar*, 1:121–9. On the rebel Mirzās, see pp. 103–5 below.

[78] A.N., 3:41–65/59–91; T.A., 2:261–85; M.T., 2:164–70; 167–74; T.Q., pp. 279–81; Srivastava, *Akbar*, 1:136–41.

from the Deccan. He took Baroda before Wazīr Khān, the governor of the province, and Rājah Tūdar Mal, again in Gujarat on administrative assignment, drove him off. A second effort against Ahmadabad also failed.[79] In 1583 (991), part of the contingent of Shihāb al-Dīn Aḥmad Khān, the outgoing governor of Gujarat, mutinied and made Muzaffar Khān Gujirātī, the pretender to the throne of the principality, their leader. He occupied the entire province before ʿAbd al-Rahīm, the future Khān-i Khānān, defeated him in battle on 25 January 1584 (13 Muharram 992). Muẓaffar Khān attacked Gujarat again later that year and in 1591 (999), when Khān-i Aʿzam was again the governor of the province. He was defeated, captured, and committed suicide, ending resistance to Mughal rule in the province.[80]

The Mughals had to conquer Bihar and Bengal only twice, though resistance to Mughal rule in Orissa and on the periphery of Bengal continued for several decades. Operations against Dā'ud Khān Kararānī, the Afghan ruler of the three provinces, began in October 1573 (Jumādā II 981) with a siege of Patna. The city did not fall until ten months later, when Akbar had taken personal control of operations. He then returned to the capital, leaving Munʿim Khān in charge. Munʿim Khān defeated Dā'ūd at Tukaroi, and extracted submission from him, despite the opposition of Rājah Tūdar Mal to an agreement. Munʿim Khān died seven months later, leading to confusion among the Mughal forces in Bengal. Dā'ūd renewed resistance and the Mughals withdrew to Bihar. Akbar assigned Khān-i Jahān Ḥusayn Qulī Khān to reconquer the province, with Muẓaffar Khān Turbatī as his deputy. They defeated Dā'ūd at Raj Mahal on 12 July 1576 (15 Rabīʿ II 984), which marks the definitive establishment of Mughal authority in Bengal and the effective end of the Afghan threat to the Mughals.[81]

Pure circumstance partially explains the need for repeated campaigns

[79] A.N., 3:67/93, 69/95, 206–9/292–4, 213–15/301–3, T.A., 2:330–2; M.T., 2:249–50/256–7, 253/60.

[80] A.N., 3:421–6/628–36, 452–5/678–84, 471–2/709/11, 494–5/750, 530–1/808–9, 593–5/902–6, 628–30/962–5; T.A., 2:371–83, M.T., 2:329–34, 336–46, 344–5/355–6, 358–62/370–4.

[81] This summary is derived from Srivastava, *Akbar*, 1:143–4, 147, 150–6, 166–70, 177–81. See also Tapan Raychaudhuri, *Bengal under Akbar and Jahangir*, 2nd imp. (New Delhi: Munshiram Manoharlal, 1969), pp. 49–93.

in these provinces. The escapes of Bāz Bahādur, Muẓaffar Ḥusayn Mirzā,[82] and Muẓaffar Khān Gujirātī permitted them to return to menace the Mughals. The deaths of Pīr Muḥammad Khān and Mun'im Khān opened the way for anti-Mughal ripostes. The fluid nature of the Mughal regime, especially before the arrangement of a revenue settlement and assignment of jāgīrs, and the surplus of military manpower, however, made the Mughals vulnerable to this type of counterattack. As in Hindustan itself, the initial victory in the field did not give the Mughals the relationships with the zamindars and urban notables which connected the regime to the sources of revenue and co-opted or neutralized the local military potential. Without such relationships, the regime had no local roots in the province at all. It was thus vulnerable to individuals and groups with lasting connections.

The second phase of expansion involved bringing many of the amīrs of these principalities into the Mughal ruling class. For example, Sayyid Muḥammad, the subordinate of Junayd Kararānī who held the fortress of Rohtas, chose to surrender the fort when Mughal forces under Shāhbāz Khān reached there. The commandant of the fortress of Shirgarh, near Sassaram in Bihar, also surrendered it to Shāhbāz Khān in return for a mansab without requiring a siege.[83] The cases fit the pattern of accepting the surrender of fortresses in return for concessions, but also show that this pattern affected the nature of the Mughal polity. S. A. A. Rizvi discusses the cases of several men with distinguished Sufi backgrounds who entered Mughal service from that of regional rulers and thus helped to bring about the expansion of the empire.[84]

The routine granting of concessions to officers of conquered principalities, though vital, posed a basic problem for the Mughals. Their own officers, especially those who participated in successful campaigns, expected promotions, which meant more lucrative jāgīrs, as their proper reward. The campaigns themselves were costly. The siege of Chitor, where the engineers digging the *sābāṭ* were encouraged with large sums of cash, is an extreme but not atypical example Even when they avoided lengthy and expensive sieges, the Mughals could not be certain

[82] The leader of the rebel Mirzās.

[83] A.N., 3:189/266; T.Q., pp. 359–63; Srivastava, *Akbar*, 1:180–1.

[84] Rizvi, *Intellectual*, pp. 187–90.

that conquest would be profitable. From the conquered territory, the productivity of which might have suffered from the effects of the fighting, the Mughals had to provide sufficient jāgīrs for the conquered elite which they had co-opted—usually by granting them more land revenue and higher ranks—and for the mansabdars who had participated in the campaign, and assign enough land and booty to the central treasury to defray the cost of the campaign. In Gujarat, for example, prolonged disorder before and after the Mughal conquest produced a famine, followed by an epidemic.[85] If agriculture was not disrupted and the Mughal occupation had been swift, the conquest might pay for itself within a few years. If only a few officers remained dissatisfied with what they received in the settlement after the conquest, their discontent would have no significant political impact. Apparently, none of the provincial conquests of Akbar's time caused political difficulties. But conquest involved an increase in both the revenue resources and the revenue demand, which were not necessarily balanced. This potential difficulty did not become an actuality until the Mughals began the conquest of the Deccan.

With the exception of Mewar and Orissa, the Mughals controlled all of Hindustan after Raj Mahal. Later conquests north of the Narbada, such as Kashmir and Sind, were peripheral. Akbar now dominated Hindustan. He controlled the Indo-Gangetic plain, the best area for agriculture, and the most important and prosperous commercial provinces, Gujarat and Bengal. His relationships with rulers of Amber, Jodhpur, Bikanir, and Jaisalmer eliminated any threat from them and gave him a cut of their revenue and access to their military resources. Except in Bengal, Bihar and Gujarat, his conquests had not required the type of the prolonged campaigning which severely disrupts agriculture; the establishment of order permitted an immediate return to commercial prosperity. Although they did not have the heritable *watan-jāgīrs* which distinguished the Rajputs, important Indo-Muslim groups like the famous Bārah *sayyids* and the Bukharī *sayyids* like Shaykh Farīd, later Murtażā Khān, had entered the Mughal political system, with the revenue and military resources they controlled. Although we do not see the process in the chronicles, the development of predictable relation-

[85] T.Q., pp. 319–21; T.A., 2:301.

ships with zamindars likewise neutralized their military power as a threat to the Mughal regime.

3.3 Recapitulation

The extent of Mughal military superiority, the political bargaining it engendered, and the existence of the armed peasantry affected the nature of the Mughal polity. Though the specific form of the gunpowder empires hypothesis does not fit the Mughal empire, it draws attention to military factors. The unique possession of the combination of mounted archers, effective artillery, and infantry with firearms permitted the Mughals consistently to defeat their opponents in the field. This ability led their enemies, with some imprudent exceptions, to avoid meeting the Mughals in battle, and to prefer to defend forts against them. Akbar demonstrated the ability of the Mughals to take major fortresses at Chitor, but then used that ability to force the defenders of other forts to submit to him rather than taking the forts outright. The difficulty and expense of sieges drove Akbar and his chief subordinates to make considerable concessions in order to avoid them, and thus brought many of the holders of fortresses into the Mughal ruling class. The conditions of submission became one of the determinants of the definition of mansabdar.

In the Indo-Gangetic plain which, with a few exceptions, was devoid of major fortresses, Mughal victories in the field permitted them to establish revenue settlements and to distribute the territory as jāgirs. This process involved absorbing or neutralizing the military potential of the conquered territory. Concession of a cut of the revenue and formal recognition of their status normally reconciled zamindars with only local ambitions to the Mughal presence. More powerful individuals became part of the Mughal system as mansabdars, though they had less bargaining power than individuals who held fortresses. Outside the plain, where topography facilitated the construction of strong fortresses, Mughal superiority won only what Crécy and Agincourt won, the ability to conduct sieges. The peripheral location—both distant from the Delhi-Agra region and outside the major agricultural region of the plain—of the principalities of Rajasthan and other areas of rough terrain encouraged the Mughals to leave existing dynasties in place.

One may say that the Mughal empire expanded by absorbing, to various degrees, the existing political elites. The Afghan ruling families who opposed the Mughals most directly did not survive and few of their kinsmen joined the Mughals, but the Indo-Muslim and Rajput officers usually did. The members of these groups brought their expectations into the Mughal polity and thus affected its development fundamentally.

The need to neutralize the armed peasantry and thus assure the co-operation of the zamindars determined the organization of the Mughal provincial army. The Mughals had to maintain organized units in the provinces to overawe, and occasionally defeat, the zamindars' armies. The need to maintain and pay the provincial army as units dovetailed with the expectations of the different groups which formed the Mughal ruling class. Chaghatays, Rajputs, Indo-Muslims and Afghans all expected to control their own independent contingents. Many if not most had followers with a special loyalty to their families, whom the Mughals could control only by co-opting the leaders. The Mughals fulfilled the expectations of their officers, drew on a significant proportion of the armed peasantry, and dominated the part retained by the zamindars by organizing their army as mansabdars' contingents.

Kolff overstates his case, however, when he argues that the Mughals actually had no military superiority over their opponents, so that the empire was a product of their intelligence system, wealth and the credit it generated, and ties to their officers. These factors were crucial, but if the combination of firearms and mounted archers had not enabled the Mughals to win battles they would have had no chance to operate. Kolff regards the prominence of archers in the Persian chronicles as the product of a cultural 'preference for the gentleman-warrior and the ethos of chivalry.' He presents no evidence for such a preference and ignores the superiority of mounted archers.[86]

[86] Kolff, 'Armed', p. 32, 34, 37. Karen Leonard, 'The "Great Firms" Theory of Mughal Decline', *Comparative Studies in Society and History* 21 (1979): 151--67 is the only discussion of the importance of credit to the Mughal empire. Kolff does not cite it.

CHAPTER 4

First Initiatives

At the time of Akbar's enthronement, he and his dynasty faced a desperate situation. He was less than fourteen solar years old, and probably and only the haziest goals for his reign beyond survival. The first half of Akbar's reign reveals an uneven series of initiatives which were the products of circumstances as well as of Akbar's personality. The mature Akbarī constitution and polity emerged slowly and painfully; neither its chief architect nor his associates could have foreseen the final outcome. At the beginning of the reign, Akbar, Bayrām Khān and the other senior officers could have had little in mind but defeating the remaining Sūr pretenders and restoring the Tīmūrid position in Hindustan. They had no leisure to consider the transformation of the Tīmūrid polity, but their behaviour nonetheless began it.

4.1 Bayrām Khān's Regency

Bayāzīd Bayāt provides a starting point for the study of Akbarī politics. He lists the officers who accompanied Humāyūn on the re-invasion under three headings: dependants (*mulāzimān*) of Akbar, those of Bayrām Khān, and the followers of Humāyūn of various descriptions: *khawānīn*, *salātīn*, *dīwānān*, *bakhshiyān*, *begchihā*, and *yikkah jawānān*.[1] His list suggests examining early political developments as

[1] T.H.A., pp. 176–86. These terms are the plurals of *khān*, *sulṭān*, *diwān*, *bakhshī*, *beg*, and *yikkah jawan*. The last term means single soldier, i.e. a soldier with no followers of his own, cognate with *ahadī* in later Mughal usage.

the products of the interaction of these groups.

Bayrām Khān dominated the situation after Akbar's enthronement, and used his position to install his dependants in positions of power. The hitherto unstudied *Ṭabaqat-i Tīmūrī* of Muḥammad Jabbarī Ummī, the great-grandson of Majnūn Khān Qāqshāl, leaves no room for misunderstanding:

> [Bayrām Khān] exalted his own servants and dependants with the titles of *khān* and *sultān*, with flags and drums, and with lucrative [literally cultivated] jāgīrs while the amīrs of Bābur and Humāyūn, each of whom had rendered distinguished services [were reduced to poverty and insignificance.][2]

This statement, written by a descendant of one of the leading Humayūnī officers and reflecting their attitude, shows that the conflict between Bayrām Khān and his followers and the other leading Humāyūnī officers dominated the politics of the regency. Only a few Humāyūnī amīrs, like 'Alī Qulī Khān Shaybani, later Khān-i Zamān, and his relatives, aligned themselves with Bayrām Khān. This conflict did not override the struggle to survive, but Bayrām Khān evidently identified the Mughal cause with himself. Iqtidar Alam Khan, in his insightful article on the politics of the regency, asserts that Bayrām Khān acted to ensure the unity of the Mughals against the Afghans. This requirement explains his temporary exile of most of the other leading officers to Kabul on the pretext either of reinforcing Mun'im Khān, who governed Kabul for Akbar's younger brother Mirzā Muḥammad Hakim, or of bringing Humāyūn's harem from Kabul to Hindustan.[3] The execution of Tardī Beg Khān after Hīmū defeated him at Tughluqabad had the same motivation, reinforced by longstanding enmity between the two men.[4]

[2] Muḥammad Barārī Ummī ibn Muḥammad Jamshīd ibn Jabbarī Khān ibn Majnūn Khān Qāqshāl, *Ṭabaqat-i Tīmūrī*, Ousely ms. 311, filmed by Oxford University Press, 1982, ff. 101r–102v.

[3] Iqtidar Alam Khan, 'Mughal Court Politics during Bairam Khan's Regency', *Medieval India: A Miscellany* I (1969): 24–31; T.H.A, p. 207; Sidi 'Ali Reis, *Mirat al-Mamālik*, Istanbul: Kitabkhanah-yi Aydin, 1895 (1313), pp. 39–61, trans. as *Travels of a Turkish Admiral*, by A. Vambery (London: Luzac, 1899; reprint ed., Lahore: Al-Biruni, 1975), pp. 45–66)

[4] Iqtidar Alam Khan, 'Politics', pp. 26–30; A. L. Srivastava, *Akbar*, 2nd. ed., 3 vols.

After the execution of Tardī Beg Khān, the struggle between Bayrām Khān and his friends and adherents and the other Humāyūnī officers became more intense. The members of Akbar's entourage now opposed Bayrām Khān, presumably because they could expect to receive the patronage of their master to the extent that he controlled his own government. Bayrām Khān's dominance was inherently unstable; even if Akbar had approved of everything he did the young ruler could not accept his tutelage forever. After antagonizing most of the other Mughal officers as regent, Bayrām Khān could not have accepted a lesser position in the government.[5]

Bayrām Khān made at least one effort to alter the composition of the ruling class. His appointment of Shaykh Gadā'ī Kambu as *ṣadr*, with responsibility for the distribution of revenue grants to Muslim ulama and Sufis, shows that he sought to win the support of the Muslim notables of Hindustan. The son of a well-known and wealthy Suhrawardī *shaykh*, Shaykh Gadā'ī had been affiliated with Humāyūn before his expulsion from Hindustan. He took refuge in Gujarat to avoid the retribution of Shīr Shāh and rejoined Humāyūn on his return. Bayrām Khān appointed Shaykh Gadā'ī *ṣadr* shortly after becoming regent. The appointment created a new and stronger connection between the Mughal government and the leading Muslims of Delhi, which included social interaction.[6] He became so thoroughly identified with Bayrām Khān that he had to flee after the regent's fall and never returned to government service.[7]

(Agra: Shiva Lal Agarwala, 1972), 1:21–4; Vincent A. Smith, *Akbar the Great Mogul* (New Delhi: S. Chand, 1962), p. 27; A.N., 2:30/51–2; M.T., 2:14/7; T.A., 2:130–1; T.Q., p. 77; T.H.A., pp. 220–1. Bayāzīd Bayāt emphasizes the importance of Bayrām Khān's pre-existing hatred for Tardī Beg Khān. Abū al-Fażl alone suggests that religious bigotry motivated Bayrām Khān. I accept Iqtidar Alam's dismissal of his testimony and submit that Abū al-Fażl deliberately uses sectarian conflict to explain evil and unfortunate actions in order to strengthen the justification for Akbar's proclamation of universal toleration as his sovereign cult.

[5] Iqtidar Alam Khan, 'Politics', pp. 31–6.

[6] M.T., 2:29–30/22–4.

[7] Iqtidar Husain Siddiqui, *Mughal Relations with the Indian Ruling Elite* (New Delhi: Munshiram Manoharlal, 1983), pp. 94–102. Both Siddiqui and Iqtidar Alam Khan, 'Politics', p. 30, discount the allegation of Smith, *Akbar*, p. 31, repeated in Srivastava, *Akbar*, 1:37, that Shaykh Gadā'ī was a Shī'ī and the Chaghatay officers opposed him for that reason.

Iqtidar Alam Khan states that Bayrām Khān recruited Rajput amīrs to counterbalance the power of his Chaghatay rivals, thus setting a precedent for the political pattern which Akbar established.[8] The text which he cites does not, however, support this position. 'Abd al-Bāqī Nihawandī, the panegyrist of Bayrām Khān's son 'Abd al-Rahīm Khān-i Khānān, mentions Bayrām Khān's patronage of many 'zamindars and officials' (*zamīndārān u 'ummāl*) of Hindustan, who became ranking mansabdars and whose families still had eminent status. Nihawandī makes no suggestion that Bayrām Khān was the first to sponsor Hindustanīs, and makes no explicit reference to Rajputs or Hindus at all. His comment probably refers to Bayrām Khān's patronage of Sayyid Maḥmūd Khān and the other Bārah *sayyids* rather than to support for Rajputs.[9]

Bayrām Khān faced one Mughal rebel, Shāh Abū al-Ma'ālī. A *sayyid* originally from Tirmiz on the Amu Darya (Oxus), he had been a close companion of Humāyūn, from whom he received the title of *farzand*. Bada'ūnī, describes his relationship with Humāyūn: 'To him the deceased Emperor had shown special favour and boundless condescension, so that he had honoured him by calling him his son.' He reports that Shāh Abū al-Ma'ālī had once murdered a Shī'ī in Qandahar in a drunken rage. When the heirs of the victim demanded justice from Humāyūn, Shāh Abū al-Ma'ālī came to court wearing the dead man's robe and spouting a suitable quatrain. Pleased with this piece of theatre, Humāyūn did not punish him. When serving with Akbar and Bayrām Khān in the Punjab, he complained because Akbar did not grant him the privileges of sitting at the *dīwān* and eating in his company which Humāyūn did. He refused to attend court at Akbar's accession and Bayrām Khān had him seized and planned to execute him. Akbar refused to allow an execution on that auspicious day, and Abū al-Ma'ālī escaped. He found refuge with a servant of Bahādur Khān Shaybanī, who remanded him to Bayrām Khān upon discovering him. He was permitted to go on pilgrimage, but committed another murder in Gujarat and fled to Khān-i Zamān, who returned him to Bayrām Khān's custody. He was released when Bayrām Khān fell, and sent to Mecca.

8 Iqtidar Alam Khan, 'Politics', pp. 36–8.
9 M.R., 2:59.

Shah Abū al-Ma'ālī refused to accept anything less than the exalted political status which his personal relationship to Humāyūn had given him. His opposition had no lasting relevance.[10]

The details of Bayrām Khān's dismissal, fall and death do not require recounting, only interpretation. As noted above, if Shaykh Gadā'ī's conduct of office annoyed the Humāyūnī officers, Sunnī-Shī'ī friction had nothing to do with it. More importantly, neither of the contemporary biographers has identified the source of tension between Bayrām Khān and his followers and the men attached to Akbar himself. This conflict led to the conspiracy of Māham Anagah and Shihāb al-Dīn Aḥmad Khān which led to Akbar's abandonment of his guardian.[11]

Akbar had dropped the pilot, but he remained under the tutelage of Māham Anagah, the supervisor of his upbringing. Lacking the personal retainers on whom Bayrām Khān had depended, she had made arrangements with other followers of Akbar, like Shihāb al-Dīn Aḥmad Khān, or with Humāyūnī officers. This situation was unstable; Shihāb al-Dīn Aḥmad Khān, Bahādur Khān Uzbeg, Mun'im Khān and Shams al-Dīn Muḥammad Khān Atgah, Akbar's foster-father, all served as chief officers between April 1560 (Rajab 967) and December 1561 (Rabī' II 968). Māham Anagah's son Adham Khān and Pīr Muḥammad Khān also held influential positions during this time. Bahādur Khān and Mun'im Khān, who were among the leading Humayūnī and Chaghatay officers, held the title of *wakīl*; Shihāb al-Dīn Aḥmad Khān and Shams al-Dīn Muḥammad Khān, who were Akbarī officers, did not. The first Mughal conquest of Malwa took place during this transitional period, and included one event which heralded future developments.

Pīr Muḥammad Khān and Adham Khān commanded the invasion. Adham Khān kept most of the booty, sending only a few elephants to Akbar. When the young emperor heard of this withholding of the spoils, he hastened to Malwa. Adham Khān surrendered all of his booty to Akbar except for two concubines. Māham Anagah had the two women

[10] M.U., 3:186–91/1:132–6; M.T., 2:9–12/2–4; A.N., 2:15–17/27–30, 101–9/152–6; Z.K., 1:77–9.

[11] Srivastava, *Akbar*, 1:36–45; Ishtiaq Husain Qureshi, *Akbar* (Karachi: Ma'ref, 1978), pp. 54–9. Basic textual references are A.N., 2:91–120/108–85, M.T., 2:35–45/29–40; T.A., 2:143–50; T.Q., pp. 89–101. On the identity and position of Māham Anagah, see Henry Beveridge's note, A.N., 1:134, and errata, pp. v–vi.

executed to prevent them from revealing her son's conduct.[12] The chronicles imply that Akbar responded on his own initiative. Later in 1561 (968), Khān-i Zamān 'Alī Qulī Khān Shaybanī, the leader of the Uzbegs and governor of the eastern frontier and Jaunpur failed to send the booty from a victory over a Sūrī prince to court. Akbar led his army to Jaunpur, where Khān-i Zamān submitted his plunder.[13] These incidents show that Akbar considered the plunder taken on imperial campaigns as imperial property. The value of the cash, commodities and prisoners taken was not negligible, but that was not the point. If the booty which amīrs gained belonged to the ruler, not to the taker, the amīrs were components of the imperial regime, extensions of the ruler, not chieftains in their own right acting for themselves. Whatever Akbar's motivation, and whoever—if anyone—advised him, his marches to Malwa and Jaunpur began the redefinition of the status of mansabdar.

Akbar married the daughter of Rājah Bihārah Mal during this time as well. During his first pilgrimage to the shrine of Mu'īn al-Dīn Chishtī at Ajmer, in 1562 (969), the Rājah requested an audience. The Rājah was in difficult circumstances because his nephew Suja sought to displace him with the help of Mirzā Sharaf al-Dīn Ḥusayn Ahrārī, the Mughal governor of Ajmer and Mewat, in spite of Bihārah Mal's existing relationship with the dynasty. Akbar granted an audience and Bihārah Mal sought to cement his position by offering Akbar his daughter in marriage and placing his son Bhagwan Dās and grandson Mān Singh in imperial service. Akbar accepted his petition and ordered the Mirzā to cease operations against Bihārah Mal. The marriage itself did not break precedent, though Akbar was the first Tīmūrid to marry a Rajput princess. The persistence of the Kachwaha position in Mughal politics, which was unprecedented, was not yet obvious.[14]

The instability of the political constellation focused on Māham Anagah led to its destruction. Whoever held the dominant position provoked considerable jealousy, especially among those who saw

[12] A.N., 2:137–8/214, 139–43/217–22; T.A., 2:152–3; M.T., 2:48/43–4; Srivastava, *Akbar*, 1:49–53.

[13] A.N., 2:138–9/215–16, 147–8/227–9, T.A., 2:154–5; M.T, 2:48–9/44.

[14] A.N., 2:154–8/240–4; T.A., 2:155, M.T., 2:50/45–6; Srivastava, *Akbar*, 1:55–7; Kunwar Refaqat Ali Khan, *The Kachwahas under Akbar and Jahangir* (Delhi: Kitab, 1976), pp. 8–12.

themselves in his place. When even Māham Anagah became alienated from Shams al-Dīn Muḥammad Khān, she had no difficulty in drawing her son Adham Khān, Shihāb al-Dīn Aḥmad Khān, and Mun'im Khān into a conspiracy against him. It succeeded, as Adham Khān and two of his retainers murdered Akbar's foster-father in open court on 16 May 1562 (12 Ramażān 969). The sovereign was so enraged at the murder that he struck Adham Khān with his own fist and ordered his execution. The other conspirators fled; Māham Anagah died of grief forty days later. From this time on, no single group or faction dominated Mughal politics; Akbar had considerable freedom of action, and used it.[15]

4.2 The Beginning of Administrative Reform

Akbar began extending his authority as soon as he began to rule without a regent. After the murder of Shams al-dīn Muḥammad Khān, he appointed a eunuch named Khwājah Phūl Malik, who had had administrative responsibilities under Salim Sūr, to take charge of the imperial finances, with the title I'timād Khān. At this time, the imperial government received little revenue from the provinces because the governors diverted what they collected to their own households and followers. In the vocabulary of Mughal administration, there was little *khāliṣah*, land whose revenue went into the central treasury. I'timād Khān increased revenues and reduced both expenditures and official extortion. Though it receives little attention in the chronicles and modern historians have ignored it, his appointment had significant implications. In pastoral confederations, tribal governors had effective control over all the revenues of their provinces. I'timād Khān's programme thus conflicted with Chaghatay political expectations. None of the Mughal historians connect this initiative with the Uzbeg revolt which began two years later, but a connection may exist.[16]

[15] A.N., 2:173–8/268–75; T.A., 2:158–9, M.T., 2:52–4/49–52; Srivastava, *Akbar*, 1:62–5.

[16] A.N., 2:178–9/276; M.T., 2:65/63–4. On I'timād Khān, see M.U., 1:88–90/708–9. There is no mention of I'timād Khān's appointment in the T.A., and, surprisingly Srivāstava, *Akbar*, Smith, *Akbar*, and Qureshi, *Akbar* all neglect to mention his role. Iqtidar Alam Khan mentions this initiative in *The Political Biography of a Mughal Noble, Mu'nim Khan Khan-i Khanan, 1497–1575* (New Delhi: Orient Longman, 1973), p. xviii.

A second stage of administrative reform began with the appointment of Muẓaffar Khān Turbatī as *wazīr* in 1564 (971). He had begun his career as Bayrām Khān's *dīwān* and served as the imperial *dīwān-i buyutāt* (administrator of the imperial workshops) before his appointment as *wazīr*. He recommended the appointment of Shaykh 'Abd al-Nabī as *ṣadr* to assert more control over revenue grants. He also ordered a new revenue settlement for the empire, replacing that of Bayrām Khān's time which had become obsolete and subject to abuse. Abū al-Fażl regards the new settlement as a definite improvement, though still imperfect. Most importantly, Muẓaffar Khān promulgated a regulation fixing the number of troops each mansabdar should support and how much those troops should be paid.[17] This important step towards the mansabdari system, instituted in the spring of 1564 (971), indicates a formal shift in the status of Mughal officers. They ceased to be chieftains with their own followers and became cogs in the imperial machinery, maintaining troops for their masters. The regulation did not, of course, produce immediate changes either in relationships between mansabdars and their followers, or in the self-perception of mansabdars. But it revealed Akbar's political agenda. In doing so, it may have precipitated the Uzbeg revolt.

4.3 The Chishtī Connection

Few developments in the early part of Akbar's reign suggest that he intended to alter the Tīmūrid doctrine of kingship. A. L. Srivastava emphasizes the importance of the announcement in 1562 (969) of a ban on the enslaving of the families of enemy soldiers. Only Abū al-Fażl reports this proclamation, and the results he attributed to it, 'the wild and rebellious inhabitants of India placed the ring of devotion in the ear of obedience,' did not happen. Abū al-Fażl may have fabricated the proclamation. If he did not, it probably had little significance.[18]

[17] A.A., 1:198–9/279–80; A.N., 2:197–8/305–7, 248/374, 270/402–3, M.T., 2:66/64–5; M.U. 3:221–7/359–64. Abū al-Fażl's specific description of Muẓaffar Khān's accomplishments as *wazīr* places him in the tradition of the circle of justice: 'He managed in a proper mannner the operations of Treasury, which is the capital stock of sovereignty, the improvement of the peasantry, and the control of the army. . . .'

[18] A.N., 2:159–60/246–7; Srivastava, *Akbar*, 1:58–60. The decree makes no reference to ending forced conversion to Islam, though Srivastava says it does.

Although it played no part in the final Akbarī constitution, Akbar sought to add to his prestige and broaden support for his rule by displaying reverence for the saints of the Chishtī Sufi order. The Chishtīyyah were the most prestigious Sufi *silsilah* in the subcontinent and represented the universalist aspect of Islam, including a willingness to learn from Hindu teachers and teach Hindu devotees. The tombs of Mu'in al-Din Chishtī at Ajmer and his spiritual successor Nizām al-Din Awliyā' in Delhi were major pilgrimage sites for both Hindus and Muslims. Akbar began regular pilgrimages to the tomb of Mu'in al-Din at Ajmer in 1562 (969), beginning a lasting association with the Chishtī *silsilah*.[19] The tombs of Sufi saints had great importance both in Indo-Muslim piety and in the spread of Islam in the subcontinent, for the *barakah* (spiritual charisma) of the saint was transferred to his tomb. Devotion to the saint could thus produce miracles.[20] Akbar apparently sought to co-opt some of the surplus *barakah*.

Abū al-Fażl attributes Akbar's first pilgrimage to spiritual curiosity piqued by hearing some minstrels singing the praise of the Khwājah.[21] Akbar visited Ajmer ten times between 1562 (969) and 1579 (988).[22] He extended his connection with the Chishtīyyah to the living in 1569 (977), when he visited Mu'īn al-Din Chishtī's spiritual successor, Shaykh Salim Chishtī, of the village of Sikri. He was seeking the saint's intercession for the birth of a son to one of the Rajput wives, who was pregnant. With or without such intercession, the daughter of Rājah Bihārah Mal gave birth to the future Jahāngīr on 30 August 1569 (16 Rabī' II 977) at Sikri. Akbar made a pilgrimage to Ajmer in gratitude. Akbar's second son Murād was also born at Sikri the next year and the

[19] On the Chishtīyyah, see Annemarie Schimmel, *Mystical Dimensions of Islam* (Chapel Hill, N.C.: University of North Carolina Press, 1975), pp. 344–51; Sayyid Athar Abbas Rizvi, *A History of Sufism in India*, 2 vols., (New Delhi: Munshiram Manoharlal, 1978–83), 1:114–89, 2:264–318; J. Spencer Trimingham, *The Sufi Orders in Islam* (New York: Oxford University Press, 1971), pp. 64–5.

[20] Richard M. Eaton, 'Approaches to the Study of Conversion to Islam in India', in *Approaches to Islam in Religious Studies*, ed. Richard C. Martin (Tucson: University of Arizona Press, 1985), p. 117.

[21] A.N., 2:154–6/237–40.

[22] A.N., 2:324/477, 349–51/510–11, 356–7/516–17, 364–5/530, 3:44–63/65–91, 79–81/111–13, 110–55/153–220, 164–5/233–4, 185–259/212–13/298–9, 250–1/361–3, 275–9/402–6.

following year construction of a new capital at Sikri began.[23]

In addition to their involvement in the birth of Akbar's heirs, Abū al-Fażl claims that the Chishtī saints recognized his sovereignty and spiritual insight. Akbar intended to make a pilgrimage on foot to Ajmer in 1568 (975). On his way, he received word from the custodians of the shrine that the saint had appeared to them in a vision. The apparition told them to dissuade Akbar from going on foot, since the ruler's spiritual insight exceeded what the saint could provide.[24] If Abū al-Fażl's claim reflects what was alleged in 1568 (975) and is not his own invention, it shows that Akbar used his devotion to the Chishtīyyah to support his claim to spiritual insight and charisma of his own. Although Abū al-Fażl does not put the relationship with the Chishtīyyah into his elaboration of Akbar's status, it probably helped to spread the belief in Akbar's position as spiritual teacher and sovereign.[25]

4.4 The Revolt of Mirzā Sharaf al-Dīn Ḥusayn Ahrārī

Mirzā Sharaf al-Dīn Ḥusayn Ahrārī was a great-grandson of Khwājah 'Ubaydullah Ahrār and thus a member of a Sufi family with great perstige among the Chaghatays.[26] His maternal grandmother was a Tīmūrid princess and in 1560 (967) he had married Akbar's half-sister, Bakhshī Bānū Begum. He had jāgīrs near Ajmer and Nagaur and the exalted title of Amīr al-Umara' when, in October 1562 (Ṣafar 970), he fled from court to his jāgīrs. None of the chroniclers explains his departure beyond saying that he developed groundless suspicions of Akbar after his own father Khwājah Mu'īn al-Dīn came to court from Kashgar. Flight from court meant revolt. Akbar sent Bayrām Khān's nephew Ḥusayn Qulī Khān, who later received the title Khān-i Jahān, against the rebel. The imperial expedition occupied Mirzā Sharaf al-

[23] A.N., 2:343–48/502–8, 365/530–1.

[24] A.N., 2:324/477.

[25] J. F. Richards, 'The Formation of Imperial Authority under Akbar and Jahangir', in *Kingship and Authority in South Asia*, ed. idem, South Asian Studies, University of Wisconsin Madison 3 (Madison. Wi.: University of Wisconsin-Madison South Asian Studies, 1978), pp. 256–8, is the first historian to examine the Chishtī connection in the context of political doctrine.

[26] On this family, see Trimingham, *Orders*, pp. 92–5; Schimmel, *Dimensions*, p. 365.

Dīn's jāgīrs without difficulty. He fled to Jalaur and joined Shāh Abū al-Ma'alī, who had just returned from Mecca. The two rebels decided that Shāh Abū al-Ma'ālī would proceed to Kabul and get control of Mirzā Muḥammad Hakim as a figurehead against Akbar. The imperial forces prevented Mirzā Sharaf al-Dīn from making much headway against the Mughal regime. Shāh Abū al-Ma'ālī's intrigues in Kabul eventually ended in his own death.[27]

Both Shāh Abū al-Ma'ālī and Mirzā Sharaf al-Dīn Ḥusayn perceived themselves as Tīmūrid officers deserving of the highest level of status and influence. Dissatisfied with what they received or could expect from Akbar, they chose to resist him. Their opposition to Akbar took place too early to be a result of his political innovations. Iqtidar Alam Khan asserts that Chaghatay officers showed little enthusiasm in operations against the two rebels while the 'Persian' officers like Ḥusayn Qulī Khān were enthusiastic. The text he cites, however, refers to a minor mutiny by some Chaghatay and Badakhshī troopers in the contingents of Aḥmad Beg and Iskandar Beg, relatives of Ḥusayn Qulī Khān. It thus does not support his point.[28]

4.5 Akbar, Delhi, Agra, and Fathpur Sikri

The dismissal of Shaykh Gadā'ī Kambu as *ṣadr* along with Bayrām Khān interfered with Mughal efforts to develop a positive relationship with the Muslim notables of Hindustan, i.e. of Delhi. According to Bada'ūnī, Akbar attempted to establish marriage alliances with the leading Muslim families of the city in 1563 (971). He married the wife of one Shaykh 'Abd al-Wāsī, who divorced her at his request and departed for the Deccan, and sought to make other marriages as well. During a pilgrimage to the tomb of Niẓām al-Din Awliyā' in Delhi, on 12 January 1564 (27 Jumādā I 971), Akbar was wounded by an arrow. The injury was not serious and the assassin was slain on the spot. Abū al-Fażl attributes the attempt to Shāh Abū al-Ma'ālī and Mirzā Sharaf al-Dīn Ḥusayn Ahrārī, but Bada'ūnī states that the resentment of the

[27] A.N., 2:198–200/308–11, 202/314, 204–7/316–21; M.T., 2:59–60/57–9; T.A., 2:164–5; M.U. 3:232–8/808–12; Srivasatava, *Akbar*, 1:70–3.

[28] A.N., 2:199/200–310; Iqtidar Alam Khan, 'The Nobility under Akbar and the Development of his Religious Policy', *Journal of the Royal Asiatic Society* (1968) p. 31.

notables towards Akbar's attempts to conscript their women led to the incident.[29] Bada'ūnī's version explains Akbar's decision to abandon Delhi. J. F. Richards, the first historian to explain the significance of Akbar's establishment of new capitals, writes:[30]

> For two and a half centuries, Delhi had been the unassailable redoubt, the refuge for Indian Muslims and the seat of the Sultans of Hindustan. By moving...to Agra, and later to...Fathepur Sikri...Akbar reduced existing associations of legitimate rulership with Delhi. Neither Akbar nor a possible rebel could henceforth claim the imperial throne by virtue of possession of the citadels, the palaces, or the active support of the volatile population of the old imperial city.

Akbar abandoned Delhi and modified the political idea which Delhi had represented. It goes far beyond the evidence to suggest that Akbar set aside the idea of justifying his position as a Muslim ruler when he ended his effort to establish ties with the groups most interested in this form of legitimacy. The hostility of the Muslim notables of Delhi must, however, have affected Akbar's attitude towards the Muslim establishment.

Akbar's imperial construction programme began in 1565 (972) with the Agra fort, which took four years to complete. The building of Fathpur Sikri began in 1571 (979), but Akbar reportedly had decided to build there two years earlier, when Jahāngīr was born.[31] Historically and geographically, Agra was the logical alternative to Delhi; Akbar's massive citadel—fortified city—there stated, if nothing else, his intention to create a new imperial structure. The decision to build at Sikri meant something more, an attempt to incorporate the Chishtī *barakah* into his imperial prestige.[32] The construction of an entirely new city, in a new and uniform architectural style with a distinctive ground plan focused on the *jharūkā*, *dīwān-i khaṣṣ*, and *dīwān-i 'am*—the focal points of the royal routine, put the establishment of a new form of kingship in stone.[33] The buildings of Fathpur Sikri, and the surviving

[29] A.N., 2:201–2/312–13; M.T., 2:60–2/59–61.

[30] Richards, *Formation*, p. 255.

[31] A.N., 2·246–7/372–3, 365/531–6; M.T., 2:108–9/112.

[32] Richards, 'Formation', pp. 255–6.

[33] I discuss these three structures in the section on court rituals in the next chapter.

Akbarī structure inside the Agra fort, known as the Jahāngīrī Mahal, represent a deliberate synthesis of Hindu and Indo-Muslim architectural styles into a distinctively Akbarī form. The new style made a conscious political statement. It was not a random mixture of styles nor the product of a merging of Hindu and Muslim craft traditions.[34] The Akbarī synthesis in architectural style stated, and thus adumbrated, the mature Mughal constitution, which combined Muslim and Hindu elements in a new political order which derived its unity and underlying pattern from the sovereign. The construction of Fathpur Sikri thus reveals that Akbar had defined the central aspects of his programme in the early 1570s (980s), although the new political and administrative pattern was not complete for another decade.

4.6 The Uzbeg Revolt

The Uzbeg revolt represented the beginning of Chaghatay opposition to Akbar's political agenda. The appointment of Muẓaffar Khān and his proposals indicated that the young emperor did not intend to

[34] See Oleg Grabar, 'The Architecture of Power: Palaces, Citadels and Fortifications', in George Michell, *Architecture of the Islamic World* (New York: William Morrow, 1978) pp. 48–9, 72; Gary Martin 'Key Monuments of Islamic Architecture: the Subcontinent', ibid., pp. 265–6, 271; Gavin Hambly, *Cities of Mughal India* (New York: G. P. Putnam's Sons, 1968), pp. 63, 74; Saiyid Athar Abbas Rizvi and Vincent John Adams Flynn, *Fathpur Sikri* (Bombay: Taraporevala, 1975), pp. 16, 25, 32–3, 37, 39, 48, 59–64, 66–9, 73–5, 85–6. The references in Rizvi and Flynn are descriptions of individual buildings; they do not interpret the style of the city as a whole or discuss its political significance. Their descriptions of Hindu, Jain, and Iranian influences do not help the reader decide if the style is eclectic or synthetic, perhaps because the authors do not understand the distinction. Some observers consider the style eclectic. My view is derived from that of Michael Willis in an informal slide presentation in 1977. I do not know if he ever published his views. I found that I agreed with him when I visited Agra and Fathpur Sikri in 1983. Paul Wheatley, *The Pivot of the Four Quarters* (Chicago: Aldine, 1971), discusses the conception of cities as ceremonial complexes and cosmological symbols. The combination of his approach with the detailed archaeological studies now being done at Fatehpur Sikri by R. C. Gaur, Jamal Siddiqui, and K. K. Muhammad would dramatically enhance our understanding of Akbar's political programme. Both the plan and the style of the city require further study. For Wheatley's general approach, see xiii–xv. He discusses cities as ceremonial centres on pp. 225–40, 477–82. On p. 225, he writes, 'Operationally, they were instruments for the creation of political, social, economic, and sacred space at the same time as they were symbols of cosmic, social and moral order.'

satisfy his father's Chaghatay adherents. But the Uzbeg clan, not the Chaghatays as a group, opposed Akbar. The Uzbegs were a family of Shaybanī Uzbegs (i.e. descendants of Chingiz Khān through his son Juchī and grandson Shayban), who had entered Humāyūn's service. Iqtidar Alam perceives the Uzbegs as a clan, or extended family of officers. Their behaviour, however, suggests they were a tribe, i.e. a ruling clan with a people attached to it, not just a family.[35] Khān-i Zamān 'Alī Qulī Khān was one of the leading Chaghatay officers and effective chief of the clan, though Ibrāhīm Khān was actually the senior member. Akbar's regulations would have severed the connection between the Uzbeg officers and their hereditary followers, giving the Uzbegs a special motivation to oppose the new rules.

Akbar's struggle with the Uzbegs began with a confrontation with 'Abdullah Khān Uzbeg, a step-brother of Khān-i Zamān's uncle.[36] He led the Mughal re-occupation of Malwa in 1562 (969) and became governor of the province. In the late spring of 1564 (972) Akbar became suspicious of him. Abū al-Fażl suggests that 'Abdullah Khān intended to revolt; Badā'ūnī refers to a financial offence, possibly a refusal to forward *pīshkash*. Akbar proceeded towards Malwa in July, 1564 (Ẑū al-Hijjah 972), in spite of the monsoon. He apparently intended to treat 'Abdullah Khān as he had Adham Khān and Khān-i Zamān three years earlier, to obtain his personal submission and the rectification of the fault in question. He twice sent emissaries to bring 'Abdullah Khān to court, offering to leave him in office and unpunished, as Mun'im Khān desired. 'Abdullah Khān again refused to accept Akbar's mercy as genuine. On 6 August (27 Ẑū al-Hijjah) Akbar's advance guard clashed with and defeated 'Abdullah Khān's forces. 'Abdullah Khān eventually escaped to Gujarat. Akbar returned to Agra after appointing Qarā Bahādur Khān governor of Malwa.[37]

35 For Iqtidar Alam Khan's view, see *Biography*, p. xvii.

36 For this relationship, see T.H.A., 87, 244; A.N., 1:142/319; Iqtidar Alam Khān, *Biography*, p. 74.

37 Qarā Bahādur Khān was a cousin of Mirzā Haydar Gurgan, the author of the *Tārīkh-i Rashidī*, and had been a servant of Mirzā Kāmrān. M.U. 3:48–50/2:492–3. For the whole incident, A.N., 2:221–35/341–56, M.T., 2:67–8/66–8; T.A., 2:171–4; T.Q., 124–7; M.U., 2:764–9/1:82–4; Srivastava, *Akbar*, 1:85–7; Iqtidar Alam Khan, *Biography*, pp. 77–8. Nizām al-Dīn Aḥmad mentions only one attempt at negotiation and names Muqim Khān as Akbar's representative. I assume Muqim Khān was the

This episode resembled Akbar's responses to Adham Khān's and Khān-i Zamān's withholdings of spoils. Akbar wanted to demonstrate unmistakably that these provincial governors had behaved in an unacceptable manner, but did not punish them even by transfer. He sought instead to re-define the relationship between provincial governors and the central authority. If we assume that 'Abdullah Khān would have submitted to Akbar if his position in Malwa remained unchanged, that re-definition—a reduction in autonomy and security—caused him to prefer flight.

Bada'ūnī asserts that 'Abdullah Khān's conduct made Akbar suspicious of the Uzbegs as a group.[38] During Bayrām Khān's regency, Khān-i Zamān's infatuation with a young man had alienated Akbar from him. Akbar attempted to separate the two men and ordered the transfer of the town of Sandilah in Oudh from Khān-i Zamān's jāgīr. Khān-i Zamān almost confronted the new jagirdar in battle but thought better of it. Bayrām Khān encouraged Akbar to forgive Khān-i Zamān; Pīr Muḥammad Khān wanted him punished and had his agent at court killed. Khān-i Zamān's appointment as governor of Jaunpur in 1559 (966) shows that Bayrām Khān prevailed. After his success there, Khān-i Zamān did part with his paramour.[39]

Fighting began in 1565 (972), when Akbar was informed that Iskandar Khān Uzbeg planned some form of rebellion. He sent Ashraf Khān to reconcile Iskandar Khān and bring him to court, but Iskandar Khān effectively kidnapped Ashraf Khān under the pretext of bringing him to negotiate with Ibrāhīm Khān. The Uzbeg officers then joined Khān-i Zamān and planned rebellion. Iskandar Khān and Ibrāhīm Khān were to occupy Lucknow while Khān-i Zamān and Bahādur Khān proceeded against Majnūn Khān Qāqshāl at Manikpur on the Ganges. Ultimately, the Uzbegs apparently hoped to imprison Akbar and take effective control of the empire.[40] Srivastava surmises that the Uzbegs felt that,

man who received the title Shujā'at Khān for distinguishing himself in this campaign (M.U., 2:557–60/850–3).

[38] M.T., 2:75/85.

[39] This account combines M.T., 2:20–4/14–17 and A.N., 2:67–9/104–7, 83–5/127–9. Akbar evidently detested male homosexuality; Muẓaffar Khān Turbatī was temporarily disgraced for the same reason, see M.U., 3:221–7/359–64; A.N., 2:286/427.

[40] A.N., 2:248–50/375–6; T.A., 2:180; M.T., 2:74–5/75–6; T.Q, p. 129; Iqtidar

because of their crucial roles in Humāyūn's return to Hindustan and in the defeat of the Sūrī claimants after Akbar's succession, they deserved a more central role in the regime, and that they resented Akbar's claim to the spoils of victory.[41] South of the Ganges, the Uzbeg advance met with immediate resistance from the local jagirdars, including Shāham Khān Jalayir, but the Uzbegs drove them back to Manikpur, which Majnūn Khān Qāqshāl defended. The loyalty of Shāham Khan and Majnūn Khān, the leaders of Chaghatay clans, shows that there was no general opposition to Akbar among Chaghatays at this time. He requested and received help from Āṣaf Khān, who was returning from his invasion of Gondwanda. When Akbar received their report, he sent an advance force under Mun'im Khan and proceeded later in the spring of 1565 (972). He joined Mun'im Khān at Qanauj before the monsoon.[42]

Iskandar Khān and Khān-i Zamān withdrew at Akbar's approach. The emperor joined Āṣaf Khān and Majnūn Khān at Manikpur and the imperial forces then proceeded towards Jaunpur.[43] When the imperial forces reached there on 13 July 1565 (13 Zu al-Hijjah 972), the Uzbegs had fled across the Ganges. Akbar sent Majnūn Khān and Āṣaf Khān in pursuit. Mun'im Khān had wanted to command this force himself, but Khwājah-yi Jahān Harawī wanted Āṣaf Khān to receive the post. Akbar gave the task to Āṣaf Khān because he presented an army of five thousand well-equipped troops. Khwājah-yi Jahān and Āṣaf Khān were both Persian bureaucrats from Herat; Mun'im

---

Alam Khan, *Biography*, pp. 78–9. Iqtidar Alam asserts that Akbar planned to eliminate the Uzbegs and sent Ashraf Khān only to attempt to delay an open break. He cites Abū al-Fażl's report that Akbar opened negotiations with Fath Khān, who held the fortress of Rohtas in Bihar but refused to submit to Sulaymān Kararānī, in order to gain his support in the coming clash with Khān-i Zamān (A.N., 2:243/365–6). Niẓām al-Dīn Aḥmad asserts that Fath Khān saw Akbar's progress east to suppress the Uzbegs as an opportunity to save himself from Sulaymān by submitting to the Mughals (T.A., 2:185–6). Niẓām al-Dīn's version is more believable because Abū al-Fażl had a motive for revision. Akbar had no exoteric means of knowing that he would need help against the Uzbegs when Abū al-Fażl says he opened negotiations to receive it.

[41] Srivastava, *Akbar*, 1:91.

[42] A.N., 2:251–2/378; M.T., 2:75–6/76–7; T.A., 2:181–2; Iqtidar Alam Khan, *Biography*, p. 80.

[43] Āṣaf Khān submitted the booty from Chauragarh at this time.

Khān was a Chaghatay. Mun'im Khān sympathized with the Uzbegs, from kinship and from shared political assumptions. He sought at this juncture what he arranged later as mediator, the preservation of the Uzbeg clan within the Mughal system. Also, Khwājah-yi Jahān had been Akbar's *bakhshī* before Humāyūn's death. Mun'im Khān and Khān-i Zamān had had ties with Humāyūn. Mun'im Khān spoke for the tradition of the pastoral confederation while Khwājah-yi Jahān and Āṣaf Khān represented Akbar's political programme.[44]

Āṣaf Khān's flight shows that he did not accept Akbar's insistence on the forwarding of booty to the imperial treasury. Muẓaffar Khān, another Persian bureaucrat, had made repeated inquiries about the booty from Chauragarh. Āṣaf Khān remained insecure; his jāgīr was changed at this time as well. He fled with his brother Wazīr Khān on 16 September 1565 (19 Ṣafar 973). Akbar appointed Mun'im Khān to replace Āṣaf Khān and Shujā'āt Khān to pursue him.[45] Āṣaf Khān and Wazīr Khān accepted an invitation from Khān-i Zamān to join the rebels, but had no common cause with them. The two brothers deserted the Uzbegs at the first opportunity and rejoined imperial service through the intercession of Muẓaffar Khān.[46]

The appointment of Mun'im Khān, who began an advance, encouraged Khān-i Zamān to open negotiations even though he had begun to receive assistance from Sulaymān Kararānī. Most likely, Khān-i Zamān felt that he could obtain the intercession of Mun'im Khān for favourable terms. He sent an old maidservant to remind Mun'im Khān of their old friendship. Mun'im Khān responded by urging Khān-i Zamān to seek forgiveness from Akbar and to avoid reliance on the Bengal Afghans. Khān-i Zamān eventually agreed to meet with him on a raft in the middle of the Ganges, which separated the two armies. Bayāzīd Bayāt attended the meeting, and reports that the two men met as old friends, mourning Humāyūn, and that Khān-i Zamān emphasized his services to the dynasty. After this meeting, negotiations became general with Khwājah-i Jahān and Khwājah Ghiyās

[44] A.N., 2:252–3/378–80; M.T., 2:76/76–7; T.A., 2:182–3; T.H.A., p. 186; Iqtidar Alam Khan, *Biography*, p. 81. On Khwājah-yi Jahān, see M.U., 1:630–2/823–4.

[45] A.N., 2:255–6/381–3; T.A., 2:184–5; M.T., 2:77/78; T.H.A., p. 288; Iqtidar Alam Khan, *Biography*, pp. 81–2.

[46] A.N., 2:271–2/404–5, 283–4/418; M.T., 2:85/86–7, 87–8/89; T.A., 196–7, 207.

al-Dīn 'Ali (later the second Āṣaf Khān) representing Akbar. Khwājah-yi Jahān apparently opposed giving amnesty and Akbar did not wish to grant it without his consent, but eventually agreed. Khān-i Zamān sent his mother and Ibrāhīm Khān, the senior Uzbeg, to submit to Akbar. The Qāqshāl officers were also reconciled to Khān-i Zamān at this time. Akbar pardoned the Uzbegs and restored their jāgīrs, but forbade Khān-i Zamān to cross the Ganges.[47]

The imperial officers in Oudh had also opened negotiations with Bahādur Khān and Iskandar Khān, but reached no agreement. Akbar sent Rājah Tūdar Mal and Lashkar Khān with reinforcements and instructions to fight or pardon the rebels at their own discretion.[48] They gave the rebels an ultimatum to attend Akbar, but lost the ensuing battle. The Uzbegs took some imperial elephants. Hearing this news, Mun'im Khān and Khān-i Zamān wrote to Bahādur Khān ordering them to return the elephants. When the imperial officers reported their discomfiture, Akbar extended the amnesty to the Uzbeg force and forgave his loyal subordinates for failing to reach a settlement.[49]

As soon as Akbar left Jaunpur for Varanasi on 24 January 1566 (3 Rajab 973), Khān-i Zamān violated the conditions of the settlement by crossing the Ganges and occupying the forts at Ghazipur and Muhammadabad. Akbar blamed Mun'im Khān for interceding for the Uzbegs. Iqtidar Alam surmises that Khān-i Zamān believed that Akbar had pardoned him out of weakness and hoped to gain the support of the Bengal Afghans. In order to wean Mun'im Khān away from his sympathy for the Uzbegs, Akbar awarded him part of the jāgīrs of Khān-i Zamān and Bahādur Khān. He then accompanied his commander-in-chief into the field. Akbar sought to make a surprise attack on Khān-i Zamān at Muhammadabad but Mun'im Khān betrayed the plan. The imperial army pursued the Uzbeg leader north to the fort of Chillupur near Gorakhpur; meanwhile the Uzbeg forces returning from Oudh re-took Jaunpur. Akbar hastened there to prevent them

[47] A.N., 2:257–60/384–8; T.A., 2:187–8; M.T., 2:78–9/80–1; T.H.A, pp. 290–3. Iqtidar Alam Khan, *Biography*, pp. 83–6.

[48] Lashkar Khān Muḥammad Ḥusayn Khurasanī, presumably a Persian bureaucrat since he held the posts of *mīr-i 'arz* and *mīr bakhshī*, M.U., 3:161–3/830–1.

[49] A.N., 2:260–3/389–92; T.H.A., pp. 292–3; M.T., 2:78–82/80–3; T.A., 2:190–1; Iqtidar Alam Khan, *Biography*, pp. 86–7.

from looting the imperial camp. At Gorakhpur, he made arrangements for a major campaign to put an end to the Uzbegs. Faced with that prospect, Khān-i Zamān again asked Mun'im Khān to intercede for him. Mun'im Khān approached Akbar through Shaykh 'Abd al-Nabī, Makhdūm al-Mulk, Mīr Murtażā Sharīfī and Mīr 'Abd al-Latīf Qazwīnī. Akbar accepted their pleas, possibly because he feared that continued operations against the Uzbegs would lead to a clash with Sulaymān Kararānī.[50]

Following this second amnesty, Akbar began to return to Agra via Kara, leaving Mun'im Khān, Muzaffar Khān, Khwājah-yi Jahān, and Lashkar Khān with most of the imperial army to arrange a definitive settlement with Khān-i Zamān. Bahādur Khān and Iskandar Khān apparently intended to break the agreement but Mun'im Khān dissuaded them without reporting their intentions to Akbar. Either because of Mun'im Khān's sympathy for the Uzbegs or some disagreement over jāgīrs, there was a major dispute between Mun'im Khān, who was supported by Khwājah-yi Jahān and Lashkar Khān, and Muẓaffar Khān. Muẓaffar Khān took the situation seriously enough to leave his assigned post to report to court and Akbar responded by dismissing Lashkar Khān as *mīr bakhshī* and depriving Khwājah-yi Jahān of custody of the imperial seal. Mun'im Khān was not punished but, according to Abū al-Fażl, behaved circumspectly as a result. Nonetheless, when Akbar proceeded to the Punjab to deal with Mirzā Muḥammad Hakim in November 1566 (Jumādā I 974), he left Mun'im Khān in charge at Agra. During this interlude, 'Abdullah Khān Uzbeg joined his relatives.[51]

The last act of the Uzbeg rebellion came in the spring of 1567 (974). While Akbar was in the Punjab, Mun'im Khān reported that Khān-i Zamān, Bahādur Khan, and Iskandar Khān had proclaimed their allegiance to Mirzā Muḥammad Hakim, whom Akbar had just driven back to Kabul. The emperor returned to Agra. The Uzbegs had taken Lucknow and the entire region north of the Ganges, with Bahādur Khān attacking Manikpur, Iskandar Khān and Ibrāhīm Khān invading

[50] A.N., 2:264–8/393–9; T.H.A., pp. 294–8; T.A., 2:192–5; M.T., 2:83–4/84–6; Iqtidar Alam Khan, *Biography*, pp. 87–90.

[51] A.N., 2:268–71/398–403/ 276/411, 279/413; M.T., 2:84/86; T.A., 2:195; Iqtidar Alam Khan, *Biography*, pp. 90–2.

Oudh, and Khān-i Zamān attacking Qanauj. Majnūn Khān and Āṣaf Khān, who had now returned to imperial service, defended Manikpur.[52] Akbar left Mun'im Khān in Agra, sent an advance force to relieve Qanauj, and departed east on 6 May 1567 (24 Shawwāl 974). Khān-i Zamān raised the siege of Qanauj. Akbar sent a large force to Oudh and proceeded toward Kara and Manikpur. Receiving a report that Khān-i Zamān had crossed the Ganges to attack Gwalior, Akbar forded the river with only a small force and joined Āṣaf Khān and Majnūn Khān.[53] They made a surprise attack on the Uzbeg camp. In a hard-fought battle on 9 June (Ẕū al-Hijjah), Khān-i Zamān was killed and Bahādur Khān captured and executed. When he heard of the defeat of his relatives, Iskandar Khān took refuge with the Afghans of Bengal and Akbar forbade pursuit. Ibrāhīm Khān appealed to Mun'im Khān to intercede for him and obtained a pardon and a post in Mun'im Khān's entourage, but not an imperial mansab.[54] Iskandar Khān eventually sought pardon through Mun'im Khān as well and re-entered imperial service as *fawjdār* of Lucknow.[55]

The Uzbeg rebellion marked the passing of the Chaghatay and Humāyūnī elite from the centre of the political stage. Khān-i Zamān's relationships with Humāyūn and Bayrām Khān had made him one of the leading officers of the regime. His posting to Jaunpur, then the eastern frontier, symbolized this position but placed him on the periphery of politics. The deaths of his patrons must have left him alienated from the new order, though his old friendship with Mun'im Khān mitigated the situation. It became apparent, however, that Mun'im Khān held the pre-eminent titles of *khān-i khānān* and *sipāh salār* because of his seniority among the surviving Humayūnī officers. Possession of the title, and even the post of *wakīl*, did not give Mun'im Khān control of the political agenda. His loss of the post to Muẓaffar Khān

[52] A.N., 2:283/418–19, 288–9/424–5; T.Q., p. 151; M.T., 2:92–4/94–6; T.A. 2:209.

[53] Akbar's first cousin, Mirzā Kāmrān's son Abū al-Qāsim, had been a prisoner in Gwalior, but Akbar had ordered his execution before leaving Agra. If Khān-i Zamān had gained custody of the prince, it would have transformed the struggle from a rebellion against the Tīmūrids to a contest between Tīmūrid rulers. T.Q., p. 145.

[54] A.N., 2:289–96/426–34; M.T., 2:94–8/95–101; T.A., 2:209–14; T.Q., pp. 151–68.

[55] A.N., 2:367–8/532–4; T.Q., pp. 244–7.

Turbatī reduced him to irrelevance.[56] Khān-i Zamān had to see Mun'im Khān's loss of status as a blow to his own position. The loss of revenue and autonomy which the new administrative measures meant had to increase the Uzbeg leader's estrangement. Mun'im Khān was not disloyal to Akbar, but was loyal to the political order he understood. This attitude explains his behaviour. The officers who opposed the acceptance to Khān-i Zamān's submissions were all Persian bureaucrats who had begun their careers in the service of Akbar or Bayrām Khān.[57] The Uzbeg officers and Mun'im Khān were all Humāyūnī officers. Ethnicity did not determine political behaviour; expectations did.

Khān-i Zamān's two submissions and Akbar's willingness to pardon him reveal that Akbar appreciated conciliation as a political weapon and probably preferred it personally. He faced enough external enemies, especially the Afghans, to make a peaceful settlement desirable. Mun'im Khān represented the entire Chaghatay establishment at court; Akbar could not lightly disregard his entreaties. Khān-i Zamān submitted to Akbar only to gain time, hoping that Akbar would suffer a reverse elsewhere or that Sulaymān Kararānī would come to his assistance in full force. Akbar finally put an end to the Uzbegs because tolerating their continued breaking of solemn covenants could lead only to anarchy. Because of Mun'im Khān's continuous intercession for the Uzbegs and passing of information to them, Akbar could not trust him and left him behind. Mun'im Khān's appointment to Jaunpur gave him a position worthy of his rank but outside the capital.

4.7 The Mirzās and the Atgah Khayl

Iqtidar Alam Khan classifies the Uzbegs with three other groups, the Mirzās, the Atgah Khayl, and the Qāqshāls. This classification is misleading because the Uzbegs and Qāqshāls were tribal groups and the Mirzās and the Atgah Khayl were families of officers.[58] When the Uzbegs and Qāqshāls revolted, Akbar had to respond with major expeditions and fight battles. The opposition of the Mirzās to his rule never posed a real threat; the Atgah Khayl never opposed him. His

[56] Iqtidar Alam Khan, *Biography*, pp. 68–74.

[57] Āṣaf Khān Harawī had been a servant of Humāyūn, but received rapid advancement after his death. M.U., 1:77–83/36–40.

[58] Iqtidar Alam Khan, *Biography*, p. xvii.

dealings with both families deserve mention.

Muḥammad Sultān Mirzā was a Tīmūrid on both sides, a great-great-great grandson of Tīmūr's second son 'Umar Shaykh and, through his mother, grandson of Sulṭān Ḥusayn-i Bayqarā, the last Tīmūrid ruler of Herat, himself a great-grandson of 'Umar Shaykh.[59] Muḥammad Sulṭān Mirzā had been a servant of Sulṭān Ḥusayn, Bābur, and Humāyūn. Because of his age, Akbar had permitted him to retire to a jāgīr at Azampur in the sarkar of Sambhal, east of and across the Ganges from Delhi. Muḥammad Sulṭān Mirzā had two older sons, Ulugh Mirza and Shāh Mirzā, and in retirement had a second family consisting of Ibrāhīm Ḥusayn Mirzā, who married a daughter of Mirzā Kāmrān, Muḥammad Ḥusayn Mirzā, Maṣ'ud Ḥusayn Mirzā, and 'Āqil Ḥusayn Mirzā. After the end of the Mirzās' rebellion, Ibrāhīm Ḥusayn Mirzā's son Muẓaffar Ḥusayn Mirzā married Akbar's eldest daughter, Sulṭān Khānūm, and his sister Nūr al-Nisā' Begum married Sulṭān Salim, the future Jahāngīr.[60]

The Mughal sources do not explain the repeated uprisings of Muḥammad Sulṭān Mirzā's younger sons, but the marriages give a good indication. We do not know whether the maternal or paternal descent of Muẓaffar Ḥusayn and Nūr al-Nisā' determined their status, but Akbar's marriage of them to his own children served two purposes. Especially in the case of Sulṭān Khānūm, a Tīmūrid spouse meant no dishonour to the emperor's child and no favour to a family outside the ruling clan. Moreover, the offspring of these marriages, if any, would bring their share in the sovereign gene pool into Akbar's own family. If Akbar treated Muẓaffar Ḥusayn Mirzā as a relative, it suggests that the Mirzās revolted as rival Tīmūrid claimants to sovereignty. Until his death in 1506 (911), Sulṭān Ḥusayn Mirzā of Herat, not Bābur, had been the pre-eminent Tīmūrid. Whether they felt that they had the same rights as Akbar as fellow descendants of Tīmūr, or that they represented an older 'Umar Shaykhī/Sulṭān Ḥusaynī dispensation against the

[59] For a recent genealogical table of the Tīmūrids, see H. R. Roemer, 'The Successors of Timur', in *The Cambridge History of Iran Volume 6: the Timurid and Safavid Periods*, ed. Peter Jackson and Lawrence Lockhart (Cambridge: Cambridge University Press, 1986) p. 139. For information on Sulṭān Ḥusayn, see ibid., pp. 121–5.

[60] The most convenient reference on the family as a whole is Blochman's A.A./ 1:513–6.

Miranshahi/Baburi dispensation, the Mirzās resistance to Akbar was a conflict between different clans or dispensations of the Tīmūrid family.[61]

With that interpretation in mind, the activities of the Mirzās require only a brief recounting. Muḥammad Sulṭān's four younger sons revolted while Akbar was in the Punjab in the spring of 1567 (974). They plundered Sambhal and when driven off by the jagirdars fled to Khān-i Zamān, whose rebellion was in remission. The Mirzās could come to no agreement with the Uzbegs, and proceeded towards Delhi. Tātār Khān, the governor there, drove them off, but the Mirzās escaped him and gained control of Malwa. Preoccupied with Mirzā Muḥammad Hakim and the Uzbegs, Akbar took no immediate action beyond ordering the imprisonment of Muḥammad Sulṭān Mirzā.[62] After the final defeat of the Uzbegs, Akbar turned his attention to the conquest of Chitor, but sent Shihāb al-Dīn Aḥmad Khān with Hajjī Muḥammad Khān Sistanī and others who held jāgīrs in Malwa, to deal with the Mirzās. The errant Tīmūrids fled at the approach of the imperial forces and took refuge in Gujarat.[63]

Driven from Gujarat temporarily, the Mirzās tried and failed to establish themselves in Malwa in 1568 (974), fleeing back into Gujarat when Akbar sent large forces against them.[64] When Akbar invaded Gujarat late in 1572 (981), the Mirzās, who held a substantial part of the province, opposed him. Their resistance continued throughout Akbar's operations in Gujarat; after the conquest of the province and the suppression of a revolt in April 1573 (Ẕū al-Hijjah 980) Ibrāhīm Ḥusayn Mirzā and Muḥammad Ḥusayn Mirža had been killed and the rest of

[61] For the concept of this type of clash, see John E. Woods, *The Aqquyunlu: Clan, Confederation, Empire* (Chicago: Bibliotheca Islamica 1976), pp. 12–16; Martin B. Dickson 'Uzbek Dynastic Theory in the Sixteenth Century', *Proceedings of the 25th International Congress of Orientalists*, 4 vols. (Moscow: 1963), 3:208–16.

[62] A.N., 2:279–81/413–15; M.T., 2:85–6/87–8, 91/93; T.A., 2:204–6, Srivastava, *Akbar*, 1:97–8.

[63] A.N., 2:313/462–3; M.T., 2:102/105; Srivastava, *Akbar*, 1:105.

[64] A.N., 2:330–1/484–6; M.T., 2:106–7/110; T.A., 2:221–3; Srivastava, *Akbar*, 1:111–12.

the family had fled to the Deccan.[65] Muẓaffar Ḥusayn Mirzā made a final effort in 1577 (985), was defeated twice, and fled to Khandesh. Rājah 'Ali Khān, the ruler of Khandesh, imprisoned Muẓaffar Ḥusayn Mirzā and sent him to Akbar. Akbar eventually pardoned him and ordered his marriage to Sulṭān Khānūm.[66]

Unlike the Uzbegs, the Mirzās had no supporters at court or constituency broader than their own followers. They were no more than a minor irritant. The Atgah Khayl differed from the Mirzās in that they owed their position entirely to Akbar. Atgah Khayl means foster-family; Shams al-Dīn Muḥammad Khān Atgah had been the husband of Akbar's nurse Jījī Anagā and had gained the position of *wakīl* through that connection. His brothers Mīr Muḥammad Khān Khān-i Kilān, Quṭb al-Dīn Muḥammad Khān and Sharīf Khān Atgah and son Khān-i A'zam Mirzā 'Azīz Kūkah constituted the Atgah Khayl. All four men had jāgīrs in the Punjab, which they had held for some time. Khān-i Kilān was governor of the province. In September 1568 (Ramażān 976), Akbar summoned all four men to court and assigned his three foster-uncles to different jāgīrs. Khān-i Kilān received Sambhal, Quṭb al-Dīn Muḥammad Khān became governor of Malwa, and Sharīf Khan received Qanauj. Khān-i A'zam alone kept his jāgīr, Dipalpur. These transfers do not appear important, but Abū al-Fażl and Bayāzīd Bayāt do not allow us to ignore them. Bayāzīd reports that Akbar told Mun'im Khān that he considered the removal of the Atgah Khayl from the Punjab and dispersal of them to different jāgīrs his greatest accomplishment.[67] Abū al-Fażl uses a marvellous metaphor of the king as a gardener, carefully weeding his plot, to describe Akbar's action. Just as the gardener weeds,[68]

so do just and far-seeing kings light the lamp of wisdom by regulating

[65] A.N., 3:16–19/24–8, 23–6/32–5, 34–8/49–54, 41–60/59–84; M.T., 2:143–5/146–8, 147–9/151–3, 149–61/152–64; 164–70/167–73; T.A., 2:235–55, 261–73; T.Q., pp. 259–67, 274, 287–8; Srivastava, *Akbar*, 1:127–9, 132–3, 136–9.

[66] A.N., 3:206–9/292–4, 213–15/301–2, 233/330, 261–2/379–80, 266/366–7, 386/571, 644/990; T.A., 2:331–2, 336; M.T., 2:249–50/256–7, 253/260, 266/274; T.Q., p. 397.

[67] T.H.A., p. 253.

[68] A.N., 2:332/487. The full discussion is on pp. 332–3/486–8; see also T.A., 2:223, M.T., 2:106/109.

> and instructing their servants, and so uprear the standard of guidance. Whenever a large body is gathered together of one mind and speech, and show much push and energy, it is proper to disperse them, firstly for their own good, and secondly for the welfare of the community. Even if no improper act in consequence of the aggregation be seen or suspected, such dispersion is the material of union, for peace cannot be established when there is damage from the man-throwing wine of the world, and the weak-headed drinkers of the cup of its intoxication! Especially when strife-mongers and tale-bearers abound. Negligence is implanted in the human constitution. Accordingly the wisdom and statesmanship of the Shahinshah demanded that the loyal members of the Atga Khail, who had for a long time been gathered in the Panjab and been administering that province, should leave it, and after appearing at Court should have charge of another territory.

The transfer of the Atgah Khayl, without opposition, demonstrated that all jāgīrs assigned by the ruler were transferable and established the policy of dispersing powerful groups of officers.

4.8 Summary

Developments during this period reveal Akbar's political intentions. He greatly expanded central control over events in the provinces, enriched the central treasury, and began the process of circumscribing the status and obligations of his officers. Muslim and Hindu provincial potentates had, tacitly or explicitly, negotiated niches in the polity, altering the character of the ruling class and adding to the resources and flexibility of the regime. The Mughal polity had lost the characteristics of the Tīmūrid pastoral confederation. Though still numerically predominant, the Chaghatay officers had neither the central political position nor the autonomy in the provinces which they expected. Because the different ethnic groups in the Mughal regime did not function as ethnic factions, the idea that Akbar brought in other groups to counterbalance the Chaghatays distorts the situation. He had to bring the Hindustani officers into his government in order to gain access to their military resources and some of the revenue from their homelands. Their adherence made his position more secure. Perhaps because their expectations were more fluid, they accepted political changes which the Uzbegs did not.

Akbar had also changed the geographic, and by extension the constitutional, centre of the empire. He had failed to win the allegiance of the Muslim notables of Delhi, i.e. the group which provided the leading ulema and was the repository of Muslim opinion in Hindustan. He had abandoned Delhi as a political centre and begun new foundations at Agra and Fathpur Sikri. The layout and architectural style of these new cities demonstrated that the departure from Delhi was more than geographical. The synthesis of Hindu and Indo-Muslim architectural styles to form a new, specifically Akbarī style demonstrated that Akbar intended to turn away from the political programme of Muslim dominance and make the Hindu, mostly Rajput, potentates who had submitted to him full participants in his government.

CHAPTER 5
The Definitive Reforms

Between 1572 (980) and 1580 (988), Akbar's empire became recognizably Mughal. The mansabdari system, pattern of provincial administration, and court rituals and the constitution which they actualized all became apparent during this period. The chronicles provide good coverage of some aspects of this development, but leave others obscure.

5.1 The Mansabdari System and Provincial Administration

In 1572–73 (980), Akbar propounded sweeping administrative changes: 'the branding regulations, the conversion of the imperial territories into crown-lands, and the fixing of the grades of the officers of the state.' Shāhbāz Khān Kambū, who as *mīr bakhshī* had control of the payment of the officers, proposed branding regulations in 1573 (981). Akbar appointed Muẓaffar Khān Turbatī *wakīl* on 19 November (24 Rajab) of that year, showing his intention to institute administrative centralization. Muẓaffar Khān did not execute this programme, however, and lost both influence and office as a result. The reason for his inaction is unclear.[1] His failure to carry out these reforms explains

[1] A.N., 3:67–9/93–5; M.T. 2:171/174, 190–3; T.A., 2:276; T.Q., p. 195; A. J. Qaisar, 'Shahbaz Khan Kambu', *Medieval India: A Miscellany* 1 (1969): 53–5. On the office of *mīr bakhshī*, see Ishtiaq Husain Qureshi, *The Administration of the Mughal Empire* (Patna: N.V. Publications, n.d.), pp. 77–9; Ibn Hasan, *The Central Structure of the Mughal Empire* (London: 1936; reprint ed., New Delhi: Munshiram Manoharlal, 1980), pp. 210–34.

the description of these reforms twice in the *Akbār-nāmah* and the *Muntakhab al-Tawārīkh*. Bada'ūnī's first reference specifies that Shāhbāz Khān initiated branding, but precedes his notice of the appointment of Muẓaffar Khān as *wakīl*.

In 1574 (982), Akbar placed four officers in charge of administering the mansabdari system and a new system of provincial government: Shāhbāz Khān Kambū, Āṣaf Khān Ghiyās al-Dīn 'Alī, Ray Purakhutam and Ray Rām Dās. Of these men, Shāhbāz Khān was an Indo-Muslim, Āṣaf Khān a bureaucrat from a prominent Iranian family, Ray Purakhutam obscure, and Ray Rām Dās, though he was a Kachwaha, apparently a bureaucrat who began his career in the service of Rajput officers. The two Hindus were most likely members of the Hindu administrative castes.[2]

The mansabdari sytem executed the assumptions of the military patronage state to perfection. It placed Mughal officers in a hierarchy with numerical ranks. The ranks (mansab) simultaneously specified an officer's place in the imperial hierarchy, his military obligation, and his salary. The number of the rank was the number of cavalrymen and horses the officer had to support. In accord with the abandonment of collective sovereignty, Mughal princes held the highest ranks, becoming imperial servants. They had a special status with the title *sulṭān* reserved for them, but the break with earlier Tīmūrid practice was decisive. An officer had to maintain a number of draft horses, elephants, and camels in proportion to his rank. *Dāgh* (branding) stood for the system of mustering men and horses to verify that mansabdars met their obligations. Until he presented the required number of troops and horses for branding, he received a proportion of his pay called *bar-awardī* (estimated). He received full pay only on presenting his full contingent for inspection.[3]

This system allowed many officers to collect their *bar-awardī* pay without ever supporting all the required troops, though they had to bring the entire contingent for their current rank in order to be eligible

[2] A.N., 3:116–18/165–6; Qaisar, 'Shahbaz Khan'; M.U., 1:90–3, 2:155–7/587–9. The identification of Ray Rām Dās with Ray Rām Dās Kachwaha is not certain.

[3] The translation of *bar-awardī* is based on the definitions of *bar-award* in John Platts, *A Dictionary of Urdu, Classical Hindi and English* (1884, reprint ed., New Delhi: Oriental Books Reprint, 1977) because none of the Persian definitions fit the usage.

for promotion. The continuing discrepancies between mansab requirements and actual contingents led to the separation of *zāt* and *sawar* ranks in 1596–7 (1005).[4] They involved more than the compulsory branding of horses and mustering of men; they also set financial penalties for failing to maintain enough troops, including salary reductions and repayment of excess funds collected.

The new provincial regime involved a massive increase in central authority and reduction in the autonomy of mansabdars. It involved the division of the provinces of the empire into tracts which produced a *krur* (ten million) of *tankas* (copper coins) in revenue. Each of these tracts had a collector, known as a *karurī*, in charge of collecting the revenue. Simultaneously, all the land was made *khāliṣah*. Jāgīrs were eliminated. This change did not take place immediately; the administrative difficulties must have been formidable and recently conquered Gujarat, Bihar and Bengal were exempted. Apparently the conversion of jāgīrs into *khāliṣah* began with territories of Jaunpur, Varanasi, and Chunar. How far the process went is uncertain, but many if not most jāgīrs were resumed. As Afzal Husain has demonstrated, the correspondence of Hakīm Abū al-Fath shows that at least the assignment of new jāgīrs had ceased because he states that Shāhbāz Khān began to do so again in 1581 (989), confirming Bada'ūnī.[5]

Bada'ūnī, a mansabdar himself, condemns Muẓaffar Khān and his colleagues in the central administration in no uncertain terms. He suffered from these regulations himself.[6] He uses *ẓālim* (tyrant, oppressor) as a chronogram for Muẓaffar Khān's appointment as *wazīr* and cites a witticism that a Rājah's dog is better than Muẓaffar Khān even though a dog is a hundred times better than a Rājah, and gives a similar

[4] This analysis follows Shireen Moosvi, 'Evolution of the Mansab System under Akbar', *Journal of the Royal Asiatic Society* (1978), pp. 171–83; I have checked all references.

[5] A.N., 3:117–18/166–7; T.A., 2:296, 300–1; M.T., 2:189–91/192–4, 296/305; T.Q., p. 317; Hakīm Abū al-Fatḥ Gīlānī, *Ruq'āt-i Hakīm Abū al-Fath*, ed. Dr. Mohd. Bashir Ahmad (Lahore: Idarah-tahqiqat-i Pakistan, 1968), pp. 26–7, 34, 37–8; Afzal Husain, 'The Letters of Hakim Abul Fateh Gilani—An Unexplored Source of Akbar's Reign', *Proceedings of the Indian Historical Congress* 44 (1983): 189–93. Husain's research invalidates M. P. Singh, 'Akbar's Resumption of *Jagir*, 1575', *Proceedings of the Indian Historical Congress* 27 (1966):208–11.

[6] M.T., 2:206–7/209–10.

comment about Rājah Tūdar Mal, the third great Akbari administrator. He refers to Muẓaffar Khān's greed in discussing his desire for an accounting of the treasure Āṣaf Khān took at Chauragarh.[7] Of several officers appointed to financial posts in Bihar, he writes, 'they were loyal neither to God nor their Emperor. They perpetrated all sorts of oppression and tyranny...'[8] Of Muẓaffar Khān's actions as governor of Bengal, he writes, 'he began a course of great strictness in his administration, and commenced wrongdoing and oppressing the Amirs of that district and confiscated many of their *jāgīrs*. He practised the *dāgh-u-mahall* in the Court fashion and the settlement of accounts in the old manner...'[9] Jagirdars, not peasants, suffered the tyranny and oppression to which Bada'ūnī refers.

Not surprisingly, Bada'ūnī considers the system unsuccessful as well as unjust:

> The condition of the soldiers grew worse because the Amirs did as they pleased. For they put most of their own servants and mounted attendants into soldiers' clothes, brought them to musters, and performed everything according to their duties. But when they got their *jagirs* they gave leave to their mounted attendants, and, when a new emergency arose, they mustered as many 'borrowed' soldiers as were required and sent them away again when they had served their purpose. Hence while the income and expenditure of the *mancabdar* remained [in statu quo], 'dust fell into the platter of the helpless soldiers... the shop of real military-service was deserted.' But notwithstanding all this His Majesty's good luck overcame all enemies, so that large numbers of soldiers were not really necessary, and the Amirs had no longer to suffer from the inconvenient reluctance of their followers.[10]

Just as the financial interests of the recipients of revenue grants influenced his view of Akbar's religious policy, his sympathy for his fellow jagirdars led him to regard Akbar's programme of centralization as injustice and its enforcers as oppressors. This comment shows the

[7] M.T., 2:66/64–5, 77/78.
[8] M.T., 2:266/274.
[9] M.T., 2:280/288.
[10] M.T., 2:190–1/193–4.

intent of *dāgh*, requiring mansabdars to retain the number of soldiers for their rank. Doubtless some mansabdars did as Bada'ūnī says, but the record of military success indicates that the capability of the army did not suffer.

The sources do not discuss the immediate reaction of the mansabdars to the promulgation of the branding regulations except for Akbar's dismissal of Muẓaffar Khān because of his reluctance to enforce the regulation. On 8 October 1575 (4 Rajab 983), Khān-i 'Aẓam Mirzā 'Azīz Kūkah arrived at court in response to Akbar's summons. The sources differ on the reason for his coming. Abū al-Fażl states that Akbar wished to begin the process of branding with the leading officers and also wanted Khān-i 'Aẓam to be present for the arrival of Mirzā Sulaymān, the former Tīmūrid ruler of Badakhshan. Bada'ūnī does not explain the summons at all, but states that Khān-i 'Aẓam made negative comments about the entire set of new administrative regulations spontaneously. Shāh Nawāz Khān, essentially a secondary source, asserts that Akbar brought Khān-i 'Aẓam to Fathpur in order to gain his support for the new regulations but found that he became a leader of the opposition. Whatever Akbar's original intention, he did not tolerate the opposition of his foster-brother but banished him from court to Agra, deprived him of his rank, and confined him to lodgings in the garden of his own house there.[11]

Shortly afterwards, Akbar sent a number of officers who also opposed *dāgh* to join Mun'im Khān in the conquest of Bihar and Bengal. The list included Shujā'āt Khān, Qāsim Khān Mīr-i Baḥr, Mīr Mu'izz al-Mulk, Dūst Muḥammad Bābā Dūst, Mirzā 'Abdullah, and Muḥammad Amīn. I can identify only the first four names. Shujā'āt Khān was the sister's son and son-in-law of Tardī Beg Khān; Qāsim Khān a hereditary servant of the Tīmūrid dynasty who had supervised the construction of the Agra fort; Dūst Muḥammad Bābā Dūst a former retainer of Mun'im Khān; and Mīr Mu'izz al-Mulk a Musawī *sayyid* from Mashhad

[11] A.N., 3:147/208–9; M.T. 2:214–15/218; T.Q., p. 174; M.U., 1:675–93/319–34. Srivastava, *Akb'ar*, 1:174, asserts without the explanation that Akbar recalled Khān-i 'Aẓam for the reception for Mirzā Sulaymān, Khān-i 'Aẓam had failed to meet his obligations as a mansabdar, and expressed his opposition to the reforms in improper terms.

who had served in the suppression of the Uzbeg rebellion.[12] Three of these four men were thus Chaghatays like Khān-i Aʿẓam. Moreover, most of the officers already on the eastern expedition and thus temporarily not affected by the new regulations were Chaghatays.[13] The Chaghatay officers thus resented the new restrictions on their security and autonomy more than other groups did. Assigning them to the eastern front put their military capabilities to use while removing them from central political activity and insulating them from the effects of the reforms. Conversely, the officers associated with the new reforms, Rājah Tūdar Mal and Shāhbāz Khān, came from a Hindu clerical caste and from a Muslim group with Sufi leanings and perhaps a clerical or legal role as well.[14] The political crisis of Akbar's reign occurred when he extended the branding and muster regulations to the eastern provinces.

Akbar and his advisers completed the reorganization of the provincial regime in 1580 (988), with division of the empire into twelve provinces. Each province had a *sipāh salār* (governor), *dīwān* (collector of central government revenue), *bakhshī* (in charge of the mansabdari system), *mīr-i ʿadl* (magistrate), *ṣadr*, *kutwal* (prefect of police in the provincial capital), *mīr-i baḥr* (in charge of riverine communications and flotillas), and *waqʿī nawīs* (newswriter). This reform established the structure of provincial administration which persisted throughout Mughal history. It severely restricted the autonomy of provincial governors. Although they commanded the mansabdars stationed in the province when the army mobilized, they had little administrative control over them. They had no control over *khāliṣah* land revenue and knew that the ruler had the means of monitoring their behaviour. The difference between this situation and the position of provincial governors in pastoral confederations is stark.[15]

[12] A.N., 3:147–8/209–10, /476 n.; M.U., 2:708–11/853–5, 3:62–6/511–14, 3:227–31/238–40. The information on Dūst Muḥammad is Beveridge's footnote; his source is the *Iqbal-namah-yi Jahangiri*. Oddly enough, Shāh Nawāz Khān does not mention this episode in any of the three relevant biographies, but Shujāʿāt Khān, Qāsim Khān, and Mīr Muʿizz al-Mulk held their titles before and after 1575. Abū al-Fażl calls Qāsim Khān Mīr-i Kuhbahr.

[13] For the participants in this campaign, see A.N., 3:104/145, 118–19/169, 122–3/1–75.

[14] Qaisar, 'Shahbaz Khan Kambu', pp. 48–50.

[15] A.N., 3:282/412–13. One must be aware that although there were seven offices, it

Abū al-Fażl states that Akbar entrusted Rājah Tūdar Mal and Khwājah Shāh Manṣūr Shīrāzī with the execution of this programme, but because the Rājah was sent to the eastern provinces the Khwājah bore most of the burden.[16] Significantly, both men were bureaucrats, the champions of centralization.

5.2 Constitutional Developments

Constitutional developments between 1572 (980) and 1579 (987) receive little attention in the chronicles. Most likely, the distinctive pattern of court rituals developed during this time. Bada'ūnī attributes the *sijdah* (prostration before the emperor) to Ghazī Khān Badakhshī, who came to court from Badakhshan in 1574 (982). He had a post in the eastern provinces at the end of the decade, so the use of the *sijdah* began between 1574 (982) and 1579 (987).[17]

A, perhaps the, major transition took place in that year, with the remittance of the *jizyah*, the *maḥżar* (the so-called Infallibility Decree) and Akbar's recitation of the *khutbah*. The 1579 (987) date for the elimination of the *jizyah* comes from Bada'ūnī; Abū al-Fażl puts it in 1564 (971).[18] Abū al-Fażl states that earlier rulers had levied the *jizyah* as a means of discouraging and demonstrating their contempt for other religions and increasing their revenue at the same time. Akbar made no distinction between religions and needed no extra revenue, so he eliminated the tax. Bada'ūnī gives no explanation. As K. A. Nizami argues, Abū al-Fażl's statement does not fit conditions in 1564 (971), when Akbar had not conquered Gujarat, taken Chitor and Ranthambor,

---

was unusual for there to be more than five appointees and there might have been only three. The *bakhshī* normally was also the *waq'ī nawīs* and in some cases was also the *dīwān*; one man normally held the offices of *mīr-i 'adl* and of *sadr*. Not all provinces had a *mīr-i baḥr*. On provincial organization and the responsibilities of these offices, see Ishtiaq Husain Qureshi, *The Administration of the Mughul Empire* (Patna: N.V. Publications, n.d.,), pp. 227–47; P. Saran, *The Provincial Government of the Mughals, 1526–1658*, 2nd. ed. (Bombay: Asia, 1973), pp. 157–91. For general information on the structure of the Mughal regime, see Sir Jadunath Sarkar, *Mughal Administration*, 3rd. ed. (1935), reprint ed., Bombay: Orient Longman, 1972, pp. 15–50; Qureshi, *Administration*, pp. 45–70; Ibn Hasan, *Central Structure*.

[16] A.N., 3:283/414.

[17] M.T., 2:183/185–6, 3:153/214–15; M.U., 1:2:872–9/1:583–7.

[18] A.N. 2:203–4/316–17; M.T., 2:276/84.

defeated the Afghans in Bengal, or demonstrated his ability to deal with rebellious factions of officers. Moreover, Abū al-Fażl has a motive for changing the date. He interprets all of Akbar's actions as the results of his patron's own inspiration and gradual revelation of his nature. In doing so, he seeks to minimize his own influence, and that of his father, Shaykh Mubarak Nagawrī, on Akbar. Since Shaykh Mubarak did not come to court until 1567 (975) and his son did not meet Akbar until the next year, they could not have influenced Akbar in 1564 (971).[19] But there is no indication that Akbar envisaged *sulḥ-i kull* that early. Abū al-Fażl's comments fit the situation in 1579 (987) much better.[20]

The *jizyah* divided a society into dominant Muslims and subordinate non-Muslims. When Akbar ended collection of it, he abandoned the standard Muslim doctrine of kingship represented by Dawānī because he ceased to enforce the Sharī'ah. He thus abandoned Islam as a sovereign cult. Surprisingly, there was little response. The Muslim revivalist leader Shaykh Aḥmad Sirhindī asserted that the *jizyah* should be levied to humiliate Hindus, but there is no evidence of political opposition to its abolition.[21]

There is no doubt that Akbar promulgated the *maḥżar* in 1579 (987) and we know far more about reaction to it. The document was controversial in its own time and has caused disagreement among historians since then. Allowing the text to speak for itself, it designates Akbar as *mujtahid* (one capable of independent legal reasoning), *sulṭān-i 'adil* (just ruler), *sulṭān-i Islam* (ruler of Islam), *amīr al-Mu'minīn* (commander of the faithful), *ẓil-ullah 'ala al-'alamayn* (shadow of God over the two worlds). It states that Akbar had the right to impose

[19] A.N., 3:39/55–6, 83–5/116–19.

[20] K. A. Nizami, *On History and Historians in Medieval India* (New Delhi: Munshiram Manoharlal, 1983), pp. 158–9. Iqtidar Alam Khan, 'The Nobility under Akbar and the Development of His Religious Policy', *Journal of the Royal Asiatic Society*, p. 35, mechanically interprets the two dates as two attempts to end collection of the *jizyah*.

[21] Yohanan Friedman, *Shaykh Ahmad Sirhindi: An Outline of His Thought and a Study of His Image in the Eyes of Posterity*, McGill Islamic Studies, vol. 2 (Montreal: McGill-Queen's University Press, 1971), pp. 73–4, 85; S. A. A. Rizvi, *History of Sufism in India*, 2 vols. (New Delhi: Munshiram Manoharlal, 1978–83), 2:365; idem., *Muslim Revivalist Movements in Northern India in the Sixteenth and Seventeenth Centuries* (Agra: Agra University, 1965), p. 249.

agreements on other *mujtahids* when they did not agree, and that he had the right to introduce new laws provided they are in accord with the Qur'ān and the general welfare of the people.[22] In addition to Shaykh Mubarak Nagawrī, the leading ulama at the court signed the document. They were Shaykh 'Abd al-Nabī, the *ṣadr*; Qāẓī Jalāl al-Dīn Multanī, the chief *qāẓī*; Mīrān, Ṣadr-i Jahān Pihanī, the chief *muftī*; Mulla 'Abdullah Makhdūm al-Mulk Sultānpūrī; and Ghazī Khān Badakhshī. Of the signers who did not hold offices, the *Ṭabaqat-i Akbarī* says that Makhdūm al-Mulk was the leading *'ālim* of the time, that Ghazī Khān was distinguished in *kalām* and medicine (or philosophy) and that Shaykh Mubarak Nagawrī was the greatest master of the narrative and rational sciences of the time.[23]

Akbar's recitation of the *khutbah* for himself came almost simultaneously with the promulgation of the *maḥẓar*, so the two steps must be interpreted together. The *khutbah* and the *sikkah*—mentioning the monarch's name in the sermon at the Friday prayer and on the coinage—were standard indicators of sovereignty in the Islamic world. But giving the *khutbah* was unusual. Doing so in the *jama'* mosque in the capital had been one of the basic duties of the caliphs.[24] Niẓām al-Dīn Aḥmad and Bada'ūnī state that in addition to the caliphs Tīmūr and his grandson Ulugh Beg had given their own *khutbahs*.[25] Akbar gave the *khutbah* on 26 June 1579 (1 Jumādā I 987), in the *jama'* mosque at Fathpur

[22] I accept the interpretation of the term *nass* as text, meaning the Qur'ān. The word *hukm*, translated as law, has a broad range of meanings, from a legal verdict or decision to a governmental institution or regime. M.T., 2:271–2/279–80; T.A., 2:345–6; S. A. A. Rizvi, *Religious and Intellectual History of the Muslims in Akbar's Reign* (New Delhi: Munshiram Manoharlal, 1975), pp. 146–7.

[23] T.A., 2:345. For biographical information see, for Shaykh 'Abd al-Nabi, M.T., 3:79–83/127–31, M.U. 2:560–4/1:41–4. For Qazī Jalāl al-Dīn, M.T., 3:78/124–5. For Mīrān Sadr-i Jahān, M.T., 3:141/198–200, M.U. 3:348–51/78–80. For Makhdūm al-Mulk, M.T., 3:70–2/113–18, M.U. 3:252–7/1:93–7. For Ghazi Khān, M.T., 3:153/ M.U., 2:872–9/1:583–7. For Shaykh Mubarak, M.T., 3:73–5/188–20.

[24] *Encyclopedia of Islam*, 2nd. ed., s.v. 'Khalifa', by Dominique Sourdel.

[25] T.A., 2:343–4; M.T., 2:268/276–7. A.N., 3:270–1/395–6 does not mention the specific precedents. I have seen no other report that Tīmūr and Ulugh Beg read the *khutbah* themselves. Vasilii Vladimirovitch Bartol'd *Sochineniia*, ed. A. M. Belenitskii, vol 2 pt. II: *Raboti Po Otd'el'im Probl'emam Istorii Azii Ulugh Beg i Yezovrem'a*, p. 160, trans. as V. V. Barthold, *Four Studies on Central Asia*, vol. 2: *Ulugh Beg* (Leiden: E. J. Brill, 1958), p. 161, states that Ulugh Beg's son 'Abd al-Laṭīf did so.

Sikri, reciting a brief verse composed by Abū al-Fażl's brother Shaykh Fayzī, and the *fātiḥah* (first verse of the Qur'ān), and then performed prayer.[26]

Judging from content rather than context, the recitation of the *khutbah* and the *maḥżar* indicates that Akbar sought to strengthen his legitimacy in the Islamic tradition. The imitation of the caliphs in giving the *khutbah* and the use of the term *amīr al-mu'minīn* in the *maḥżar* suggests that he was taking the position of a caliph in the older sense of a universal Islamic emperor, not just a ruler who enforced the Sharī'ah. Although the early, Umayyad, and 'Abbāsid caliphs were most often called *khalifah*, they called themselves *amīr al-mu'minīn* in documents. Muslim rulers after 1258 (656) used the term *khalifah* frequently but almost never called themselves *amīr al-mu'minīn*.[27] In and of themselves, these two initiatives resemble Muḥammad ibn Tughluq's designation of himself as a *mujtahid* and seeking recognition from the 'Abbāsid shadow caliph in Cairo. If we knew nothing else of Akbar's political agenda, we would conclude that he sought to project himself as a Muslim sovereign, capable enough in jurisprudence so that he did not require guidance—criticism—from the ulama and could bring about agreement among them. But the historical context requires a different interpretation.

Akbar had tried and failed to make the Indo-Muslim elite, from which most of the ulama came, his active supporters tied to him by marriage. He nonetheless had to employ them in the governmental positions concerned with Shar'ī matters, as *ṣadr* (religious administrator) and *qāẓī* (Sharī'ah judge). The *ṣadr* had an extremely influential position because he controlled the allotment of revenue grants to religious figures for their maintenance.[28] Personally, Akbar was fascinated by all religions and appalled by religious prejudice or fanaticism,

[26] Rizvi, *Intellectual*, pp. 145–6. I follow Rizvi in discounting Bada'ūnī's testimony that Akbar stammered nervously and could not complete his task.

[27] Sir Hamilton Gibb, 'Some Considerations on the Sunni Theory of the Caliphate', in *Studies on the Civilization of Islam*, ed. Stanford J. Shaw and William R. Polk (Boston: Beacon, 1962), pp. 144–8.

[28] Qureshi, *Administration*, pp. 79–80, 207–12; Ibn Hasan, *Central*, pp. 254–88. On revenue grants, see Irfan Habib, *Agrarian System of Mughal India* (Bombay: Asia, 1963), pp. 298–316.

especially when it led to violence.[29] In the famous discussions among the representatives of all religions in the Ibādat-khānah at Fathpur Sikri, which began on 3 October 1578 (1 Shah'bān 986), Akbar found the actions and opinions of the ulama, both Sunnī and Shī'ī, inadequate, petty and narrow-minded.

Bitter and selfish disagreements among the ulama also annoyed him.[30] Akbar found the 'Muslim establishment wanting, both politically and personally. Shaykh 'Abd al-Nabī had alienated his sovereign by ordering the execution of a Brahmin for reviling the Prophet and by allegedly mismanaging revenue grants; Makhdūm al-Mulk had sought to discredit his rival and discredited himself.'[31]

At this point Shaykh Mubarak Nagawri suggested that Akbar, as an *imām* and *mujtahid*, did not need the guidance of the ulama, for they had only knowledge, not wisdom. Akbar responded by asking the Shaykh to free him from the domination of the Mullas. Shaykh Mubarak directed the discussion of the assembly of ulama to the issue of *ijtihād* (independent legal reasoning) and to the desirability of having an *imām-i 'ādil* (just leader) who could resolve disagreements on all legal questions. His skilful management of the discussions led to production of the *maḥżar*. Bada'ūnī asserts that Shaykh 'Abd al-Nabī and Makhdūm al-Mulk ended their differences in order to oppose the *maḥżar* and had to be coerced into signing it, and that only Shaykh Mubarak was not reluctant to sign.[32]

Because he is the chief contemporary critic of Akbar's religious activities, one would expect Bada'ūnī to condemn the *maḥżar* as contrary to Islam if he connected it with *sulh-i kull* or with religious innovations. He does not. Abū al-Faẓl, the architect of *sulh-i kull* and

[29] This sentiment, and Akbar's lack of emotional commitment to the cause of Islam, in addition to his abandonment of Muslim public rituals, justifies the perception of Akbar's apostasy, but that view is not useful for political analysis.

[30] S. A. A. Rizvi, *Religious and Intellectual History of the Muslims in Akbar's Reign*, (New Delhi: Munshiram Manoharlal, 1975), pp. 105–40, is the best discussion of the Ibadat Khanah. Basic textual references are M.T., 2:198–204/200–207, 207–13/210–16, 216–219/20, 255–64/262–72; A.N., 3:112–13/157–60, 241–2/347–8, 252–6/364–72, see also Pierre Du Jarric, *Akbar and the Jesuits*, trans. C. H. Payne (New York: Harper, 1926); Srivastava, *Akbar*, 1:213–16.

[31] A.N. 3:234/311–12; M.T., 2:255–6/262–3, 3:79–83/127–30.

[32] M.T., 2:270, 272/278–280, 3:83/130–31.

the son of the framer of the *maḥżar*, does not quote the document or mention his father's role. He explains the recognition of Akbar as a *mujtahid* as a means of communicating Akbar's status to those who could understand his perfection only imperfectly.[33] The *maḥżar* thus did not fit into the mature Akbari programme, though Srivastava and Qureshi, from their opposed perspectives, interpret it as such.[34] It may represent an initiative to gain higher legitimacy as a Muslim ruler which he abandoned for *sulḥ-i kull*, as Iqtidar Alam Khan asserts.[35] But the abandonment of the *jizyah* in the same year and the physical evidence of Fathpur Sikri suggest that Akbar had already decided on a different path. The *maḥżar* probably had two purposes, to attempt to justify Akbar's abandonment of the Shar'ī element of Islamic kingship and to demonstrate his right to control revenue grants to the ulama.[36]

Discussion of the response to the *maḥżar* approaches two of the most controversial aspects of Akbar's reign, his policy towards Islam and whether or not he sought to found a new religion. Even Abū al-Fażl admits that the promulgation of the *maḥżar* provoked considerable opposition and misunderstanding. He explains the opposition in three ways. The verse by Fayzī which Akbar used as a part of his *khutbah* included the phrase 'Allahu Akbar', which meant literally God is Great but might also be taken to mean God is Akbar. The ambiguity of the phrase suggested to some that Akbar claimed to be either an expression of God or a prophet. His treatment of the ulama as mere equals of the representatives of other religions in the Ibādat-khānah suggested that he was hostile to Islam, especially because he ridiculed the ulama for their failures in debate. In addition, Abū al-Fażl states that Akbar's favourable treatment of *sayyids* (descendants of the Prophet) and willingness to appoint Iranians, many of whom were

[33] A.N., 3:268–70/390–4.

[34] Srivastava, *Akbar*, 1:222–5; Qureshi, *Akbar*, pp. 152–64.

[35] Iqtidar Alam Khan, 'Nobility', pp. 34–5.

[36] I have made considerable use of the Rizvi's discussion of the *maḥżar*, in *Intellectual*, pp. 141–74. He disposes of several inadequate interpretations, including that of F. W. Buckler in 'A New Interpretation of Akbar's Infallibility Decree of 1579', *Journal of the Royal Asiatic Society* (1924), pp. 590–608, reprinted in *Legitimacy and Symbols: The South Asian Writings of F. W. Buckler*, ed. M. N. Pearson, Michigan Papers on South and Southeast Asia No. 26 (Ann Arbor: Center for South and Southeast Asia Studies, The University of Michigan, 1985), pp. 131–48.

Shīʿīs, to high office led some Sunnīs to consider him a Shīʿī. Likewise his patronage of Brahmins and employment of Hindus led some observers to believe he had Hindu sympathies.[37]

Bada'ūnī states that Akbar intended to proclaim his prophethood by changing the *shahadah* to 'there is no God but God and Akbar is his Prophet' but that resistance forced him to restrict the phrase to a few intimates. Badaʿūnī also characterizes Akbar's religious actions as an abandonment of *taqlīd*, adherence to an established *mażhab* (sect or legal school). The oath which Bada'ūnī quotes for officers who accepted Akbar's spiritual guidance includes the abandonment of *taqlīdī* Islam.[38] Two of his leading officers, his foster-brother Quṭb al-Dīn Muḥammad Khān and Shāhbāz Khān Kambū, opposed this change. Quṭb al-Dīn Muḥammad Khān asked what other rulers like the Ottoman sulṭān (*khūnkār-i rūm*) would say if they heard of Akbar's views, for all had the same religion whether it was *taqlīdī* or not (*hamah hamīn dīn dārad khwāh taqlīdī khwāh nah*).[39] Akbar reproached Quṭb al-Dīn Khān bitterly in his presence, but took no action against him.

The charge that Akbar suppressed Islam, or at least Sunnī, Sharʿī Islam, rests primarily on his hostility to the Sunnī ulama, specifically his reduction of their revenue grants. Shaykh ʿAbd al-Nabī and Makhdūm al-Mulk felt his wrath several months after the promulgation of the *maḥżar*, in November 1579 (Shaʿbān 987). He appointed them jointly to the office of Mir-i Hajj, responsible for the gifts and funds he sent to the Hijaz in the pilgrimage season, and forbade them to return. Abū al-Fażl attributes his master's action to the ignorance, selfishness and arrogance of the two men. In view of the timing, their opposition to the *maḥżar*, and probably Shaykh ʿAbd al-Nabī's position as *ṣadr*, influenced the decision.[40]

Concerning the revenue grants, Bada'ūnī writes: 'And any piece of orthodox learning which [a man] might have acquired became his bane, and the cause of his degradation. And the 'ulama and Shaikhs, the leaders

[37] A.N., 3:272–4/398–400.

[38] M.T., 2:304, trans. Rizvi, *Intellectual*, p. 391. I discuss the oath at length below.

[39] M.T., 2:273–4/281–2. On the concept of *taqlīd*, see Marshall G. S. Hodgson, *The Venture of Islam*, 3 vols. (Chicago: University of Chicago Press), 2:406, 448.

[40] A.N., 3:277–8/405–6. Bada'ūnī's comments, in his biographies of the two men, do not give additional insight.

of thought to all around, [Akbar] sent for to court, and enquired into their grant-lands and pensions.' He alleges that Akbar awarded revenue grants in accord with his own judgement of the recipients and punished legitimate ulama and Sufis with imprisonment or banishment to different provinces.[41] Abū al-Fażl states that because many earlier *ṣadrs* had approved grants in return for bribes and engaged in other corrupt practices, Akbar appointed Shaykh 'Abd al-Nabī as *ṣadr* to revoke improper grants and make the necessary inquiries. When he heard similar allegations about the Shaykh, Akbar took matters into his own hands and personally reviewed all grants.[42] Qureshi asserts that Akbar reduced or eliminated grants in order to penalize those ulama who refused to accept and spread his religious beliefs. The poverty and hardship which resulted implied persecution.[43]

The resumption of land grants on a large scale did not mean religious persecution. No modern historian has accused the Ottoman Sulṭān Meḥmed II of hostility to Islam, but the conqueror of Constantinople ordered a thorough examination of all land grants and the resumption of many. The ulama suffered a considerable loss of income as a result, and opposition to this policy coalesced around the Conqueror's son Bayāzīd. Meḥmed II had no religious objective, though the ulama accused him of impiety; he resumed land grants in order to increase government revenue and thus the size of his army.[44] Although they were very different men, Meḥmed II and Akbar had similar political and administrative goals. Both sought to expand their empires and

[41] M.T., 2:278–9/286–7.

[42] A.A., 1:/278–80.

[43] Qureshi, *Akbar*, pp. 161–2.

[44] Halil Inalcik, 'The Rise of the Ottoman Empire', in P.M. Holt, Ann K.S. Lambton, and Bernard Lewis, eds., *The Cambridge History of Islam* 2 vols. (Cambridge: Cambridge University Press, 1970), 1:304–5. The 'standard' history, Franz Babinger, *Mehmed the Conqueror and his Time*, trans. Ralph Manheim, ed. William Hickman (Princeton: Princeton University Press, 1978), mentions this point on p. 454. It should not be consulted without Halil Inalcik, 'Mehmed the Conqueror (1432–81) and his Time', *Speculum* 35 (1960), pp. 408–27, which mentions the resumption of grants on p. 426. See also Halil Inalick, 'Rice Cultivation and Celtukci-reaya System in the Ottoman Empire', *Turcica* 14 (1982), p. 77n.; Tursun Bey, *History of Mehmed the Conqueror*, trans. with facsimile text by Halil Inalcik and Rhoads Murphy (Chicago: Bibliotheca Islamica, 1978), f. 18a.

their own power—i.e. that of the central government—within them. For this reason, I submit that Akbar examined and resumed revenue grants primarily for fiscal and administrative reasons, not as a religious purge.[45]

The issue of Akbar's alleged hostility to Islam cannot be separated from the question of the Dīn-i Illahī. I. H. Qureshi states that Akbar punished the 'orthodox' ulama for refusing to serve as missionaries for his own new faith, the Dīn-i Illahī. S. A. A. Rizvi and J. F. Richards have invalidated this argument by showing that the Dīn-i Illahī was not a new religion but a sort of Sufi order focused on Akbar.[46] Dīn-i Illahī did not replace Islam as Akbar's sovereign cult; *sulḥ-i kull* (general peace) did. The political meanings of *sulḥ-i kull*, Dīn-i Illahī, and of Akbar's personal religious observances are among the topics of the next chapter.

[45] Although the circumstances differed enormously, the Muḥammad Reza Shah Pahlavi's 'White Revolution' also involved expanding state power and influence at the cost of land revenue for the ulama.

[46] Qureshi, *Akbar*, pp. 134–70, esp. pp. 161–62. Rizvi, *Intellectual*, pp. 374–437; Richards, 'Formation', pp. 267–71.

CHAPTER 6
The Akbari Constitution

The complex array of tacit and explicit beliefs and assumptions which made up the Mughal constitution evolved slowly. In a sense, each individual in the Mughal system had his own view of the constitution, modified by his view of his own place in the structure. The constitution which was Mughal in the restricted sense found expression in the rituals of the Mughal court and the writings of Abū al-Fażl.[1]

6.1 Court Rituals

Court rituals had a central place in Mughal politics and society. Sir Thomas Roe discussed Jahāngīr's court, but his comments apply to Akbar's reign as well:

> This course is unchangeable, unless sickness or drink prevent yt; which must be known, for as all his subjects are slaves, so he in a kynd of reciprocal bondage, for he is tyed to observe these howres and customes so precisely that if hee were unseene one day and noe sufficient reason rendred, the people would mutinie; two days noe reason can excuse, but that he must consent to open his doores and bee seene by some to satisfye others.[2]

[1] I use the term constitution with the specific meaning described on p. 14 of the introduction.

[2] Sir Thomas Roe, *The Embassy of Sir Thomas Roe to India, 1615–19*, ed. Sir William Foster (London: Humphrey Milford, 1926), pp. 86–7.

Without the rituals which surrounded it, Mughal sovereignty did not exist. The nature of the rituals propounded the nature of sovereignty. To begin with ordinary court routines, Abū al-Fażl and Roe describe the routines of Akbar and Jahāngīr in similar form. Akbar began his day with personal religious devotions, and then came to the *jharūkā*, the famous small balcony from which Akbar showed himself to the general public. The general population, 'soldiers, merchants, peasants, tradespeople and other professions,' gathered at dawn in order to see him.[3] Jahāngīr also began his public day by visiting the *jharūkā*.[4] The custom was called *jharūkā darshan*. *Darshan*, literally seeing, is a basic feature of the interaction between Hindu spiritual teachers and their disciples.[5] The individuals who received *darshan* acknowledged the sovereign by performing the *kurnīsh*, the placement of the palm of the right hand on the forehead and bending the head downwards. The *kurnīsh* 'signifies that the saluter has placed his head (which is the seat of the senses and the mind) into the hand of humility, giving it to the royal assembly as a present, and has made himself in obedience ready for any service that may be required of him.'[6]

From the *jharūkā*, Akbar went to the *dīwān-i khaṣṣ u'am* (hall of public audience). There he conducted the primary business of his office, giving justice in criminal and civil matters, including official misconduct, and examining the merits of officers. Various functionaries presented reports and made requests. The ruler's visits to the hall of public audience were called *darbār* (usually transliterated durbar). Abū al-Fażl describes the time in the *dīwān-i khaṣṣ u'am* as the second occasion during the day 'when people of all classes can satisfy their hearts with the light of [Akbar's] countenance.'[7] The responsibility of the king to make himself accessible to all persons for the redress of grievances is an important part of the Iranian tradition of kingship.[8] The beating of a drum announced

[3] A.A., 1: 155/164–5.

[4] Roe, *Embassy*, pp. 84–7.

[5] Richard Lannoy, *The Speaking Tree* (London: Oxford University Press), p. 366.

[6] A.A., 1:166/167.

[7] A.A., 1:155/165.

[8] E.g. Abū 'Alī Hasan Ṭūsī, Niẓām al-Mulk, *Siyāsat-nāmah* or *Ṣiyār al-Mulūk*, ed. H. Darke (Tehran: B.T.N.K., 1962), trans. H. Darke (London: Routledge & Kegan Paul, 1978), pp. 13–14. See also J. R. Perry, 'Justice for the Underprivileged: the

Akbar's presence in the audience hall. Abū al-Fażl describes what occurs as follows:

> His Majesty's sons and grandchildren, the grandees of the Court, and all other men who have admittance, attend to make the *kurnish* and remain standing in their proper places. Learned men of renown and skilful mechanics pay their respects; the *darūghas* and *bitikchīs*... set forth their several wants; and the officers of justice give their reports.

Akbar dealt with all the matters presented to him and, if he desired, viewed wrestlers, other pugilists, tumblers, jugglers, or musicians.[9]

The men who attended each *darbār* stood in a particular arrangement. Salim, the eldest prince, stood one to four yards from the throne, or sat two to eight yards from it. Murād stood from one and a half to six yards away or sat three to twelve yards away, as did Dānyāl, but the younger prince sometimes was permitted to come closer. Akbar frequently permitted his grandsons to be even closer to him. The highest ranking officers, 'worthy of the spiritual guidance of His Majesty,' came after the princes in proximity, standing within three to fifteen yards and sitting within five to twenty yards of him. The next two groups of officers began at a distance of three and a half and then at ten or twelve and a half yards from the throne. Others attending the *darbār* stood further away, in the proper arrangement. On one side stood the mansabdars, *ahadīs*, and others charged with holding of the *qūr* (literally quiver), the selection of the ruler's weapons held in readiness. Abū al-Fażl does not state just how many men and weapons were involved, but says that 'every four of them carry four quivers, four bows, four swords, four shields; and beside which they take up lances, spears, axes, pointed axes, *piyāzī* war-clubs, sticks, bullets, bows, pestles and a footstool....'[10]

Ombudsman Tradition of Iran', *Journal of Near Eastern Studies* 37 (1978): 203–15; Lambton, 'Justice'.

[9] A.A., 1:156/166.

[10] A.A., 1:157, 188/116, 169. Abū al-Fażl states that others stood in *yasal*, which Blochman defines as the wing of an army, but Gerhard Doerfer, *Turkische und Mongolische Elemente im Neupersichen*, 4 vols., Akademie der Wissenschaften under der Literatur Veroffentlichungen der Orientalischen Kommision, vols. 16, 19–21 (Wiesbaden: Franz Steiner Verlag, 1963–1975), 4:82–92, gives the general meaning of

Persons attended the *darbār* for spiritual guidance, medical assistance, or resolution of personal or familial problems. But most outsiders sought some form of patronage, employment as a soldier or elsewhere in the imperial establishment. Senior officers brought forward their friends for whom they sought employment.[11] Although Abū not al-Fażl does not mention it directly, officers coming to court had audience at the *darbār*, promotions and appointments were announced, and mansabdars and others presented and received gifts on these occasions.

The royal throne, as the centrepiece of the *darbār*, deserves attention. The ruler sat above the assembly, on a platform, pile of cushions or throne, called a *masnad*. Akbar's thrones (*awrang*) were platforms, normally hexagonal, either made of precious metals or inlaid with precious stones, with an umbrella (*chatra*), above them.[12] Later thrones became more elaborate, reaching their final form with the famous Peacock Throne.[13] Akbar used two other insignia of royalty at the *darbār*, the *saya-bān* (the Persian word for shadow with an occupational suffix) or *aftāb-gīr* (literally sun taker), an oval or circular parasol, and the *kawkabah*, a polished metal ball suspended from a long pole. Abū al-Fażl specifies that only Akbar used these insignia.[14]

The discrimination among different strata of individuals extended to the forms of prostration to the emperor. Deeper prostration meant higher status. Above *kurnīsh* was *taslīm* (literally submission). It began with placing the back of the right hand on the ground, 'and raising it gently till the person stands erect, when he puts the palm of his hand upon the crown of his head, which pleasing mode of salutation signifies that he is ready to give himself as offering.' Upon being given permission to leave court, being presented to the ruler for the first time, or receiving a mansab, jāgīr, robe of honour, elephant, or horse, the person being

---

ordering, specifically of an army, a procession or of a government. I have followed his definition. Abū al-Fażl's statements are negative in form, but Blochman's positive translation does retain the meaning.

[11] A.A., 1:157–8/169–70. This passage makes clear that some private soldiers who served under mansabdars passed through the imperial establishment. *Ahadīs* were private cavalry soldiers who served the ruler directly.

[12] A.A., 1:45/52 and plate VII; Abdul Aziz, 'Thrones, Chairs and Seats Used by Indian Mughals', *Journal of Indian History* 16 (1937): 186–8.

[13] Ibid., pp. 194–225.

[14] A.A., 1:45/52, 1:118–19/116.

honoured made three *taslīms*; on lesser occasions like being paid or receiving a lesser gift, only one *taslīm* was required. The highest form of submission, the *sijdah*, was not used in the hall of public audience.[15]

Returning to the royal routine, Akbar spent roughly four hours in the *darbār* before going into the harem to deal with the business of its inhabitants. He also inspected the animals of the imperial stables and dealt with related issues at this time of day. He then took lunch and a siesta. A. L. Srivastava states that Akbar held a private *darbār*—a session in the *dīwān-i khaṣṣ* or *ghuslkhānah*—after the siesta, and after a second rest he returned to the private audience hall for discussions with Sufis, philosophers, and historians, but his authorities do not explain the afternoon activities.[16] According to Roe, Jahāngīr watched an elephant fight after the morning *darbār*, went into the harem for his siesta, and then held an afternoon *darbār* and, after supper, went into the *ghuslkhānah*, so Srivastava is probably correct.[17]

The *dīwān-i khaṣṣ* was a special, private court, which only princes and the highest officials, and the spiritual followers of the ruler, attended. Rather than *kurnīsh* or *taslīm*, they performed the complete prostration (*sijdah*).[18]

Naturally the routine varied during travel and on special occasions. Abū al-Fażl reports that heavy commitments forced Akbar to rotate specific duties on different days.[19] When Akbar came forth from the capital, to hunt or for other purposes, he and his party proceeded ahead of the men transporting the *qūr*, which was accompanied by elephants in all their trappings, flags, camels, carriages, *kawkabahs*, drums, and other imperial insignia. In addition to the sovereign's insignia, five flags or standards accompanied the *qūr*, wrapped in scarlet cloth but unfurled only in battle or for festivals. The ensigns included two types of yak tail standards, the *chatrtūq* and the *tumantūq*.[20]

[15] A.A., 1:156–7/167–8.

[16] A. L. Srivastava, *Akbar*, 2nd ed. 3 vols. (Agra: Shiva Lal Agarwala, 1972), 2:28–30; A.A., 1:154–6/164–5; A.N., 3:257/372–3.

[17] Roe, *Embassy*, pp. 84–7.

[18] A.A., 1:157/167–8. I discuss the issue of spiritual guidance in the section on Akbar as spiritual guide.

[19] A.N., 3:717/1069.

[20] A.A., 1:45/52, 116/117–18. The Turkish word *tūq* means yak or horsetail standard (Doerfer, *Elemente*, 2:618–22); *chatr* is the same word as used for the imperial umbrella

The Mughals had three major festivals a year: the solar and lunar birthdays of the monarch and Nawrūz, the Iranian new year on the vernal equinox. The Mughals used the solar Illahī calendar for administrative and court purposes. On his birthdays, the monarch had himself weighed against various commodities. On the solar birthday, they were gold, mercury, silk, perfumes, copper, *rūh-i tutiyā* (probably pewter), drugs, ghee, iron, rice-milk, seven grains and salt, in order of cost. On the lunar birthday, they were silver, tin, cloth, lead, fruits, mustard oil, and vegetables. The commodities weighed were distributed as charity.[21] The imperial princes were also weighed on their birthdays. Called *wazn* in Persian, from the Arabic root pertaining to weight, the weighing ceremony is a common practice among Hindus even in the twentieth century, but its precise significance in Mughal times is unclear. Abū al-Fażl describes the purpose of the weighing as gaining good fortune and making an opportunity to distribute charity.

In response to the usurpation of imperial prerogatives by Islām Khān Chishtī, governor of Bengal, in 1612 (1020), Jahāngīr promulgated a regulation listing imperial prerogatives forbidden to governors. We have three versions of the list, Jahāngīr's own in the *Tūzuk-i Jahāngīrī*, Mirzā Nathan's in the *Bahāristān-i Ghaybī*, and a report in the later *Mir'at-i Ahmadī*. The *Mir'at-i Ahmadī* specifies that the regulations applied especially to princes. The list helps to put the customs of the *darbār* in context. Governors could not construct a *jharūkā*, hold *darbārs* of their own, compel men to perform *taslīm*, or require imperial officers to remain standing in their presence, or to mount guard duty. They could not require imperial officers to do obeisance to their gifts as they did to imperial gifts, or give titles to their own servants. The list also states that governors should not have a kettledrum beaten in front

---

and *tuman* the Mongol word for ten thousand, and thus a corps of ten thousand men. William Irvine, *The Army of the Indian Moghuls* (London: n.p., 1903; reprint ed., New Delhi: Eurasia, 1962), pp. 31–4, does not give concrete descriptions of either of these ensigns—or perhaps more accurately whisks. I speculate that the *chatrtūq* was an Indian version and the *tumantūq* was a central Asian form. I have had access to a chapter draft by Bernard S. Cohn, 'The Mughal, Court Rituals, and the Theory of Authority in the Sixteenth and Seventeenth Centuries', which has been extremely useful in composing this section.

[21] A.A., 1:197/276–7; T.J., pp. 45–6/1:78, Roe, *Embassy*, pp. 378–9. On the *nawrūz* celebration, see Roe, *Embassy*, pp. 125–7.

of them on expeditions or stage elephant fights.[22] The *jharūkā*, demanding *taslīm* and *sijdah*, viewing elephant fights, the customs surrounding the *qūr*, requiring mansabdars to stand, the use of the *chatr*, *sayā-bān*, and *kawkabah*, and the specific forms of other symbols made Mughal sovereignty palpable.[23]

Different elements of the symbolic package reveal various aspects of the Mughal constitution. The umbrella had been a symbol of kingship in India for a millennium. The umbrella serves two purposes: it gives physical form to the function of the sovereign as *axis mundi* and separates the radiance of the sun from that of the sovereign.[24] The physical arrangements of the *darbār*, focused on the sovereign, mirrors his status as the heart of the society. Because the king determines the ranks and posts of his officers, he gives order to the society. The inclusion of the princes among the subordinates of the imperial focus of sovereignty, rather than as secondary foci, demonstrates the repudiation of collective sovereignty. The different forms of submission—bowing—show that the degree of subordination to the sovereign determined the individual's status in the Mughal hierarchy; the deeper the bow the higher the position and the greater the proximity to the ruler. The *jharūkā* and the provision of the *sijdah* for the spiritual disciples of the ruler demonstrates that Akbar posed as—or was perceived as—a spiritual guide.

6.2 Abū al-Fażl's Doctrine of Sovereignty and Society

In the *Akbar-nāmah*, especially its most famous component, the *Āyīn-i Akbarī*, Abū al-Fażl explains the political and social order which

[22] T. J., p. 117/1:205; Mirzā Nathan, *Baharistan-i Ghaybi*, ed. and trans. M. I. Borah, 2 vols. (Gauhati: Government of Assam, 1936), 1:213–14; M.A.G., 1:190; M.U., 1:118–20/692–3; J. F. Richards, 'The Formation of Imperial Authority under Akbar and Jahangir', in *Kingship and Authority in South Asia*, ed. idem., South Asian Studies, University of Wisconsin Madison 3 (Madison. Wi.: University of Wisconsin-Madison South Asian Studies, 1978), p. 257 mentions Islām Khān's usurpation of imperial prerogatives, citing Sir Jadunath Sarkar, ed., *History of Bengal, Muslim Period, 1200–1750* (reprint ed., Patna: 1973), p. 282 as his source. I assume that Sarkar's information comes from the M.U.

[23] Cohn, 'Rituals', makes a similar statement.

[24] Ronald Inden explained the second function to me.

the court rituals represented. As S. A. A. Rizvi, in perhaps his most important single contribution as a historian, states, Abū al-Fażl combines the Tīmūrid model of kingship and the Sufi doctrine of illuminationism.[25] In brief, Shihāb al-Dīn Suhrawardī al-Maqtūl, 1153 (549)–1191(587), merged the Neo-Platonic doctrine of emanation with the Zoroastrian view of light as the unseen but underlying essence of creation. God emanates light. Existence is the possession of light. Purer light means a higher level of existence.[26] This view dovetails with the myth of the impregnation of Ālan-qū'ā, the mythic ancestress of Chingiz Khān and Tīmūr, by a heavenly radiance. It suggests that sovereignty is a special emanation from God. Abū al-Fażl writes in the preface of the *Āyīn*:

> Kingship is a refulgence from the Incomparable Distributor of justice . . . and a ray from the sun, the illuminator of the universe and the receptacle of all virtues. The contemporary language calls it *farr-i izidi* (the divine effulgence) and the tongue of antiquity calls it *kiyan khura* (the sublime halo). It is communicated by God to the holy face (the king) without the intermediate assistance of anyone; and men, in its presence, bend the forehead of praise towards the ground of submission. Again, many excellent qualities flow from the possession of this light.[27]

Abū al-Fażl's version of the story of Ālan-qū'ā appears early in the *Akbar-nāmah*:

> One night this divinely radiant one was reposing on her bed when suddenly a glorious light cast a ray into the tent and entered the mouth and throat of that fount of spiritual knowledge and chastity. The

[25] S. A. A. Rizvi, *The Religious and Intellectual History of the Muslims in Akbar's Reign* (New Delhi: Munshiram Manoharlal, 1975), pp. 80, 87–8, 91, 340–1, 344–6, 352, 358–62, 381–2; see also Richards, 'Formation', pp. 260–6.

[26] On Shihāb al-Dīn Suhrawardī, and Illuminationism, see Fazlur Rahman, *Islam* (New York: Doubleday Anchor, 1968), pp. 147–9; Annemarie Schimmel, *Mystical Dimensions of Islam* (Chapel Hill, N.C: University of North Carolina Press, 1975), pp. 259–63; Seyyed Hossein Nasr, *Three Muslim Sages* (Delmar, New York, 1976), pp. 52–82; Henry Corbin, *Sohrawardi d'Alep, fondateur de la doctrine illuminative* (Paris: Societe des Etudes Iraniennes, 1939).

[27] A.A., 1:3/3, also Rizvi, *Intellectual*, p. 354. The tongue of antiquity is Middle Persian or Pahlavi.

cupola of chastity became pregnant by that light in the same way as did Hazrat Miryam the daughter of 'Imram.

He makes clear that others saw the ray of light penetrate the tent so there could be no less exalted explanation of her pregnancy.[28] Although Chingiz Khān was not a paternal ancestor of Akbar, Abū al-Fażl includes a notice of him in his genealogy because 'as he was a ray of the divine light of Alanqū'ā a brief account of him is indispensable.'[29] Ālan-qū'ā forms a decisive break in the genealogy of Akbar, which Abū al-Fażl extends from Adam to Jū'īnā Bahādur (Ālan-qū'ā's father) and from her son Buzānjār Qāān to Tīmūr. Of the descendants of Tīmūr, only Bābur and Humāyūn receive special notice. Abū al-Fażl describes Bābur as 'the carrier of the world illuminating light' and states that Humāyūn 'was illuminating the world with the power of this Divine light, which through so many cycles and epochs had been concealed under various garbs, and the time of apparition was now at hand.'[30]

Of his own master, Abū al-Fażl writes:

> the same light which took shape, without human instrumentality or a father's loins, in the pure womb of Her Majesty Alan-qūā, after having, in order to arrive at perfection, occupied during several ages the bodily wrappings of other holy witnesses, is manifesting itself at the present day, in the pure entity of this unique God-knower and God-worshipper.[31]

Indeed, the light came to Ālan-qū'ā in order to cause Akbar's eventual advent; the exploits of Chingiz Khān and Tīmūr were mere wayside ventures in the journey of the light of sovereignty.[32]

As the pure and perfect expression of sovereignty, Akbar has the

[28] A.N., 1:65/179. Hazrat Miryam is the Virgin Mary.

[29] A.N., 1:72/191–2. Abū al-Fażl mentions that Bābur's mother, Qutluq Nigār Khānum, was a descendant of Chingiz Khān through his second son Chaghatay, but apparently does not consider it a cause or proof of Akbar's sovereignty (1:86/224).

[30] A.N., 1:52–86/155–222 covers Akbar's ancestors from Adam to 'Umar Shaykh; 1:86–120/223–82 covers Bābur, and 1:270–370/283–667 covers Humāyūn. The quotations are from 1:97/246 and 1:122/287.

[31] A.N., 1:12/39.

[32] A.N., 1:166/353. The phrase 'mere wayside ventures' is borrowed from Sir Arthur Conan Doyle.

attributes of the Perfect or Universal Man, as conceived by another Sufi thinker, Muhīyy al-Dīn Ibn al-'Arabī, 1165 (560) – 1240 (638). The Perfect Man is a microcosm of the universe, an assemblage of all the Platonic ideas from which reality emanates, an embodiment of the wisdom of man. Ibn al-'Arabī uses the phrase *al-haqīqat al-muḥammadiyyah* (the Reality of Muḥammad) for the Perfect Man, and cites the Prophet as the realization of the idea.[33] After Muḥammad's death other men fitted the ideal of the Perfect Man, but not as prophets with broad public recognition. They were instead *quṭb* saints, part of a secret hierarchy of Sufis on which the existence of the world depends.[34] Abū al-Fażl blends the Perfect Man with al-Fārābī's Platonic conception of a perfect ruler and finds the actualization of this ideal in Akbar.[35] This status distinguishes Akbar from ordinary Muslim rulers. Abū al-Fażl's brother Fayzī wrote of Akbar: 'Although kings are the shadow of God on earth, he is the emanation of God's light. How then can he be called a shadow?'[36] 'The shadow of God on earth' is a standard description of Muslim rulers in the middle periods of Islamic history.[37]

In Abū al-Fażl's eyes, the maturation of the light of sovereignty in the form of Akbar begins a new age in the history of the world, coinciding with the second (lunar) millennium of Islam.[38] Bada'ūnī mentions (and condemns) the belief that Akbar was the Lord of the Age (*ṣāḥib-i zamān*), who would 'remove all differences of opinion among the seventy-two sects of Islam and the Hindus.'[39] The term *ṣāḥib-i zamān* designated the leading *quṭb* saint of the time, but has another meaning as well. For Ithna-'Asharī (Twelve) Shī'is, it designates the Twelfth

[33] On Ibn al-'Arabī and the Perfect Man, see Fazlur Rahman, *Islam*, pp. 174–6; Schimmel, *Dimensions*, pp. 187–227, Nasr, *Sages*, pp. 83–121.

[34] Marshall G. S. Hodgson, *The Venture of Islam*, 3 vols. (Chicago: University of Chicago Press, 1974), 2:227–30. *Quṭb* means pole or axis and is best translated *axis mundi*.

[35] Rizvi, *Intellectual*, pp. 352–7.

[36] A.A., 1:241/631.

[37] Eg. Abū Hāmid Muḥammad ibn Muḥammad Ghazālī Tūsī, *Naṣihat al-Muluk*, ed. Jalāl al-Dīn Humā'ī (Tehran: Silsilahyi Intishārat-i Anjuman-i Millī), 1972 (1351) [solar]), p. 81, trans. F. R. C. Bagley as *Ghazali's Book of Counsel for Kings* (London: Oxford University Press, 1964), p. 45.

[38] A.N., 2:380/551; Rizvi, *Intellectual*, p. 360.

[39] M.T., 2:287/95.

Imām, who is currently in occultation, but will return as the Mahdi.[40] Calling Akbar the *sāḥib-i zamān* did not mean he claimed to be the Mahdi, but showed the type of status and expectations he claimed and inspired.

His claim to mark the advent of a new age led Akbar to promulgate a new solar calendar, known as the Illahī era, which remained in official use into Awrangzīb's reign. Because the Islamic calendar did not coincide consistently with the seasons, Islamic rulers routinely used solar calendars for administrative purposes. For example, the Saljūq *sulṭān* Malik Shāh sponsored the calculation of the Jalali calendar by a group of astronomers including 'Umar Khayyām for this purpose.[41] But these administrative calendars did not compete with the Hijrī era in formal usage; the Mughals used the Illahī era for more than convenience. The new era began with the first *nawrūz* after Akbar's accession, though it was not introduced until the twenty-ninth year of Akbar's reign.[42] Amir Fathullah Shīrāzī developed the calendar.[43] The sources differ on its significance. Bada'ūnī asserts that Akbar promulgated the new calendar because he believed the era of Islam would expire in its thousandth year and expected his new era to replace it.[44] Shāh Nawāz Khān states that the Hijrī era had become impractical because of its age, and that Akbar introduced a replacement for that reason. But because of the common belief that calendars expressed confessional allegiance, the new era did not win broad acceptance.[45] The institution of a new calendar supports the idea that Akbar claimed to represent a new era in history. In connection with the introduction of the new calendar, Akbar ordered composition of a chronicle, the *Tarīkh-i Alfī* (loosely The Thousand Year History).[46]

[40] 'Allamah Sayyid Muhammad Husayn Tabataba'i, *Shi'ite Islam*, trans. and ed. Seyyed Hossein Nasr (Albany: State University of New York Press, 1975), p. 210.

[41] Hodgson, *Venture*, 2:122, 166; E. S. Kennedy, 'The Exact Sciences in Iran under the Saljuqs and Mongols', in *The Cambridge History of Iran, Volume 5: the Saljuq and Mongol Periods*, ed. J. A. Boyle (Cambridge: Cambridge University Press, 1968) 670–2.

[42] A.N., 3:431/645; M.T., 2:306/16; Srivastava, *Akbar*, 1:302–3.

[43] M.U., 2:105/1:546.

[44] M.T., 2:306/16.

[45] M.U., 2:105/1:546.

[46] M.T., 2:301/10., 318–19/327–9. For discussions of this work see Rizvi, *Intellectual*,

As the quintessence of sovereignty, Akbar had special qualities: wisdom, patience with the folly and imperfection of others, and justice. Justice has a broad range of meaning; Abū al-Fażl refers to the importance of fairness: '[to] place the familiar friend and the stranger in the same balance and...comprehend the affairs of creation's workshop... without being weighted by personal considerations.'[47] Another list of Akbar's unique qualities includes a paternal love of his subjects, a large heart (which includes equal justice), increasing love of God, and prayer and devotion. The paternal love of the ruler prevents sectarian differences from disturbing his subjects.[48] His goals separate him from ordinary monarchs. They share the requisites of government and the status of kings: 'a large treasury, a numerous army, clever servants, obedient subjects, an abundance of wise men, a multitude of skilful workmen, and a superfluity of means of enjoyment.' But the true emperor retains these objects far longer and is less attached to them, for they are merely the means of removing oppression and providing for the good: 'security, health, chastity, justice, polite manner, faithfulness, truth, an increase in sincerity....'[49]

Like other writers on kingship, Abū al-Fażl propounds a view of society with his theory of sovereignty. Connecting each class of men with one of the Aristotelian elements, he writes of warriors, who have the nature of fire and may burn the rubbish of rebellion or light the lamp of disturbance. Artisans and merchants are air, the breeze which nourishes the tree of life. The learned are water, irrigating the world with knowledge. Husbandmen and labourers are earth, nourishing the grain of life. 'It is therefore obligatory,' he writes, 'for a king to put each of these in its proper place, and by uniting personal ability with due respect for others, to cause the world to flourish.'[50]

Abū al-Fażl employs a similar division in describing the imperial servants. The *nuyanīn-i dawlat* (nobles of the empire) serve the ruler

pp. 253–62; K. A. Nizami, *On History and Historians of Medideval India* (New Delhi: Munshiram Manoharlal, 1983), pp. 234–6; Harbans Mukhia, *Historians and Historiography During the Reign of Akbar* (New Delhi: Vikas, 1976), pp. 107–8.

[47] A.N., 2:173/268, also 216/334.

[48] A.A., 1:2–3/3. Equal justice does not imply equal distribution of worldly goods.

[49] A.A., 1:2–3/2.

[50] A.A., 1:2/2.

on the battlefield, consuming their foes like fire.[51] The *wakīl* heads this group, controlling affairs of state, especially 'promotion and degradation, appointment and dismissal.'[52] Other members of this group include court functionaries like the *mīr-i tūzuk* (master of court ceremonies), heads of household departments like the stables and news, and the *mīr bakhshī*.[53] The second class, the *awliyā'-yi nuṣrat* (fathers or assistants of victory) represents the wind, 'at times a heart rejoicing breeze, at other times a hot, pestilential blast.'[54] They are the financial officials, including the *wazīr*. The *aṣḥāb-i suḥbāt* (companions of conversation) are the king's wise advisers, including judicial and religious officials, astrologers, poets, and philosophers. They represent water because they drown wrath with their wisdom. The last group includes the personal servants of the king, who represent the earth.[55]

Abū al-Fażl's typologies of men and of imperial servants fit the view of Akbar as microcosm, for his servants and ultimately his subjects are extensions of himself. He combines all four elements in himself; his subordinates embody each independently. There is no explicit link between Abū al-Fażl's notion of the king as Perfect Man and the doctrine of king as microcosm expressed in the *rajyabhiseka*, and no Mughal ritual comparable to the Hindu ritual bath, unless the weighing ceremony is one. Perhaps the king's body was the symbolic source of the materials with which it was equated in the balance. The arrangement of the persons attending the *darbār* represented the society in microcosm, and, through Abū al-Fażl's imagery, the world, just as the Hindu king's audience hall did. Akbar and his successors did not become Hindu rulers;

[51] *Nuyan* is the Mongol *noyon*, similar to the Turkish *beg* and the Arabic amīr.

[52] *Wakīl* refers to the highest subordinate of the ruler, or one who acts for the ruler in his absence. See Ishtiaq Husain Qureshi, *The Administration of the Mughul Empire* (Patna: N.V. Publications, n.d.,), pp. 71–2; Ibn Hasan, *The Central Structure of the Mughal Empire* (London: 1936; reprint ed., New Delhi: Munshiram Manoharlal, 1980), pp. 124–40, for the office under the Mughals.

[53] The *mīr bakhshī* was the chief military administrator, in charge of managing the mansabdari system. See Qureshi, *Administration*, pp. 77–9; Ibn Hasan, *Central*, pp. 210–33.

[54] The translation of *awliyā'* as fathers is Rizvi's; Blochman uses assistants. Neither is the normal translation of *awliyā'*, the plural of *wali*. *Walī* normally means friend (of God), i.e. a Sufi saint.

[55] A.A., 1:4–5/4–7; Rizvi, *Intellectual*, pp. 369–72.

only the adoption of the *rajyabhiseka* could have made them so. But the rituals and underlying assumptions made the Mughals appear more like Hindu kings, or what Hindus expected kings to be like, than their Muslim predecessors in the subcontinent had.

Akbar's one personal religious ritual fitted this conception. It involved worship of the sun at dawn, noon, dusk and midnight. The noon worship involved the reading of the 1001 Sanskrit names for the sun. Akbar showed his devotion to the sun by 'devoutly turning toward the sun . . . hold[ing] both ears and turning himself quickly round about [and] striking his ears with his fists.'[56] Abū al-Fażl quotes Akbar as saying that 'a special grace proceeds from the sun, the exalted, in favour of kings, and for this reason they pray and consider it worship of the Almighty.' Akbar understands that many perceive reverence for the sun as contrary to Islam, but cites Surah 91 of the Qur'ān, Shams (the sun) in response.[57] Abū al-Fażl justifies his master's custom by saying that every flame is derived from divine light and 'the fire of the sun is the torch of God's sovereignty.'[58] The connection between this sentiment and the doctrine of the light of sovereignty needs no elaboration.

Abū al-Fażl's conception of Akbar as the complete and mature manifestation of the light of sovereignty placed him on a different level from that of his predecessors, even Chingiz Khan and Tīmūr. In the language which Dickson and Woods use in their analyses of collective sovereignty, Akbar began a new dispensation; he received afresh the divine mandate to rule.[59] In the context of the subcontinent in the sixteenth century, this new claim gave Akbar and his dynasty a higher and more durable legitimacy, a lasting prestige, which no Delhi Sultan ever achieved. Not everyone read Abū al-Fażl, but the political theater of the Mughal court communicated his perspective as well as his words did.

[56] M.T., 2:322/332.

[57] A.A., 1:235/3:435.

[58] A.A., 1:43/50.

[59] Martin B. Dickson, 'Uzbek Dynastic Theory in the Sixteenth Century', *Proceedings of the 25th International Congress of Orientalists*, 4 vols. (Moscow: 1963), 3:208–16; John E. Woods. *The Aqquyunlu: Clan, Confederation, Empire* (Chicago: Bibliotheca Islamica), 1976, pp. 12–16.

6.3 Sulh-i Kull as Sovereign Cult

The new model of kingship included a new sovereign cult. It was not the Dīn-i Illahī, but *sulḥ-i kull* (general peace), the principle of universal toleration. When Akbar ended collection of the *jizyah* in 1579 (987), he eliminated the social distinction between Muslims and non-Muslims and ceased to enforce the Sharīʿah in regard to non-Muslims. The second major Sharʿī limitation on *zimmīs* banned the construction of new places of worship. The Mughals did not enforce that ban. The Mughal constitution did not coincide with the standard model of Islamic kingship codified by Dawānī; it did not make the fundamental distinction between Muslim and *zimmī* and thus could not include enforcement of the Sharīʿah as an element of legitimacy. Abū al-Fażl clearly recognized the importance of ending the collection of the *jizyah*. He considers this action 'the foundation of the arrangement of mankind.' The *jizyah* was unnecessary in Akbar's time because members of all religions joined in his service as if they were of the same religion. Only misguided dissenters held back.[60] Abū al-Fażl presents religious strife as a basic cause of human misfortune and upholds *sulḥ-i kull* as a fundamental good.[61] The treatment of adherents of all religions as equals forms a part of his conception of equal justice.

Akbar's non-participation in the public rituals of Islam reinforced the position of general peace as the sovereign cult because it removed him from the category of Muslim. Right practice in the public cult—orthopraxy—is a matter of consensus in Islam, while right belief—orthodoxy—is harder to establish. There has never been an official mechanism to establish orthodoxy or denounce heterodoxy in Islam.[62] To a degree, Akbar's avoidance of Muslim ritual did constitute an abandonment of Islam. He became an uncommitted arbiter of the relations of Muslims and non-Muslims, above sectarian conflict and

[60] A.N., 2:213–14/316–17.

[61] E.g., A.N., 2:32/51, in which Abū al-Fażl makes the only reference to sectarian differences as the cause of Bayrām Khān's ordering the execution of Tardī Beg Khān.

[62] W. Montgomery Watt, *The Formative Period of Islamic Thought* (Edinburgh: Edinburgh University Press, 1973), pp. 5–6. Wilfred Cantwell Smith, *Islam in Modern History* (Princeton: Princeton University Press, 1957), p. 20, first suggested the application of the term orthopraxy to Islam.

equipped with independent spiritual insight. Abū al-Faẓl explains Akbar's stance: 'Among monarchs, divine worship is expressed by their justice and good administration,' he asserts.[63]

The Mughal doctrine of kingship thus asserted that the dynasty held sovereignty as a special emanation from God, which reached complete fruition in Akbar after many centuries of maturation. He transmitted sovereignty to his descendants just as he had received it. Possession of the light of sovereignty made the Mughal emperor a microcosmic Perfect Man, who subsumed all of the elements of the universe, and thus of society, in his body. This doctrine resembles the 'standard' model of Hindu kingship expressed in the *rajyabhiseka*, which presumably facilitated Hindu acceptance of the Mughal ruler as an actual (i.e. legitimate) monarch. Recognizable rituals such as *jharūkā darshan* and the weighing ceremony also contributed to acceptance. Mughal rituals and texts articulated kingship of a higher order than that of earlier Muslim rulers in the subcontinent; the common practice of calling the Mughal emperors as opposed to the Delhi sulṭāns thus has validity. The same rituals and texts expressed a new social and political framework. It made no political distinction between Hindu and Muslim and equated political rank—proximity to the ruler at the *darbār*—with depth of submission of him, as demonstrated by the hierarchy of bows. The *darbār*'s function as a model of society and thus of the world also corresponded to Hindu practices.

6.4 Emperor and Officers

The form of the *darbār* articulated the relationship of the emperor and his mansabdars. The institutional outline in the previous chapter gives only the skeleton of the mansabdari system; the ritual interaction defined the relationship which made it work. The change in identity and sense of honour which J. F. Richards considers the keystone of the mansabdari system and the Mughal polity found expression in the rituals.[64] The relationship depicted in the court rites differed in many cases from the actual self-perception of the individuals involved. Rajput mansabdars affected by the bardic and genealogical tradition perceived

[63] A.A., 1:244/3:451.

[64] Richards, 'Formation', pp. 254, 271–7.

their position as Rajputs as a result of their ancestry, not of Akbar's favour. But the rituals stated the relationship as Akbar wanted it to be. F. W. Buckler's comments on the relationship of sovereigns and officers applies:

> the king stands for a system of rule of which he is the incarnation, incorporating into his own body by means of symbolical acts, the person of those who share his rule. They are regarded as being parts of his body . . . and in their district or their sphere of activity they are the King himself. . . .[65]

As the definer of status and distributor of power, the king determines the nature and position of his subordinates.

As one would expect from this background, the status of mansabdar resembled military slavery. The mansabdars referred to themselves as the slaves of the ruler and claimed exaltation as such.[66] When a mansabdar died, the central government resumed his property; it was a mark of unusual favour for a Mughal ruler to permit an officer's sons to inherit a major portion of his property.[67] The tie of the subordinate to his master superseded, but did not obliterate, all other ties. Unlike military slaves or *nawkar*, mansabdars did not lose their own identities. Like *nawkar*, they were at the physical disposal of the sovereign, had a direct relationship with him, and were responsible for guarding his person.

The ritual exchange of gifts at the *darbār* gave the relationship form. Mansabdars presented two categories of gifts to the ruler, *naẕr* and *pīshkash*. The ruler presented various types of gifts to the mansabdars. They included robes of honour, swords, daggers, horses, saddles and related accoutrements, flags, drums, elephants, elephant gear, turbans, turban ornaments, and cash. Unfortunately, Abū al-Faẓl devotes less

[65] F. W. Buckler, 'The Oriental Despot', *Anglican Theological Review* 10 (1927–8) p. 239, reprinted in *Legitimacy and Symbols*, p. 177. See also A. M. Hocart, *Kings and Councillors*, ed. with an introduction by Rodney Needham and a Foreword by E. E. Evans-Pritchard (Chicago: University of Chicago Press, 1970), pp. 86–128.

[66] E.g. *Baharistan*, 1:27; T. J., passim.

[67] Richards, 'Formation', pp. 271–2 puts forward the connection between the status of mansabdar and military slavery. On escheat, see M. Athar Ali, *Mughal Nobility under Aurangzib* (Bombay: Asia, 1966), pp. 63–8.

attention to the exchange of gifts than later chroniclers do, but his emphasis is different. For this reason, what he reports is supplemented with data from the reign of Shāh Jahān.

Only the princes and ranking officers presented *naẕr*. The term comes from a Semitic root and literally means vow, but in the Mughal empire it came to mean a gift of gold coins (*muhrs*), which did not generally circulate. On most occasions, both princes and mansabdars submitted one hundred or one thousand coins.[68] The first ten pages of Lahawrī's account of Shāh Jahān's fourteenth year, 1640–1 (1050), include the following examples of *naẕr*: Wazīr Khān, the governor of the Punjab with the rank of 5000/5000, presented a thousand *muhrs*, as did Āṣaf Khān Yamīn al-Dawlah, who was the highest officer of the empire at 9000/9000, and Murād Bakhsh, Shāh Jahān's youngest son.[69] Mansabdars presented *naẕr* only when they attended *darbār*. The presentation of coins probably represented the vow of loyalty to which its name refers.

In addition to mansabdars, foreign ambassadors and subordinate rulers presented *pīshkash* to the Mughal emperor. *Pīshkash* literally means (that which is) drawn forward, and is the most common Persian term for a gift to a political superior signifying subordination. Apparenlty, mansabdars had to present *pīshkash* annually, but did not always do so and were not necessarily punished for omissions. After Mahābat Khān's last and greatest victory, the conquest of Dawlatabad, he wrote to Shāh Jahān saying that he had not presented *pīshkash* for three years and now was making Dawlatabad his *pīshkash*.[70] Unlike *naẕr*, *pīshkash* normally was not a cash gift and was sent to the ruler when the sender was not at court. Subordinate princes, like the Quṭb Shāh of Golconda and the ʻAdil Shāh of Bijapur, always sent their *pīshkash* with their ambassadors to the Mughal court. Those ambassadors brought *pīshkash* of their own, as did the emissaries of rulers not subordinate to the emperor.[71] When an officer arrived at court, he presented *pīshkash* if

[68] My comments on both who submitted *naẕr* and how many coins they gave differ from the Cohn draft. See also Buckler, 'Despot', pp. 243–4.

[69] B.N.L., 2:207–17.

[70] Z.K., 2:153, repeated in M.U., 3:/2:24.

[71] On the *pīshkash* of ambassadors, see Riazul Islam, *Indo-Persian Relations* (Tehran: Islamic Culture Foundation, 1970), p. 223. B.N.L., 2:177, gives a normal instance of the submission of the ʻAdil-Shah's *pīshkash*.

he did not present *naẕr*. Princes and officers also gave *pīshkash* when they had the honour of entertaining the sovereign.[72] Both officers and princes frequently gave elephants or horses as *pīshkash*, if they had access to them.

To give some examples, again in Shāh Jahān's fourteenth regnal year, Allah Qulī Khān, the son of Yilangtush, who was the regent of Balkh and thus effectively a subordinate prince, presented a horse as *pīshkash*. Sayyid Ḥusayn, a servant of the Quṭb Shāh, presented three elephants as his own *pīshkash*. 'Alī Mardan Khān presented *pīshkash* in gratitude, as mentioned above. Awrangzīb, who was then governor of the Deccan, sent six elephants which he had received from the Quṭb Shāh and Adil Shāh as his own *pīshkash*. A'zam Khān, the governor of Gujarat, sent *pīshkash*, including thirty horses.[73] Mukramat Khān, the Khan-i Sāmān submitted sixty Turki horses.[74] Shāh Jahān visited Āṣaf Khān Yamīn al-Dawlah, who presented *pīshkash* worth Rs 300,000.[75] Since both *pīshkash* and *naẕr* denoted subordination, the same logic applied to them as to the modes of prostration: the larger the gift the deeper the subordination and thus the higher the status.

Turning to the gifts from the emperor to the mansabdars, the types of gifts given form a hierarchy parallel to that of rank. The basic gift of a *khilat* (robe of honour) transformed the mansabdar into an extension of the king. In Buckler's words:

> Robes of Honour are symbols of some idea of continuity or succession . . . that continuity rests on a physical basis, depending on the contact of the body of the recipient with the body of the donor through the medium of clothing . . . the donor includes the recipient within his own person through the medium of clothing.[76]

In the Mughal case, only a few of the robes distributed were actually worn by the sovereign, but the principle was the same. The robes were

[72] E.g., B.N.L., 2:216, when 'Alī Mardan Khān entertained Shāh Jahān.

[73] On this officer, see Z.K., 2:200–1; M.U., 1:174–80/3215–19.

[74] M.U. 3:460–77/2:264–76. Though he apparently was the *khān-i samān* at this time, it appears from the text that he came from Gujarat and perhaps brought A'ẓam Khān's *pīshkash*. Because it was on the sea route of the horse trade from the Middle East, it was natural for officers stationed in Gujarat to send horses as *pīshkash*.

[75] B.N.L., 2:207–17.

[76] Buckler, 'Despot', p. 241.

actually entire costumes, the simplest consisting of a turban, long gown or coat, and belt. More elaborate five- and six-piece outfits included a *sarpīch* (turban ornament), and band for the turban (*bālāband*), and a tight short-sleeved jacket.[77] According to the European traveller Tavernier, a seven-piece outfit included a cap, the long gown and short jacket, two pairs of trousers, two shirts, two girdles (probably belts), and a scarf.[78] Clothing which the emperor had worn had a higher status than any other, but I suspect that only the more elaborate robes had graced the imperial form. The chronicles do not normally specify whether the emperor had worn a given robe or not.

Other gifts depended on and transmitted the status of the recipient. When Akbar appointed Sulṭān Murād governor of Malwa in 1591 (1000), Akbar awarded him a flag, drum, umbrella (*chatr*), and whisk (*tūgh*).[79] When Mirzā Rustam Ṣafavī, the grandson of Bahrām Mirzā, the brother of Shāh Ṭahmasp, who was the Ṣafavī governor of Zamīn Dawar in Afghanistan, sought refuge with Akbar, the Mughal ruler sent tents, screens, carpets and a jewelled dagger to him in response to his request for sanctuary. When he reached court, Akbar gave him the rank of 5000, a substantial jāgīr, and later a flag and drum. Neither Abū al-Fażl nor Shāh Naważ Khān mentions gifts to Mirzā Rustam at his first audience with Akbar; one must assume he received at least a robe of honour. The gifts which Akbar sent were practical in that they were useful in the journey from Zamīn Dawar to Lahore, especially in making the journey in style. In this way, the gifts indicated that Mirzā Rustam would retain his high position in Mughal service.[80]

In 1599 (1007) when Akbar sent Abū al-Fażl to the Deccan, Shāhbāz Khān against the Rānā of Mewar, Mirzā Shāh Rukh to Malwa, and Mirzā Rustam Ṣafavī to Raisin (a *sarkār* in Malwa), he gave each officer a robe of honour and a horse. They held different ranks and posts, and had already received various gifts indicating their status. The presentation of a horse and robe on their departure reinforced their connection to

[77] Irvine, *Army*, p. 29. For some reason Irvine translates *kamrband* as scarf for the waist rather than belt.

[78] Jean-Baptiste Tavernier, *Travels in India*, trans. W. Ball, rev. William Crook, 2 vols. (London: Humphrey Milford, 1925), 1:132.

[79] A.N., 3:598/911.

[80] A.N., 3:644–6/992–4; M.U., 2:434–442/2:631–37.

their master and stated that they were military—cavalry—servants.[81]

Mirzā Nathan gives an example of the gifts normally given to the newly appointed governor of a major province. When Jahāngīr appointed Ibrāhīm Khān Fath-i Jang, the son of I'timād al-Dawlah, governor of Bengal in 1617, he granted him a robe, a jewelled sword, a flag and a kettle drum.[82] The Shāh Jahānī chronicles give far more details on gift transactions. Between 21 October and 9 November 1637 (1–19 Jumādā I 1047), the following officers received imperial gifts: Shāh Nawāz Khān Ṣafavī, the *gush begī* (Superintendent of the Imperial Aviary) received a robe of honour, a horse with saddle and harness, and an elephant. Muḥammad Zamān and Sāḥib Dād, who had revolted in Afghanistan and were descendants of Bayāzīd Ansarī, the founder of the Rawshaniyyah movement, were forgiven and received robes of honour and horses. The children of Rājah Anup Singh Badgujar came to court following his death, and his eldest son Jay Rām received a robe, the rank of 1000/800, the title Rājah, and an elephant. His four younger brothers received suitable ranks. Hakīm Ṣaliḥ, the brother of Hakīm Fathullah and a new arrival from Iran, received a robe, a gift of Rs 3000, and became an imperial servant. The account of these gifts, and of *pīshkash* which arrived at court at the same time, covers two pages of the chronicle.[83] The steady exchange of *nazr* and *pīshkash* for *khilat* and other gifts continuously actualized the distribution and exercise of imperial authority and the place of the mansabdars within the system.

When not at the court, mansabdars still received and sent gifts regularly. The receipt of imperial orders and gifts involved its own rituals. Mansabdars performed obeisance to imperial orders as if the documents were the emperor himself.[84] When officers received robes and promotions, they put on their *khilats* and placed their diplomas on their heads, and rewarded the imperial messenger.[85] When Mirzā

[81] A.N., 3:749/1119–20. On Shāhbāz Khān, see A. J. Qaisar, 'Shahbaz Khan Kambu', *Medieval India: A Miscellany* 1 (1962): 48:–60. On Mirza Shah Rukh, see M.U., 3:329–35/779–83.

[82] *Baharistan*, 1:263.

[83] B.N.L., 2:3–4.

[84] E.g. *Baharistan*, 1:261.

[85] Ibid., 1:297–8.

Nathan received a portrait of Jahāngīr to wear on his turban, he put it in place and performed the *sijdah* as if his sovereign had been present.[86] When granted an elephant, Mirzā Nathan placed the elephant-goad on his shoulder to show his grateful submission.[87] Roe reports that when the governor of Gujarat received an imperial letter, 'the ceremony and joy tooke up the day.'[88] The rituals which reinforced the ties between the emperor and his mansabdars thus went on.[89]

Because the mansabdars were king's men, the booty they took on campaign was his, not theirs. In practice, the ruler required only a proportion of booty taken to be sent to him as *pīshkash*. As already noted, Akbar established this regulation early in his reign and it ceased to be a matter of contention. The booty which the officers collected had considerable real value. Akbar and his successors had good uses for gold, jewels and elephants, not to mention women of the harem. But the economic or erotic value involved does not explain the importance of imperial jurisdiction over booty. The transmission of booty to court as *pīshkash* stated and demonstrated the relationship of ruler and officer. The failure to send it meant disruption of the relationship which the gift exchange stated.

The anlaysis of the issue of gifts raises two issues. Dirk Kolff, in discussing the relationships of Rajput leaders to Muslim rulers, uses the term gift economy to describe the exchange of gifts in this context.[90] If Kolff means that economic factors—the cost of the goods and animals exchanged—determined the significance of the transaction, he misunderstands the situation.[91] The second issue concerns corruption.

[86] Ibid., 1:74. See also Richards, 'Formation', p. 270.

[87] Ibid., 1:228.

[88] Roe, *Embassy*, p. 46.

[89] Richards, 'Formation', p. 273, discusses this issue.

[90] Dirk Kolff, 'An Armed Peasantry and Its Allies' (Ph.D. dissertation, Rijksuniversiteit te Leiden, 1983), p. 37. Because the term is in single quotation marks and possibly translated from a Dutch expression, I do not know exactly what Kolff means by it.

[91] Kolff is not the only historian or anthropologist to deny that the exchange of gifts has the symbolic functions which I ascribe to it. John R. Perry, whose study of *Karim Khan Zand*, Publications of the Center for Middle East Studies 12 (Chicago: University of Chicago Press, 1979) is a standard work, denies that the exchange of *pīshkash* and robes of honour had a similar meaning in eighteenth century Iran. His views are a

Such outsiders as Roe found frequent demands for gifts exasperating and sometimes embarrassing proofs of the corruption and rapacity of the Mughal emperor and his officers.[92] Their views became part of the overall Western perception of Islamic empires in general. The Mughals and their servants were certainly no less greedy than other humans—the entire species is noteworthy on that score. Some demands for gifts were extortion; some gifts were bribes. But the established structure of the exchange of gifts involved not corruption but the definition and reinforcement of political relationships. To equate the regular exchange of gifts with abuse of the system or corruption misses the point entirely.[93]

In addition to the exchange of gifts, several other aspects of the relationship between the emperor and his officers deserve attention. Even when not at court, mansabdars were at the physical disposal of their master. Abū al-Fażl gives a complex set of regulations for mounting guard at the court. In theory all mansabdars served at court for a month, mounting guard duty once a week, so as to have an 'opportunity to come to Court and to partake in the liberality of his Majesty. But those who are stationed on the frontiers, or told off for any important duty, merely send in reports of their exact condition. . . .' The guard changed daily, at the evening *darbār* when the *qūr* was in the *dīwān-i khaṣṣ*, with the relieving watch on the right and the relieved watch on the left.[94] Akbar inspected each soldier personally. This ceremony doutbless enhanced the personal relationship of the ruler with his officers.[95]

The monarch determined the physical location of his officers even when they were stationed elsewhere. Most mansabdars spent their careers either in a court post or in attendance at court, in a post in the provinces, or in transit between court and a post. Officers rarely received permission to be anywhere else—their *watans* or jāgīrs most frequently—and departure from their posts without permission, even

salutary reminder that rituals and political terms do not have a single permanent meaning, but change in content and significance with time and place.

92 Roe, *Embassy*, pp. 105, 251, 305, 378–9.

93 Both Bernard Cohn and Halil Inalcik have drawn my attention to this issue.

94 A.A., 1:/267–8. The reference to those attending the *darbār* standing in the proper order may refer to this regulation.

95 See also Athar Ali, *Nobility*, p. 138.

to go to court, was an offence. Flight from court constituted rebellion, as in the case of Mirzā Sharaf al-Dīn Ḥusayn Ahrārī. The chronicles do not refer to departures from court, only to receiving permission to leave. When a disagreement with Islām Khān Chishtī, the governor of Bengal, placed Mirzā Nathan in an impossible situation, he rejected the advice of his followers to bring the matter to Jahāngīr at court because he and his father had official positions in Bengal. 'If I turn my face and proceed to the imperial court,' he wrote, 'then it will prove my ungratefulness.'[96]

Political loyalty involves calculation as well as emotion, but many Mughal mansabdars had strong emotional ties to their masters. Mirzā Nathan's refusal to show ingratitude reveals his feelings, as does his vision of Jahāngīr in a dream. The Mirzā came to Bengal as an adolescent, with his father Ihtimām Khān. He became ill, and on the seventh night of his fever, he dreamed. Jahāngīr ('the king of the spiritual and temporal domain') spoke to him—

> O Nathan! Is this the time for a tiger to lie down? Arise, we have granted you security from pain and trouble by our prayers to the Almighty and Omnipresent Lord. Be quick and placing the foot of manliness and sincerity in your devoted work be a comrade to your great father and be his support.[97]

Mirzā Nathan awoke free from illness, and through his father and Islām Khān petitioned Jahāngīr for an imperial mansab and inclusion as an imperial disciple. In response, Jahāngīr sent him a robe of honour and a miniature portrait for his turban.[98] Even if Mirzā Nathan embellished his experience, he leaves no doubt about his deep personal loyalty to and affection for his sovereign.

Mizā Nathan had a special bond to the emperor as a *khānahzād*. The term literally means 'son of the house' or 'household born one', and referred to the sons of mansabdars and lesser officials who grew up in Mughal service.[99] Originally *khānahzād* meant exactly what it

[96] *Baharistan*, 1:150.

[97] Ibid., 1:17.

[98] Ibid., 1:74.

[99] Richards, 'Conduct', pp. 288–9, makes the point that officials below mansabdar status considered themselves *khānahzāds*.

said, a child who had grown up in the imperial camp or court, and then came to mean the son of any imperial official. The Mughal historians do not identify Rājah Mān Singh as a *khānahzād*, though his father and grandfather were in Akbar's service, but Lahawrī describes his great-grandson Jay Singh as 'one of the trusted *khānahzāds* of this court.'[100]

Mughal texts frequently refer to *khānahzādagī* (being a *khānahzād*) as an explanation of influence, qualification for an office, or a justification for an appointment. For example, Shāh Nawāz Khān says of Multafat Khān Mīr Ibrāhīm Ḥusayn, whose father, Aṣālat Khān, had been *mīr bakhshī*, 'Though his rank during that reign was not more than 700, but in view of his being a *khānazād* . . . which is an important consideration with appreciative sovereigns—he had precedence over his equals.'[101] In the notice of Tarbiyat Khān's appointment as ambassador to Naẕr Muḥammad Khān, the ruler of Balkh, Lahawrī describes him with the same words as he uses for Jay Singh.[102] He later gives more detail, saying *abā 'an jad az khānazādān-i in dargah* (whose family had been *khānazāds* for generations).[103] Several officers received the title Khānazād Khān, all the sons of great amīrs. Mirzā Amānullah, the eldest son of Mahābat Khān, gained that title while governing Kabul for his father during the campaign against the rebel Shāh Jahān and held it until he became Khān-i Zamān at Shāh Jahān's accession.[104] I'tiqād Khān Mirzā Bahman Yār, the son of Āṣaf Khān Yamīn al-Dawlah, held the title briefly.[105] Sa'id Khān Bahādur Ẓafar-i Jang, a provincial governor in the north-west for many years under Shāh Jahān wanted the title for his eldest son, Mirzā Shaykh. After he and his son

[100] B.N.L., 1:492. Court is the literal translation of *dargāh*; dynasty would probably be more accurate. Richards, 'Formation', p. 272 comments that *khānahzād* apparently referred to actual residence at court, and the definition changed in the course of the century.

[101] M.U., 3:611/2:281. On Aṣālat Khān, see M.U., 1:167–72/295–9. The reign referred to is that of Shāh Jahān.

[102] B.N.L., 1:465.

[103] B.N.L., 1:470. Hans Wehr, *A Dictionary of Modern Written Arabic*, ed. J. Milton Cowan, 3rd ed. (Ithaca, N.Y.: Spoken Language Service, 1976) defines *aba 'an jad* as from father to son, but the expression does not fit syntactically.

[104] M.U., 1:740–8/212–19.

[105] M.U., 1:232–4/354–5.

had distinguished themselves in the Qandahar campaign of 1637–8 (1047), Shāh Jahān granted the request. Mirzā Shaykh held the title until he was killed in the Balkh and Badakhshan campaign.[106] The use of the term as a title indicated that it implied honour to both the recipient and the family.

6.5 Akbar as Spiritual Guide

S. A. A. Rizvi and J. F. Richards describe the Dīn-i Illahī (literally divine faith or faith of God) as a spiritual tie between the ruler and those of his officers who accepted him as their spiritual guide, much as Sufi novices followed the teachings of their *pīr*.[107] Dīn-i Illahī is one of four terms which Bada'ūnī uses in this connection. The others are *tawhīd-i Illahī* (unity of God), *ikhlas-i chahārgānah* or *marātib-i chahārgānah* (fourfold loyalty or four ranks) and *murīdī* (discipleship, the common term for that status in Sufism). Bada'ūnī applies these terms to both Akbar's personal religious conduct and to his relations with his officers. He reports that Akbar used the term *tawhīd-i Islāmī* to practices which he copied from the lamas of Tibet in the hope of extending his life. Such imitation shocked Sharī'ah-minded observers, but, as Rizvi says, was hardly unprecedented among Sufis.[108] Dīn-i Illahī, which Blochman made the standard term for Akbar's religious innovations, appears in Bada'ūnī's discussion of the oath which Mirzā Jānī Beg, the former ruler of Tatta, took when he entered Mughal service in 1593 (1001). The oath called for rejection of *islām-i majāzī u taqlīdī*, insincere and imitative Islām, not for apostasy from Islām itself.[109] Muslim reformers before Akbar's time had condemned *taqlīd*, the simple acceptance of authority in religious matters.[110]

Ikhlās-i chahārgānah and *murīdī* refer to the officers' special loyalty

[106] B.N.L., 2:40, 688–91.

[107] Richards, 'Formation', pp. 267–71; Rizvi, *Intellectual*, pp. 374–417. Our knowledge of the Dīn-i Illahī comes from two disparate sources, Abū al-Fażl and Bada'ūni. Abū al-Fażl presents Akbar as he wished to be understood, and probably as he understood himself. Bada'ūnī saw his sovereign through the lenses of personal bitterness and pious disapproval.

[108] M.Ṭ., 2:325–6/335; Rizvi, *Intellectual*, pp. 390–1.

[109] M.T., 2:305–6/314.

[110] Rahman, *Islam*, pp. 241–2.

to Akbar. Abū al-Fażl uses the first term to describe the prerequisites for the office of *wakīl*.[111] In another context, he states that the loyalty (or disinterest) of the *wakīl* should be such that he is willing to execute his own father in the interests of his master.[112] Akbar reportedly praised the loyalty of Hindus—meaning Rajputs—which found its logical conclusion in *sati*. He specifically mentions their willingness to sacrifice life, reputation, and religion.[113] Akbar's well-known interrogation of Rājah Mān Singh shows that loyalty constituted the primary element of discipleship. During a private interview with 'Abd al-Rahīm Khān-i Khānān and Mān Singh, Akbar raised the subject of *murīdī*. Mān Singh replied—

> 'If discipleship means willingness to sacrifice one's life, I have already carried my life in my hand: what need is there of further proof? If, however, the term has another meaning and refers to faith, I am certainly a Hindu. If you order me to do so, I will become a Muslim, but I know not the existence of any other path . . . than these two.' At this point the matter stopped and the Emperor did not question him any further.[114]

Vincent Smith describes this episode as Mān Singh's protest against the Dīn-i Illahī; Srivastava sees it as proof that Akbar did not require adherence to his new cult.[115] But the exchange reveals that Akbar demanded loyalty from his officers; *murīdī* in the sense of accepting his spiritual guidance was secondary. He acted as a spiritual guide primarily in order to instil loyalty.[116] Akbar accepted Mān Singh's loyalty as enough and appointed him governor of Bihar.[117]

The officers who accepted Akbar's guidance swore the oath which Bad'ūnī mentions. It goes:

[111] A.A., 1:4/5.

[112] A.N., 2:100–150. One should bear in mind the belief that a parent is more precious than a child because the child is replaceable.

[113] A.N., 3:256–371.

[114] M.T., 2:364/375.

[115] Vincent A. Smith, *Akbar the Great Mogul* 2nd. ed. rev (New Delhi, S. Chand, 1962), p. 183; Srivastava, *Akbar*, 1:288–9.

[116] Rivzi, *Intellectual*, p. 396; Richards, 'Formation', pp. 267–71.

[117] M.T., 2:364–75. Mān Singh had been recalled from the Punjab to take up his new post; Akbar examined him when he came to court.

> I so and so, son of so and so, do voluntarily, and with sincere predilection and inclination, liberate and disassociate myself from the traditional and imitative Islam which I have seen my fathers practice and heard them speak about, and join the dīn-i Illahī of Akbar Shāh accepting the four degrees of devotion, which are the sacrifice of property, life, honour, and religion.[118]

The oath makes the Dīn-Illahī an alternative to traditional Islām, but does not involve apostasy from Islām itself. Again, the new obligation consists primarily of loyalty to Akbar. Abū al-Fażl makes spiritual guidance an integral part of kingship. Since the same power underlies spiritual and temporal glory, the distinction between *dīn* (faith) and *dunyā* (the world) is artificial. Perceptive men realize that there is no distinction, and 'when a nation learns to understand how to worship truth,' it looks to the 'king, to be [the] spiritual leader as well, for a king possesses independent of men, the ray of Divine wisdom.' Hindustan has learned this lesson in Akbar's time, and through his realm persons from all elements of society seek to attain their desires through devotion to him. In some cases, miraculous healing has occurred through devotion to Akbar.[119] The devotion to which Abū al-Fażl refers resembles the adherence of disciples to a Sufi or Hindu saint, rather than the worship of a deity.

Abū al-Fażl asserts that Akbar did not actively seek disciples among his officers, but Bada'ūnī's report of the discussion with Mān Singh casts doubt on the point. Abū al-Fażl's statement that thousands of men accepted his guidance is probably exaggerated. Those who did went through an initiation ceremony. On a Sunday, the day when the sun is most splendid, the initiate approached Akbar in the *dīwān-i khaṣṣ*, and, carrying his turban, placed his head on Akbar's feet. Abū al-Fażl interprets the initiate's obeisance as symbolic of abandoment of selfishness, readiness for worship, and desire for the means to everlasting life. Akbar responded by bringing the novice to his feet and placing the turban on his head. He then gave the initiate the *shast*, which was either a ring or a miniature portrait of Akbar which his *murīds*

[118] M.T. 2:304, trans. Rizvi, *Intellectual*, p. 391. The reasons for not accepting Lowe's translation are on pp. 391–2.
[119] A.A., 1:158–61/170–4.

wore on their turbans. Whatever it was, the *shast* was inscribed *Allahu Akbar*.[120] The disciples had several customs. They greeted each other with Allahu Akbar and responded Jallalah Jallahu (may his glory be glorified, from Akbar's *laqab*, Jalāl al-Dīn), gave feasts on their own birthdays, restrained their consumption of meat and abstained from it entirely during their birth months, and abstained from sexual intercourse with women who either could not become pregnant or already were.[121] With the exception of Shāhbāz Khān Kambū, Akbar's officers used the word *murīd* on their seals.[122]

Akbar's status as a spiritual guide fitted his imperial image as the Perfect Man. In a sense, he did claim to be a prophet, because Mḥammad, in the view of Ibn al-'Arabī, combined the spiritual status of the Perfect Man with secular leadership. Akbar made the same claim, but did not do so publicly or unambiguously enough to be recognized generally as an apostate. He used his claim to spiritual status and insight primarily to gain greater devotion from his officers, and sought loyalty rather than discipleship from those officers. As Rizvi mentions, the Ṣafavī example may have influenced Akbar. The Ṣafavī rulers had the status of *murshid-i kāmil* (perfect spiritual guide), and the Qizilbāsh tribal soldiers were, in theory, their *murīds*. This relationship did not guarantee loyalty, but it remained a potent political force.[123] In addition, Akbar's claim to be a spiritual teacher strengthened the perception that he was neither a Muslim nor a Hindu. For Bada'ūnī, and for later Sharī'ah-minded Muslims, Akbar's programme removed him from the category of Muslim sovereign and constituted political apostasy. But this view stemmed more from Akbar's public abandonment of Islamic worship and of enforcement of the Sharī'ah restrictions in *żimmīs* than from his private relationships with his officers.

[120] A.A., 1:160/174. Blochman interprets the *Āyīn* as stating that the *shast* had two inscriptions, Allahu Akbar and the great name of God (*ism-i a'ẓam*); I follow Rizvi's translation, *Intellectual*, p. 401.

[121] A.A., 1:160–1/175–6.

[122] Rizvi, *Intellectual*, p. 406.

[123] The most convenient reference is Roger Savory, *Iran under the Safavis* (Cambridge: Cambridge University Press, 1980), pp. 16–103.

6.6 Summary

The Mughal doctrine of kingship and constitution had several significant features. It broke with Tīmūrid precedents by eliminating collective sovereignty and the appanage system. The Ottoman and Ṣafavī dynasties also eventually discarded the appanage system. The elimination of collective sovereignty was a necessary element in the transformation of politics in the Islamic world in the sixteenth century. Mughal rituals and texts articulated a higher form of kingship than their Muslim predecessors in the subcontinent had projected. Although Mughal kingship had significant similarities to Hindu kingship, there is little evidence of direct Hindu influence or imitation of Hindu forms. Abū al-Fażl combined elements of Sufi theosophy with a modification of existing Tīmūrid doctrine to produce a distinctive Akbarī kingship.

Rather than receiving only a mandate to rule from God, Akbar and his successors claimed a special sovereign nature, emanating from God. It included the status of the Perfect Man, who embodied all the elements of the universe in microcosm. Because the structure of government and of society mirrored that of the universe, the king articulated the order of society in his own person. The physical arrangement of the participants in the *darbār* reflected that order. High status in the society coincided with deep submission to the ruler, reflected by the hierarchy of forms of obeisance. The Mughals deviated from the pattern of Islamic kingship by eliminating the *jizyah*, the sign of the subordinate status of non-Muslims in society. They substituted *sulḥ-i kull* for Islām as the sovereign cult. Rituals, including *jharūkā darshan*, the weighing ceremony and the pattern of *darbār* made it fit Hindu patterns enough to make Mughal kingship recognizable—in both senses—to Hindus.

The same court rituals made Mughal mansabdars symbolic extensions of the monarch and strengthened the ties between the ruler and his officers. Their gifts to him demonstrated their position as his subordinates; again the greater the present given the higher the rank of the giver. The ruler's gifts, most importantly robes of honour, transformed the officers into extensions of his body and provided outer marks of their status. A mansabdar with a low rank might receive a robe of honour alone; a high officer or prince taking up a provincial governorship might receive a more elaborate robe, a jewelled sword and dagger, a breeding pair of elephants with jewelled equipment for the male, a horse with a jewelled saddle, and a turban with a jewelled ornament. Their costumes indicated their nature and rank; receiving them from the king showed that the king determined their status and political identity. The clothes made the men.

The Akbarī constitution articulated in the court rituals and the *Akbarnāmah* and the governmental reforms described in the previous chapter formed a single, seamless fabric. To us, administrative reform and symbolic re-ordering may seem unrelated, but the participants probably were aware of no distinction. The *dāgh* regulations provided the administrative means to regulate the status of officers in accord with the doctrine stated in the rituals; the ritual interaction made the change in the status of officers in the provinces personal and immediate.

In less than three decades, Akbar and his advisers had transformed the political face of Hindustan. In the villages and localities, perhaps, the change meant little. The same zamindars and headmen collected the revenue from the peasants, transformed it into cash, and transmitted it to the more distant recipient. Akbar's reforms doubtless made the revenue demand more predictable and perhaps more fair, but did not change the overall pattern. Beyond the local level, however, the transformation was unmistakeable. A single ruler dominated the entire Indo-Gangetic plain, plus Malwa and Gujarat. Although they ruled larger provinces, his governors had less autonomy than their predecessors had. The power of the central bureaucracy had increased proportionately. Though composed of men with vastly different backgrounds, the ruling class of the new Mughal polity formed a single hierarchy, its heterogeneity not destroyed but subordinated to allegiance to Akbar. The new constitution presented not Muslims ruling over Hindus but Muslims and Hindus together, serving a ruler who, whatever his personal beliefs, was not merely a Muslim or Hindu.

The attempt to make the government and politics of Hindustan correspond with this constitution flew in the face of political, military, and economic reality. The confrontation produced the Akbarī compromise.

CHAPTER 7
Crisis and Compromise

7.1 The Great Revolt

There is a consensus of historians that the revolts of 1580–2 (988–90) caused the greatest crisis of Akbar's reign, but there is no agreement as to the causes of the revolts and their significance. Most writers view the revolts as the results of Muslim resistance to Akbar's religious innovations.[1] I. H. Qureshi, however, the best of the historians to approach Akbar's reign from a Muslim perspective, considers religion only a minor motivation, though he describes the outcome of the conflict as the end of the primacy of Islam.[2] The weight of evidence supports Qureshi's view of the causes.

The rebellions did not occur in Bengal and Bihar by accident. As previously mentioned, Akbar consistently stationed Humāyūnī Chaghatay officers on the eastern frontier of the empire. This policy served two purposes. The Chaghatay officers were generally experienced soldiers with large contingents of mounted archers. They thus formed an effective defence against the Afghan threat from Bengal and had

[1] A. L. Srivastava, *Akbar the Great*, 2nd. ed., 3 vols. (Agra: Shiva Lal Agarwala, 1972), 1:273–4; Vincent A. Smith, *Akbar the Great Mogul*, 2nd ed. rev. (New Delhi: S. Chand, 1962), pp. 132–4; Stanley Wolpert, *A New History of India* (New York: Oxford University Press, 1977), p. 132; Iqtidar Alam Khan, 'The Nobility under Akbar and the Development of His Religious Policy', *Journal of the Royal Asiatic Society*, (1968), p. 35; S. A. A. Rizvi, *A Religious and Intellectual History of the Muslims of Akbar's Reign* (New Delhi: Munshiram Manoharlal, 1975), pp. 161–2.

[2] Ishtiaq Husain Qureshi, *Akbar* (Karachi: Ma'aref, 1978), pp. 91–5, 103–4.

scope for their ambitions because they could conquer land for larger jāgīrs. Stationing them there also removed them from the political centre of the empire, leaving Akbar greater freedom of action. As the Mughal frontier zone moved eastward, Chaghatays remained at the point of advance. Khān-i Zamān 'Alī Qulī Khān, the first Mughal governor of Jaunpur, received the assignment to conquer and occupy the province from his patron and friend Bayrām Khān.[3] After the defeat of the Uzbegs, Akbar appointed Mun'im Khān governor of Jaunpur. This appointment removed the leading Chaghatay officer from the political mainstream. Most of Mun'im Khān's leading subordinates were also Chaghatays, including two who were probably clan leaders, Majnūn Khān Qāqshāl and Muḥammad Qulī Khān Barlās.[4] The Chaghatays thus led the conquest of Bihar and Bengal, and were insulated from the immediate effect of administrative reforms. The extension of those reforms brought Chaghatay opposition.

The revolts of 1580–2 (988–90) in Bihar and Bengal had the same cause and outcome, but began separately. Bada'ūnī states that the Bihar uprising had two parallel causes, the *fatwā* of Mullā Muḥammad Yazdī, the Shī'ī *qāẓī* of Jaunpur, ordering revolt against Akbar because of his religious innovations and the administrative excesses of Mullā Ṭayyib, Ray Purushuttam, Mullā Mujdī Sirhindī, and Shamshīr Khān, who had been appointed *dīwān*, *bakhshī*, and lesser financial administrators in the province.[5] None of the other historians mentions the *fatwā* and even Bada'ūnī devotes far more attention to what he considers administrative oppression.[6] Akbar responded to Yazdī's challenge by ordering his arrest and surreptitious execution. Bada'ūnī reports that Akbar had executed several other ulama whom he suspected of disloyalty, but does not name them or describe the circumstances. Shortly afterwards, Akbar transferred the ulama of the province of Lahore to other posts in Gujarat, Jaunpur, Bihar, and Malwa.[7] Akbar must have

[3] A.N., 2:82/125–6; Iqtidar Ālam Khan, *The Political Biography of a Mughal Noble: Mun'im Khan Khan-i Khanan* (New Delhi: Orient Longman, 1973), p. 53.

[4] Ibid., pp. 97–101.

[5] M.T., 2:266/274, 276/284.

[6] A.N., 3:284–7/417–23; T.A., 2:349–51; Srivastava, *Akbar*, 1:249–51; Qureshi, *Akbar*, pp. 162–8; Rizvi *Intellectual*, pp. 161–2.

[7] M.T., 2:277–8/85–6.

suspected these ulama of disloyalty, but his response hardly amounts to persecution and does not form a part of the history of the revolt.

Akbar had assigned Mullā Ṭayyib, Ray Purushuttam, Mullā Mujdī Sirhindī and Shamshīr Khān to Bihar as part of the reorganization of provincial governments in 1580 (988). They rigorously enforced his regulations.

> In the matters of reviews and drills and of branding, they exhibited harshness and malignity, and in their blindness neglected tact and the acceptance of excuses—without which the administration of the world cannot be carried on—and lost sight of prudence.[8]

Bada'ūnī states that they, by 'bending unsuitable and unfitting seasons to their wishes so annoyed the soldiery that they compelled [Ma'ṣūm Khān Kābulī] to revolt'.[9] The *Ṭabaqat-i Tīmūrī*, a late source more sympathetic to the rebels than the others, emphasizes the mastery and past success of the officers now subjected to the dominance of new officials and stresses an argument between Ma'ṣūm Khān Kābulī and Mullā Ṭayyib and Ray Purushuttam over branding.[10] None of the historians asserts that Mullā Ṭayyib and his colleagues violated or exceeded their instructions. The strict enforcement of the regulations caused major discontent among the officers. The rebels included Ma'sūm Khān Kābulī, the jagirdar of Patna; Sa'īd Beg Badakhshī and 'Arab Bahādur, the jagirdars of Sassaram; Sa'ādat 'Alī; Hajjī Kulbābī; another Sa'īd Badakhshī with his son Bahādur; and Darwīsh 'Alī Shakrū. Ma'ṣūm Khān Kābulī, a foster-brother of Mirzā Muḥammad Hakīm, had left Kabul because of local political infighting. He was a *sayyid* from Turbat in Khurasan, not a Chaghatay, but had no particular loyalty to Akbar. He had distinguished himself in the struggle with the Afghans of Bengal, as his possession of Patna in jāgīr indicates.[11] One must

[8] A.N., 3:284–5/418.

[9] M.T., 2:266/274

[10] Muḥammad Barārī Umī ibn Muḥammad Jamshīd ibn Jabbārī Khān ibn Majnūn Khān Qāqshāl, *Tabaqat-i Tīmūrī*, (Ousely Ms. 311, Bodleian Library, filmed by Oxford University Press, 1982), f. 144r.

[11] M.U., 3:292–6/2:66–9. Presumably he and Muẓaffar Khān both came from either Turbat-i Jam or Turbat-i Haydariyah, southwest and southeast of Mashhad. On 'Arab Bahādur, see M.U., 2:771–3/1:266–8.

suppose that he felt that the imposition of financial penalties by imperial clerks was not an appropriate reward for his services.

The jagirdars of the province found it difficult to meet the *dāgh* requirements and sought to satisfy the officials with bribes. Niẓām al-Dīn Aḥmad asserts that Mullā Ṭayyib and his associates deprived Ma'ṣum Khān Kābulī, 'Arab Bahādur, and other officers of Bihar of their jāgīrs. The disloyal officers showed their intentions when they tried to plunder an imperial caravan.[12] When Muḥibb 'Alī Khān, a loyal officer who had attempted to bring his contingent up to standard, realized the intentions of the rebels, he warned them against insurrection and added his own men to the convoy escort. His action saved the convoy, but the rebels looted the city of Patna instead. Muḥibb 'Ali Khān hastened to prevent the rebels from taking Rohtas.[13] The newly appointed officials also resisted the rebels, who now included another Ma'ṣūm Khān, known as Farankhūdī. He was the son of Mu'īn al-Dīn Khān Farankhūdī, who had made the revenue settlement in Malwa after 'Abdullah Khān Uzbeg had reconquered it, but we know nothing of his career before this episode.[14] Ma'ṣūm Khān Farankhūdī held Ghazipur as his jāgīr. He deceived Ray Purushuttam, who had led a force against him, and with 'Arab Bahādur, three named local jagirdars, Kamāl al-Dīn Ḥusayn Sīstānī, Sayyid Ḥasan, and Dūrāj, attacked and defeated him. Ray Purushuttam was mortally wounded. Muḥibb 'Ali Khān then led a successful counter-attack against 'Arab Bahādur.[15]

When Akbar received news of the uprising, he appointed Rājah Tūdar Mal to command an army to suppress it, including Shaykh Farīd Bakhshī (Murtażā Khan), Mihr 'Alī Khān Sildūz, Rājah Askaran, Ray Lunkarn, Naqīb Khān, Qamar Khān, Shaykh Khwājah Abū al-Qāsim,

[12] T.A, 2:349–50. The contents of the convoy included the property which Khān-i Jahān had left, the revenue of Bengal for the imperial treasury, and several important prisoners. Many merchants accompanied the imperial consignment. A.N., 3:286/420–1.

[13] This man was Muhibb 'Alī Khān Ruhtasī, not the son of Bābur's *wakīl*. See M.U., 3:277–80/226–9. His action supports the thesis that major forts in the provinces guarded against revolt rather than served as potential bases for it.

[14] M.U., 3:246–9/2:64–6; A.A., /1:480. Blochmann mentions that there was a place called Farankhud near Bukhara, but the geographic origin of the family gives little insight into their historical role.

[15] A.N., 3:285–7/420–2; M.T., 2:281/289–90; T.A., 2:349–50; Srivastava, *Akbar*, 1:249–50.

Abū al-Ma'ālī, and Bāqir or Bāqī Sufrachī.[16] He also ordered the jagirdars of the provinces of Allahabad and Oudh, including Tursun Muḥammad Khān, Ghazī Khān Badakhshī, Ray Surjan, and Ma'ṣūm Khān Farankhūdī, whose participation in the revolt was apparently not known, to join Rājah Tūdar Mal in Bihar.[17] A second group of officers, including Ṣadiq Khān, Bāqī Khān, Ulugh Khān Habashī, Ṭayyib Khān, and Mīr Abū al-Muẓaffar, approached Bihar from Chanderi and Narwar.[18]

Meanwhile, Bahādur, the son of Sa'īd Badakhshī, had assumed sovereignty in Bihar and attempted to become the leader of the revolt. Ma'ṣūm Khān Kabūlī, unable to reason with him, led many of the other rebels to join the rebellion in Bengal. 'Arab Bahādur remained in possession of Patna, but Shāham Khān Jalayir, the jagirdar of Hajjipur and leader of the Jalayirs who had at first supported the rebels, changed sides. When Muḥibb 'Alī Khān again defeated 'Arab, this time outside Patna, Sa'ādat 'Alī Khān, whom 'Arab had left in charge of his household, returned to imperial allegiance. Muḥibb 'Alī Khān took possession of Patna and then led Ghazī Khān, Ulugh Khān and several other officers to joint Rājah Tūdar Mal. Ma'ṣūm Khān Farankhūdī also joined

[16] On Mihr 'Alī Khān Sildūz, see M.U., 3:217–8/71–2; A.A., /1:481. He began his career as a subordinate of Adham Khān and then of Mir Muḥammad Khān-i Kalan, Khān-i A'ẓam Khān's uncle. Sildūz was a Chaghatay clan name, but Mihr 'Ali Khān's affiliation was with Akbar's foster family. Rājah Askaran was a brother of Rājah Bihārah Mal, A.A. /1:509 and Ray Lunkarn was also a Kachwaha, M.U., 2:116–17/1–836–7. Naqīb Khān, a Ṣafī *sayyid* of Qazwin and the son of a servant of Shāh Tahmasb Ṣafavī, was best known as a scholar. Shāh Nawaz Khān says of him: 'Because of his liberal views devoid of bigotry he was well-known as a Sunni throughout Iran, and in India he was generally accepted as Shi'a.' M.U., 3:812–17/2:381-4; Qamar Khān, M.U., 3:53–4/2:487–8, was his son. Abū al-Ma 'alī was the son of Sayyid Muḥammad Mīr-i 'Adl, a *sayyid* of Amroha, A.A., /1:485, 563. I cannot identify the other participants.

[17] A.N., 3:287–9/422–5; T.A., 2:351. Tursun Khān is called Tursun Muḥammad Khan in the M.U., 1:471–5/944–8, the son of the ruler of a principality in Garjestan and formerly a servant of Bayrām Khān. Ray Surjan is the same man who surrendered Kalinjar to the Mughals.

[18] Ṣadiq Khān was Ṣadiq Muḥammad Khān Harawī, also a former servant of Bayrām Khān, M.U., 2:724–9/658–62. I assume Baqī Khan was Bāqī Muḥammad Khān, the elder brother of Adham Khan, M.U., 1:394/384–5. Ulugh Khān Habashī had been in service in Gujarat and joined the Mughals when they conquered Gujarat, M.U., 1:87/3:970. Mīr Abū al-Muẓaffar was the son of Ashraf Khān Mīr Munshī, A.A./1–542. Unless Ṭayyib Khan was Mulla Ṭayyib I cannot identify him.

the imperial forces but planned to assassinate their commander. The rebels of Bihar did not offer battle, but Rājah Tūdar Mal, distrusting the loyalty of his supporters, halted at the fort of Monghyr on the Ganges. He greatly strengthened the fortifications there, and defended the fort against the rebels from Bengal. In the course of the siege, several imperial officers defected to the rebels.[19]

Like the newly appointed officials in Bihar, Muẓaffar Khān, who had replaced the late Khān-i Jahān as governor of Bengal, enforced the administrative regulations strictly. He followed the instructions of Khwājah Shāh Manṣūr Shīrāzī, whose biography forms the next section. Because of the inclement climates of Bihar and Bengal, Akbar had doubled the salaries of the jagirdars of Bengal and increased the salaries of the men stationed in Bihar by half. Shīrāzī had reduced the increases to 50 per cent and 20 per cent. Muẓaffar Khān put this reduction into practice. In several cases, he instituted severe punishments in order to force jagirdars to return to the treasury excess funds which they had collected. He had an officer named Khālidī Khān, whose jāgīr had been resumed because of his failure to meet the branding and muster regulations, tortured. At orders from court, Muẓaffar Khān also had one Rawshan Beg, an imperial tax collector guilty of embezzlement, executed in public. Rawshan Beg had taken refuge with the Qāqshāl officers and Muẓaffar Khān clashed with their chief, Bābā Khān, in order to take him. He had already annoyed Bābā Khān by refusing to confirm his jāgīr and waive the branding requirements. The conduct of Riżawī Khān, who had originally had charge of collection from *khāliṣah* land near Jaunpur and then been made *bakhshī*, with charge of branding, in that province, also concerned the jagirdars. He revised the assignments in the province and reduced many. Muḥammad Barārī Ummī reports that his great-uncle claimed to have expended Rs 70,000 and still had to have a hundred more troopers registered. These grievances caused the Qāqshāls to revolt.[20]

Abū al-Fażl gives several other causes, including the wickedness of the rebels and the failure of loyal men to forestall them, but only one

[19] A.N., 3:305–8/450–3; T.A., 2-351–2; M.T., 282/290–1; M.R., 1:872; Srivastava, *Akbar*, 1:255–6.

[20] A.N., 3:289–93/426–33; T.A., 348–9; M.T. 2:280–1/288–9; M.R., 1:869–70; *Ṭabaqat-i Tīmūrī*, f. 145v. Srivastava, *Akbar*, 1:251–2.

deserves comment. He states that the rebels made *sulḥ-i kull* at least a pretext for their actions. Neither Bada'ūnī nor Niẓām al-Dīn Aḥmad substantiates this allegation; Abū al-Fażl gives no specifics. Muḥammad Barārī Ummī does, however, state that the promulgation of *sulḥ-i kull* added to the main causes of discontent. Both historians have obvious motives for mentioning *sulḥ-i kull*. Abū al-Fażl's statement fits his perception of a struggle between Akbar and his supporters, in favour of *sulḥ-i kull*, and their bigoted and ignorant opponents. For Ummī, writing in the reign of Shāh Jahān, the possibility of religious motivation softens the treason of his ancestors.[21]

The Qāqshāl officers—Bābā Khān and Jabbārī Khān, the son of the late Majnūn Khān—led the uprising. Abū al-Fażl also names Wazīr Beg Jamīl as a ringleader, but his subsequent pardon suggests that he did not play a pivotal role.[22] Of the other participants whom Abū al-Fażl lists, Sa'īd Tuqbā'ī, Mirzā Hajjī Lang, 'Arab Balkhī, Ṣāliḥ, Mīrakī Khān Murtażā Qulī Turkman, and Farrakh Irghaliq, we know only their names. The *Ṭabaqat-i Tīmūrī* gives a far longer list. Virtually all of the otherwise unknown rebels had Chaghatay tribal names like Qāqshāl or Barlās, Turkic elements in their names, or the title *beg*. Abū al-Fażl condemns Qiyā Khān Gung, who was governor of Orissa, Murād Khān, who held Fathabad, and Shāh Bardī, who held Satgaon on the border of Bengal and Orissa, for their failure to join in suppressing the revolt, although they remained loyal. The revolt actually began on 19 January 1580 (1 Ẑū al-Hijjah 988), when the rebel officers left the capital of Bengal, Tanda, and crossed the Ganges.[23] Violence did not begin immediately, but the departure from the capital without permission constituted revolt.[24]

Muẓaffar Khān sent a strong force across the river to confront the rebels. Its officers included Mīr Jamāl-Dīn Ḥusayn Injū, a *sayyid* of Shīrāz who served in the Deccan before entering Mughal service; Hakīm Abū al-Fath, a distinguished physician and favourite of Akbar

[21] A.N., 3:291–3/429–33; *Ṭabaqat-i Tīmūrī*, f. 145v.

[22] On Wazīr Beg, M.U., 3:928–9/2:980–1.

[23] The main channel of the Ganges no longer passes near the site of Tanda, which has been destroyed by erosion; the distributary which flows through the old bed is called the Bhagirathi (A.N., 3:428n, 442).

[24] A.N., 3:291/428–9; *Ṭabaqat-i Tīmūrī*, f. 146r–147v.

who was the *bakhshī* of Bengal; Riżawī Khān; Ja'far Beg, who later became the third Āṣaf Khān; Ray Patr Dās, later Rājah Bikrāmjīt, who was of the same caste as Rājah Tūdar Mal and was the *dīwān* of Bengal; and Muḥammad Qulī Turkman.[25]

Before fighting began, the rebels sought a reconciliation, but the imperial officers rejected their overtures. Akbar responded to news of the situation with two orders, one to Muẓaffar Khān censuring him and ordering him to confirm the jāgīrs of the Qāqshāls because they were old servants and one to the rebels offering forgiveness.[26] Negotiations began as a result, with the mutineers hoping that one of the loyal officers would intercede for them. Riżawī Khān, Ray Patr Dās, and others acted as intermediaries. Abū al-Fażl and Ummī blame the failure of these negotiations on Ray Patr Dās, who hoped to take advantage of them to make a surprise attack on the Qāqshāls, and Rizawī Khān, who betrayed his intention. Niẓām al-Dīn Aḥmad and Bada'ūnī, however, blame only the rebels, who, they believe, were insincere. When news of the continued conflict reached Akbar, his advisers felt that he should go to Bengal himself. He declined to do so, saying that Mirzā Muḥammad Hakīm was actually responsible, and that he had to remain ready in case his brother again invaded Hindustan. If Abū al-Fażl has not invented this episode to demonstrate Akbar's foresight it is very interesting. Perhaps Akbar felt that without an alternate Tīmūrid claimant, the rebels whould not have opposed him.[27]

After the negotiations failed, the rebels re-crossed the Ganges and besieged Tanda. A second attempt at reconciliation failed. Meanwhile, the rebels in Bihar, facing Rājah Tūdar Mal's imperial force, heard of the uprising in Bengal. The two groups began negotiations and the Bihar rebels under Ma'ṣūm Khān Kābulī proceeded towards Bengal. They defeated a force under Khwājah Shams al-Dīn Khwāfī, Tīmūr Khān, and Ja'far Beg which Muẓaffar Khān had sent to block the way.[28]

25 M.U., 3:358–60/1:742–3, 1:558–62/107–10; 1:107–15/282–7, 2:139–41/1:411–12, 3:342–3/186–7.

26 The *Ṭabaqat-i Tīmūrī*, f. 145r, reports that Akbar sent a copy of the order to Muẓaffar Khan to the Qāqshāls.

27 A.N., 3:293–5/432–5; T.A., 2:349; M.T., 2:280–1/289; M.R., 1:870; *Ṭabaqat-i Tīmūrī*, f. 145r; Srivastava, *Akbar*, 1:252–3.

28 Khwājah Shams al-Dīn was one of the many Mughal officers from Khwaf, both a town and a region in Khurasan, south of Turbat-i Jām and Turbat-i Haydariyah and

Muẓaffar Khān lost the confidence of his troops, and many of them defected. The rebels took the fort, executed Muẓaffar Khān, and gained control of the treasury. This infusion of funds permitted them to raise a large army. Bada'ūnī makes this connection explicit: 'making his goods and chattels the fund from which they drew in inducing people to join them, they collected a large force.'[29]

The rebels captured all the imperial officers, but Hakīm Abu al-Fath, Ray Patr Dās, and Khwājah Shams al-Dīn escaped. Ja'far Beg did so later. Having possession of the capital, the rebels then set up a parody of the imperial administration. Ma'ṣūm Khān Kābulī took the post of *wakīl*, and the title of Khān-i Dawrān, Bābā Khān Qāqshāl became Khān-i Khānān and governor of Bengal, and Jabbārī Khān became Khān-i Jahān with the rank of ten thousand. Other officers took the titles Khān-i Zamān, Khān-i 'Ālam, Lashkar Khān, and Shujā'āt Khān. Before his escape, Ja'far Beg received the title Āṣaf Khān, then held by his uncle Ghiyās al-Dīn. Less prominent men received less exalted titles with numerical ranks. To give this new structure a top, they read the *khutbah* in the name of Mirzā Muḥammad Hakīm. As their titular leader in Bengal, the rebels installed Mirzā Sharaf al-Dīn Ahrārī. He had been a prisoner in Muẓaffar Khān's custody and received a high position because of his family's prestige, especially among Chaghatays, and his Tīmūrid descent. The rebels proceeded up the Ganges to besiege Monghyr.[30]

Akbar's response to the news of these developments shows that he understood the nature of the crisis. He reinstated Khān-i A'ẓam to the rank of 5000 and appointed him governor of Bengal, with Sayyid 'Abdullah Bārah as his deputy.[31] In spite of his foster-brother's unruly tongue, Akbar trusted his loyalty. Because he had opposed the branding regulations, Khān-i A'ẓam's appointment sent a conciliatory signal to the rebels. Making an Indo-Muslim his chief subordinate increased

almost due east of Herat. His distinguished record during the rebellion started his rise to prominence. M.U., 1:664–9/804–8.

[29] M.T., 2:282–90.

[30] A.N., 3:299–305/442–50; M.T., 2:281–2/289–91; T.A., 2:349–51; M.R., 1:871; Srivastava, *Akbar*, 1:253–5. The *Ṭabaqat-i Tīmūrī*, f. 146r–147v, gives a much more extensive list of rebels who received titles, flags and drums.

[31] M.U., 3:489–91/1:79–80.

the likelihood that his troops would fight the rebels if necessary. Akbar also recalled Shāhbāz Khān Kambū, from Mewar, and sent him to Bengal with reinforcements, and ordered the arrest and clandestine execution of Mulla Muḥammad Yazdī. Lastly, he dismissed Khwājah Shāh Manṣūr Shīrāzī as *wazīr*, had him confined in the custody of Shāh Qulī Khān Mahrām, and appointed Wazīr Khān to replace him. This action suggested that Akbar intended to redress the grievances of the rebels. Akbar kept Shīrāzī confined only a few days but intended his dismissal as a symbol.[32]

Rājah Tūdar Mal defended Monghyr effectively for two months, and the news of Khān-i A'ẓam and Shāhbāz Khān's progress eastward caused the rebels to raise the seige on 25 April 1580 (9 Rabī' al-Awwal 988). The imperial forces began pursuit. Khwājah Shams al-Dīn Khwāfī, who had escaped from rebel custody, reported that the enemy had scattered. The news that Bābā Khān Qāqshāl was mortally ill ended the unity of the rebels. Mirzā Sharaf al-Dīn Ḥusayn and Jabbārī Khān Qāqshāl returned to Bengal while Ma'ṣūm Khān Kābulī advanced into Bihar and briefly besieged Patna. 'Arab Bahādur and others plundered the countryside of the province and attacked an imperial supply convoy unsuccessfully. Bahādur Khān (or Pahār Khān Balūch) defended the fort successfully.[33] When this news reached Rājah Tūdar Mal, he sent a flying column to Patna. At his request, Ma'ṣūm Khān Farankhūdī received command, but Rājah Tūdar Mal assigned Muḥibb 'Alī Khān and Mihr 'Alī Khān to shadow him. Ma'ṣūm Khān dispersed the rebels around Patna, but then went off on his own towards Jaunpur, taking Hajjipur from the rebel Bahādur Badakhshī on the way.[34]

Khān-i A'ẓam reached the camp in late September 1580 (Sha'bān 988). Unable to co-operate with Shāhbāz Khān, he joined Rājah Tūdar Mal and Shāhbāz Khān remained behind. Shāhbāz Khān arranged garrisons to bring order to Bihar and defeated 'Arab Bahādur, who fled to

[32] A.N., 3:308–9/454–5, 314–16/459–61; M.T., 2:285–93; T.A., 2:353–4; Srivastava, *Akbar*, 1:256–7. I agree with Srivastava that although Abū al-Fażl divides his discussion of Akbar's response into two sections, he planned his actions simultaneously, as Bada'ūnī and Nizām al-Dīn imply. I discuss Abū al-Fażl's criticism of Shīrāzī in the next section.

[33] The identity of this officer is doutbtful, see A.A./1:444–5, 593–4.

[34] A.N., 3:315/460–1, 319–21/467–71; Srivastava, *Akbar*, 1:256–8.

Sarangpur. Khān-i A'ẓam and Rājah Tūdar Mal divided their forces in order to deal with the dispersed rebels. Disputes between Shāhbāz Khān and Khān-i A'ẓam, and Rājah Tūdar Mal plagued the imperial forces but the weakness of the opposition made them successful nonetheless. Abū al-Fażl blames Shāhbāz Khān, saying that he had put on airs as a result of his defeat of Dalpat and made himself popular by distributing jāgīrs. Ultimately, Shāhbāz Khān led an army to Jaunpur against Ma'ṣūm Khān Farankhūdī and the other two commanders went northeast to Tirhut against Bahādur, with Ghazī Khān Badakhshī in the vanguard. Khān-i A'ẓam and Rājah Tūdar Mal defeated Bahādur. Meanwhile in Bengal, Ma'ṣūm Khān Kābulī had had Mirzā Sharaf al-Dīn poisoned.[35]

Abū al-Fażl's reference to Shāhbāz Khan's distribution of jāgīrs requires treatment of that subject. When Akbar went to the Punjab and then to Kabul to deal with Mirzā Muḥammad Hakīm in the spring of 1581, he left Shāhbāz Khān at Agra, effectively a regent. Mirzā Muḥammad Hakīm had invaded Hindustan in response to the invitation of the two rebel Ma'ṣūm Khāns.[36] In Akbar's absence, Shāhbāz Khān had 'turned the whole of the imperial dominions right away from [Garhi] to the Punjab into people's jagirs.' Upon Akbar's return, he had chastised Shāhbāz Khān for this unauthorized largesse. Shāhbāz Khān replied:

> If I had not thus won over the soldiery, they would have revolted with one consent. Now the Empire is yours and the army is yours. You may give what you like to whom you will and take away appointments and *jagirs* from whom you please. . . .[37]

The letters of Hakīm Abū al-Fath confirm that Shāhbāz Khān was exchanging land revenue assignments for cash salaries.[38]

Shāhbāz Khān's action shows that, although discontent was most

[35] A.N., 3:322–6/472–8; *Ṭabaqat-i Tīmūrī*, f. 148r; Srivastava, *Akbar*, 1:258–9.

[36] A.N., 3:335–7/492–5; M.T., 2:291/299; T.A., 2:357; M.R., 1:877.

[37] M.T., 2:296/304–5. See also Qaisar, 'Shahbaz Khan', p. 63–4.

[38] Hakīm Abū al-Fath Gīlānī, *Ruqāt-i Hakīm Abū al-Fath*, ed. Dr. Mohd. Bashir Ahmad (Lahore: Idarah-Tahqiqat-i Pakistan, 1968), pp. 26–7, 34, 37–8; Afzal Husain, 'The Letters of Hakim Abul Fateh Gilani—An Unexplored Source of Akbar's Reign', *Proceedings of the Indian Historical Congress* 44 (1983): 189–93.

acute in the eastern provinces it was present throughout the empire. The elimination of the jāgīr system both deprived officers of an autonomous geographic base and probably cut their salaries as well. The administrative overheads and cost of transferring revenue from one place to another must have reduced the funds which the mansabdars received. Unlike Khwājah Shāh Manṣūr Shīrāzī but like Rājah Tūdar Mal, who was absent from the capital, Shāhbāz Khān was a soldier as well as a bureaucrat and probably understood the feelings of most of his fellow mansabdars well. His action created one of the cornerstones of the Akbarī compromise.

Fighting continued for some time, but had little political significance on the imperial scale. The recitation of the *khutbah* in his name induced Mirzā Muḥammad Hakīm to invade Hindustan from Kabul, as Akbar had anticipated, but the young prince received no support from any of Akbar's subordinates except the already defeated eastern rebels. He retreated hastily when the Mughal forces entered the Punjab, and Akbar occupied Kabul without difficulty. The disputes between Shāhbāz Khān and other officers culminated in Akbar's decision to relieve him of his rank and put him in the cutody of Ray Sal Darbārī. After Akbar returned to Fathpur, on 16 March1582 (19Ṣafar 990), Ma'ṣūm Khān Farankhūdī sought and received a pardon through the intercession of Khān-i A'ẓam. He was murdered, possibly at Akbar's instigation, several months later. Ghazī Khān Badakhshī captured the rebel Bahādur, who was executed at Akbar's orders. In Bengal, Ma'ṣūm Khān Kābulī joined 'Isā Khān, the Afghan leader of opposition to Mughal expansion. He continued to resist his former masters until his death in 1599 (1007), but as a participant in Bengali, rather than imperial, politics. Most of the Qāqshāl rebels submitted and were forgiven. Jabbārī Khān was incarcerated until 1594 (1002).[39]

All of the chroniclers emphasize mansabdar resistance to the harsh and inflexible application of the branding and muster regulations and

[39] A.N., 3:327–8/479–81, 329–33/483–8, 335–44/492–504, 344–9/506–13, 351–71/516–14, 374–8/549–55, 383–4/566–7, 387–9/574–5, 396–402/586–94, 405–7/600–2, 416–18/619–22, 433–4/645–51, 438–40/657–60, 448–50/672–6, 650/1000; T.A., 2:357–64, 365, 367–9; M.T., 2:289–99/297–308, 310–20, 322–332; M.U., 3:246–9/64–6, 292–6/66–9; M.R., 1:877–9; Srivastava, *Akbar*, 1:259–74; Qaisar, 'Shahbaz Khan', pp. 58–68; Qureshi, *Akbar*, pp. 93–104.

the related financial sanctions as the causes of the revolt. To use modern terms, the new regulations restricted the security and autonomy of the mansabdars, especially men with Chaghatay roots, too much. It was too easy for them to lose their jāgīrs, to face humiliation and torture for failure to return excess funds collected. Akbar's willingness to forgive the rebels, and his attempts to prevent violence in Bengal by redressing their grievances, show that he understood the reason for opposition to his policies. Although Akbar succeeded militarily and, from hindsight, never faced a serious threat to his position, he did not triumph outright, but reached a *modus vivendi*, the Akbarī compromise.

7.2 Khwājah Shāh Manṣur Shīrāzī

If a single individual represented Akbar's prgramme of political and administrative centralization, Shīrāzī did. The sources do not disclose when he or his ancestors came to Hindustan. He began his service as an accountant (*mushrif*) in the imperial perfume department. In that capacity, he clashed with Muẓaffar Khān when the latter was *dīwān* and retired from imperial service. He then sought and received employment as the *dīwān* of Khān-i Zamān in Jaunpur. He later served Mun'im Khān Khān-i Khānān as *dīwān*, and then as *bakhshī*, in Bengal.[40] When Mun'im Khān conquered Bengal, he sent Shīrāzī to court to request the transfer of his jāgīr from Bihar to Bengal.[41] After Mun'im Khān's death in 1575 (983), Rājah Tūdar Mal confined Khwājah Shāh Manṣūr in chains while Mun'im Khān's wealth was accounted for.[42]

Akbar summoned Shīrāzī to court on the basis of his previous acquaintance with him and he returned to imperial service without an intercessor.[43] In 1578 (984), Shīrāzī became *wazir*. Bada'ūnī reports that 'his excessive economy and stinginess in the army expenses and

[40] The sources do not disclose when Khwājah Shāh Manṣūr shifted employers. We do not know for certain that he was in Mun'im Khān's service until 1570 (897), so he may not have left Khān-i Zamān before his death. See Iqtidar Alam Khan, *Biography*, p. 101.

[41] A.N., 3:116/164.

[42] M.U., 1:653–6/2:750–2; A.N., 3:116/164, 193/273; *Ṭabaqat-i Tīmūrī*, f. 150.

[43] Normally individuals received mansabs and promotions on the intercession of another mansabdar.

the pitch that he reached in grasping in season and out of season, people forgot the tyrannies of . . . Muẓaffar Khān.'[44] He was later associated with Muẓaffar Khān and Rājah Tūdar Mal in an administrative triumvirate. The three officers divided the affairs of the empire in 1577 (985), each taking responsibility for one of the imperial mints; Shāh Manṣūr's charge was the Jaunpur mint. Later in the same year, Akbar made Shīrāzī and Muẓaffar Khān responsible for investigating peasant allegations of oppression by tax collectors near Delhi. In 1578 (986) the two officers again inspected the imperial treasury. Just before the eastern rebellions broke out, Akbar had Shīrāzī and Rājah Tūdar Mal make a revenue assessment for the empire based on the production of each *parganah* during the previous decade. According to Shāh Nawāz Khān, Shīrāzī was also responsible for the new arrangement of provincial government established at the same time.[45]

Shīrāzī's policies precipitated the eastern revolts. Abū al-Fażl makes the reduction of the additional salary/jagir allowances to the Bengal and Bihar officers one of the causes of the uprising in Bengal, and discusses it at greater length than the other causes. The inflexible enforcement of the branding and muster regulations, which forced many officers to spend large sums of money on their contingents without satisfying the *bakhshīs*, motivated the rebels. Shīrāzī advocated and symbolized that type of administration. Unlike Muẓaffar Khān and Rājah Tūdar Mal, he had never governed a province or commanded an army in the field. Even after the rebellions began, Shīrāzī pursued the collection of arrears from officers serving in the armies sent against the rebels. Bada'ūnī reports that Akbar dismissed Shīrāzī and had him confined because he claimed arrears from Ma'ṣūm Khān Farankhūdī even after Rājah Tūdar Mal had reported Ma'ṣūm Khān's wavering loyalty, and from Tursun Muḥammad Khān.[46]

Abū al-Fażl's criticism of Shīrāzī, written more than a decade after the event, states what Akbar and his intimates perceived as the lesson of the episode:

[44] M.T., 240/247–8.

[45] A.N., 3:193–4/273–4, 203/287, 215–16/303, 227/320–2, 250/360, 257/374, 282–3/413–14; M.T., 2:141/145, 250/57; M.U., 1:653–5/2:750–2.

[46] A.N., 3:289–93/426–32, 315–16/461–62; M.T., 2:287–88/295–96; T.A., 2:354–55; M.U., 1:655–57/2:752–53.

> From his practice in accounts, and seeking after profit, he looked narrowly into the transactions of the army, and giving his attention to one side only of a Vizier's duties he pressed forward the rules of demand. He is a Vizier who by acuteness and the strength of honesty preserves of God, and considers the mean between liberality and rigour, and between severity and softness, to be the highway, the middle course of truth. He does not abandon what is suitable for the time and place, nor does he regard the collecting of gold as the finest of occupations, but lives with an open brow, a sweet tongue, a strong heart, a gracious soul, and a constant justice. He closes the eye of envy and opens the door of wide toleration. He shuts the shop of fastidiousness and hard-bargaining and drives away from men dealing at a high tariff.... Also the accountant should have something to do besides clerking, and stirring up of strife and collecting arrears and increasing the revenue. He should remove interested motives and watch over the account-department. The Khwaja went out of the proper course and set himself to increase the revenue. Nor did he consider the disturbances of the time and the crisis of the age, but demanded payment of arrears.[47]

He does not accuse Shīrāzī of going beyond his instructions, or opposing Akbar's will. Shīrāzī, with his expertise in financial management and limited experience of politics and war, executed Akbar's programme of financial and administrative centralization without considering the political consequences. He treated mansabdars who commanded hundreds of soldiers as a household *dīwān* would have dealt with individual servants and soldiers, confident that his master's warrant put him in the right. Akbar dismissed Shīrāzī not in anger, but in order to remove the grievances of the rebels and to give the imperial forces in the eastern provinces more confidence. The swift restoration of Shīrāzī to office shows that the move was tactical. Abū al-Fażl writes: 'there was no fault of the Khwaja's except the thought of increasing the revenue and a failure to recognize the circumstances of the time.' The reappointment came within a few months.[48]

Shīrāzī's policies had already set in motion the forces which put an

[47] A.N., 3:315–16/461–2. I have deleted Beveridge's emendations and notes.
[48] A.N., 3:327/480; M.U., 1:657/753.

end to him. The *Tabaqat-i Tīmūrī*, though it gives few details, asserts that his rigorous policies caused people to think day and night of how to eliminate him.[49]

During Akbar's progress from Fathpur Sikri to Lahore to confront Mirzā Muḥammad Hakīm, a series of incriminating letters came to light. The first document, one of three letters from Mirzā Muḥammad Hakīm, was addressed to Shīrāzī and indicated that he had written to the Mirzā expressing affection and loyalty. Mān Singh had allegedly captured these letters after a victory over one of the Mirzā's generals and forwarded them to Akbar. Akbar did not act on these letters, and apparently regarded them as forgeries. Shortly after this incident, Malik Sanī Kābulī, who was Mirzā Muḥammad Hakīm's chief minister with the title Wazīr Khān, came to Akbar's camp, either as a spy or a defector, and went to the Khwājah, as an old acquaintance, and sought an introduction to Akbar. This circumstance increased suspicion of Shīrāzī, and Akbar suspended him from office and confronted him. Shīrāzī's responses did not satisfy Akbar and he was placed in close confinement. Several days later, Malik 'Alī, the *kutwal* of the imperial camp, produced more suspicious letters, this time from Sharaf Beg, the agent responsible for Shīrāzī's jāgīr near Lahore. These letters made it appear that Shīrāzī's contingent was about to join Mirzā Muḥammad Haḳīm's army and that his lands had not been required to pay taxes to the Mirzā. As a result of this evidence, Akbar decided to have Shīrāzī executed unless he could prove his innocence and find an officer who would stand as surety for him. No one, not even Khwājah Sulaymān his friend and relative by marriage, would do so, and Shīrāzī was hanged on 28 February 1581 (23 Muharram 989).[50]

All the Akbarī historians make clear the universal desire for his execution. Bada'ūnī writes: 'His numerous oppressions of the people formed the halter around his neck, and may it remain clinging there until the day of Resurrection.'[51] Niẓām al-Dīn Aḥmad sees the events differently: 'Since most of the amirs and pillars of the estate were annoyed by him,

[49] *Ṭabaqat-i Tīmūrī*, f. 150r.

[50] A.N., 3:342–4/500–5; T.A., 2:358–9; M.T. 2:292–3/300–1; M.U., 1:655–9/2:753–5; Z.K., 1:185–7; *Ṭabaqat-i Tīmūrī*, f. 150r. A.N., 3:504–5 is a valuable note by the translator bringing together all the soruces except the Z.K. and *Ṭabaqat-i Tīmūrī*.

[51] M.T., 2:293/301.

they sought his death by acclamation, so that the sovereign ordered his death.'[52] Abū al-Fażl writes,

> Inasmuch as the time was confused owing to the presence of envious people, and the season was critical, and the grandees were plotting against his life, of necessity an order was passed for capitally punishing him.... From a want of understanding and narrowmindedness, Turks and Tajik were pleased, and there was great rejoicing in the camp.[53]

When Akbar reached Kābul, he had the matter thoroughly investigated. The inquiry showed that Karamullah, the brother of Shāhbāz Khān Kambū had forged the documents on behalf of a group of officers. The last letters which had caused Shīrāzī's execution had also been forged. When this evidence came to light, Akbar greatly regretted the execution and often said afterwards that his finances were never in order after Shīrāzī's death. Different sources blame different people for the conspiracy against Shīrāzī. They include Rājah Tūdar Mal, Man Singh, and others. Akbar made no attempt to punish them.[54]

Khwājah Shāh Manṣūr Shīrāzī died because he served his sovereign loyally and to the best of his ability and judgement. By doing so, he threatened the interests of many other loyal officers, some with longstanding ties to the family of Bābur. The administrative programme which he executed corresponded to the political theory propounded in Mughal court ritual. The response to it, in the eastern provinces and in the conspiracy against Shīrāzī, showed Akbar that he could not make the political reality correspond with that theory. He had to find a political mean, the middle way between severity and softness of which Abū al-Fażl writes.

7.3 The Akbarī Compromise

Akbar's effort to centralize the administration and financial system failed for several reasons. The fundamental difficulty of collecting and

[52] T.A., 2:359.

[53] A.N., 3:343/508.

[54] T.A., 2:363, 327; M.T., 2:294–5/303; Z.K., 2:187; Srivastava, *Akbar*, 1:261–3; Qureshi, *Akbar*, pp. 99–100. Smith, *Akbar*, pp. 139–41 argues that Shirazi was guilty and was the head of a conspiracy against Akbar, but gives no real evidence.

distributing funds through the central treasury and the desire of the mansabdars, of almost all groups, for autonomous geographic bases made the elimination of the jāgīr system impossible. Th inflexible *dāgh* regulations made mansabdars too insecure and too vulnerable to humiliation and punishment at the hands of imperial bureaucrats. Perhaps most importantly, not all mansabdars perceived themselves as extensions of the sovereign. Except for individuals from the bureaucratic strata, most mansabdars, though not disloyal, did not see themselves as court rituals depicted them. They took pride in their own lineages, as Chaghatays, *shaykhs*, *sayyids*, and Rajputs, and sought to expand their autonomy, strengthen their ties to their subordinates and reduce their dependence on imperial authority.

The adjustments progressed unevenly. Shāhbāz Khān's return to the jāgīr system was the earliest and perhaps most important step. Others were more subtle. The *dāgh* regulations remained in effect, but ceased to be an instrument of bureaucratic oppression. Although it deals with a later period, R. A. Alavi's study of *'arẓ u chihrah* (literally petition and face) documents from the reign of Shāh Jahān now in the Andhra Pradesh archives reveals the nature of the change. These documents are descriptions of troopers and their horses drawn up at the inspection of mansabdar contingents in the provinces and forwarded to the central government. Alavi's analysis reveals lax enforcement of regulations. Troopers were registered with the central government three to five years after the mansabdars hired them, so there could have been no annual inspections of contingents.[55] M. Athar Ali's list of 8107 transactions involving mansabdars between 1573 and 1658 includes only 16 reductions in rank which were not the result of death, retirement, or departure from Mughal service. Failure to abide by *dāgh* regulations could explain no more than twelve of these incidents. Demotion was rare; demotion for violation of the branding regulations extremely so.[56]

The mature Akbarī regime reflected what the mansabdars wanted. In theory, their income and status depended entirely on the ruler's trust. In practice, once a man entered imperial service, as *khānahzād*,

[55] R.A. Alavi, 'New Light on Mughal Cavalry', in idem., *Studies in the Medieval Deccan* (New Delhi: Idarah-i Adabiyyat-i Delli), pp. 20–3.

[56] M. Athar Ali, *The Apparatus of Empire* (New Delhi: Oxford University Press, 1985), pp. 1–345.

an immigrant or a former officer of a principality which the Mughals conquered, he could assume that he would keep his rank and have an appropriate jāgīr as long as he remained competent and loyal, treated the inhabitants of his jāgīr fairly, and came close to meeting the military obligations of his rank. He could expect promotion if he showed competence to his immediate superiors—governors in the provinces, the various department heads in the central government—or to the sovereign or one of the princes. Of course there was never enough room at the top. Pure competence could lift an officer only so high. One could expect patronage from a superior officer, prince, or emperor only for so long and to a limited degree. But few Mughal officers had more to fear than remaining in provincial or departmental obscurity. Only obvious misconduct or disloyalty brought resumption of jāgīrs, fines, imprisonment, or execution. A mansabdar could expect his sons to receive suitable ranks when they came of age or at his death, if they were so inclined. These expectations softened the mansabdar's dependence on the emperor for his position, though they did not eliminate it.

Most officers took pride in their loyalty and service to the sovereign and his house as well as their personal achievements and positions. The flexibility of the system allowed for the heterogeneity of expectations among the mansabdars, which did not exist in the Ottoman empire. The Mughals could not use an institution like the Ottoman *devshirme* and palace school to manufacture a homogeneous ruling class over time. The mechanism of expansion and the need to tap Hindustan's enormous reservoir of military manpower forced them to assimilate disparate groups immediately. The autonomy and security which the mansabdari system allowed permitted them to do so.

CHAPTER 8
Conclusions

From the suppression of the eastern revolts to the second half of Awrangzīb's reign, mansabdars accepted their status and remained loyal to the Mughal dynasty. The response to the uprisings created a lasting *modus vivendi*, satisfactory to all parties, and thus marked the definitive establishment of the empire; changes in the relationship between emperor and officer indicated the beginning of its decline. These statements are corollaries of the broadly accepted view that the Mughal empire consisted of the ties between the emperor and the mansabdars.[1] In other words, the Mughal empire existed as long as the holders of power in the provinces defined themselves as Mughal mansabdars.

Because of its crucial importance, the status of mansabdar deserves review. Comments on it form the first section of this chapter. The remaining sections summarize the process of the formation of the empire and present a new characterization of the Mughal polity.

8.1 The Status of Mansabdar

In the Islamic world in the sixteenth century, the military slave and the pastoral tribal chief exemplified the two models for high officers. The Ottoman empire depended almost entirely on military slaves, except

[1] I dealt with Mughal decline and its interpretation in part of my original dissertation which does not appear in this work; I hope that it will eventually be published under the title 'The Interpretation of Mughal History'.

in border and tribal regions. The Ṣafavī empire began as yet another pastoral confederation dominated by tribal amīrs; the reforms of Shāh ʻAbbās made military slaves dominant.[2] The Mughals alone developed a distinctive alternative. Akbar and his close advisers may have used military slavery as a model, but circumstances prevented them from approaching it. The surplus of military manpower meant that the Mughals could not possibly import and enslave enough boys to make military slaves the main force of their army. They had to rely in part on men whose hereditary positions gave them control of armies of their own, and therefore sought to endow these men with the loyalty and steadfastness of military slaves. Simultaneously, they had to satisfy the political ambitions of these men, which required far greater autonomy and security of life and status than the pattern of military slavery provided. Akbar could dispense with, or dispose of Chaghatay officers who could not accept the loss of political centrality to the central bureaucracy and reduction in autonomy, but he could not do without the Rajputs and Indo-Muslims who had the loyalty of substantial numbers of troops. In addition, the symbolic packaging of the status of mansabdars permitted a vital degree of ambiguity.

The rituals establishing and defining the relationship of emperor and mansabdar had no ambiguity in themselves. They depicted the ruler as the absolute orderer of society, from whom all status emanated. Participation in the rituals of the *darbār* encouraged men to perceive themselves as extensions of the emperor, transformed by their robes of honour, equipped with the characteristics and capabilities denoted by their other gifts. The rituals did not, however, extinguish the existing identities and ties of these men. Rājah Bihārah Mal, Bhagwan Dās, and Mān Singh remained Kachwaha Rajputs, with their inherited ties and positions intact; Sayyid Maḥmūd Khān and his relatives continued to

[2] On the Ottoman governing elite, see Halil Inalcik, *The Ottoman Empire: the Classical Age*, trans. Norman Itzkowitz and Colin Imber (London: Weidenfeld and Nicholson, 1973), pp. 77–78; Klaus Rohrborn, *Untersuchungen der osmanischen Verwaltungsgeschichte*, Studien zur Sprache, Geschichte un Kulter des Islamischen Orients, n.s. 5 (Berlin: Walter de Gruyter, 1973), pp. 22–6. On the Ṣafavī elite, idem., *Provinzen und Zentralgewalt Persiens im 16. und 17. Jahrhundert*, Studien zur Sprache, Geschichte und Kultur des Islamischen Orients, n.s. 2 (Berlin: Walter de Gruyter, 1966), pp. 29–44.

identify themselves as Bārah *sayyids*. Even though mansabdars served at the pleasure of the monarch, they could expect to hold their positions as long as they were loyal and reasonably competent. Compared with their Ottoman and Ṣafavī counterparts, Mughal mansabdars had far greater security of life and status. They were rarely executed, even when they supported unsuccessful claimants to the throne or behaved disloyally. Even imprisonment and demotion were unusual.[3] The dependence of the Mughal emperors on their officers as links to most of the imperial army inevitably made the ranks of those officers more secure and encouraged the expectation of mansabdars that their sons would inherit their status. The gap between the theory of service at pleasure and the practice of secure status formed a necessary part of the political compromise which created the Mughal empire.

The psychological satisfaction which the ambiguity of the situation engendered created a degree of loyalty which extended beyond what the control mechanisms provided for in the Mughal administration could ensure. The intelligence system, frequent transfers of mansabdars in provincial posts, and imperial tours of the empire, which other historians have discussed at length, and the role of the fortresses in preventing successful revolts, could not have functioned if Akbar had not won the loyalty of his subordinates without depriving them of their own pride of position.[4] Akbar learned that too much control, as well as too little, could cause opposition to his regime.

One may describe mansabdars as the rulers of autonomous but moveable principalities. They collected taxes, and maintained their own armies, but the imperial government periodically changed the area from which the taxes came and the deployment of the troops. Because mansabdars frequently did not serve in their jāgīrs, the meta-

[3] The Mughal sources themselves reveal the dangers of being an Ottoman or Ṣafavī officer. The cases include Ḥusayn Pasha Islām Khān Rumī (M.U., 1:247/698–701), a governor of Basra who entered Mughal service in fear of execution after dismissal from his post; the execution of Ẕū'l Fiqār Khan, Ṣafavī *beylerbey* of Azerbayjan and father of the Mughal officer of same name (M.U., 2:85–9/1045–6); and 'Ali Mardan Khān Amīr al-Umarā, who transferred his loyalty to the Mughals in fear of execution at the hands of Shah Ṣafī (M.U., 2:795–807/1:186–94).

[4] For a convenient summary of the control measures, see Stephen P. Blake, 'The Patrimonial-Bureaucratic Empire of the Mughals', *Journal of Asian Studies* 39 (1979): 90–4.

phor is not exact, but remains useful. Before the Mughal conquest, Hindustan had been a patchwork of principalities; it remained so to a great degree. Though a prosopographical study is impractical, one would probably show that a large proportion of the mansabdar families in Mughal times held similar positions before the Mughal conquest. The Mughal polity developed so as to absorb the existing elite. The result was far from the polity envisioned by Niẓām al-Mulk Ṭūsī, but approached the model of imperial centralization far more closely than either the pastoral confederations of central Asia and Iran or earlier Muslim polities in the subcontinent had done.

8.2 The Mechanism of Formation

If one describes the Mughal empire as the product of changes in loyalty and behaviour among the Tīmūrid ruling elite and that of Hindustan, negative and positive incentives caused that change. The Mughals could not conquer Hindustan in detail, eliminating the local focuses of military and political power, i.e. the zamindars, but could and did eliminate all holders of regional power who did not submit to them. The Mughal monopoly on the combination of effective field artillery and mounted archers permitted them to exercise a monopoly on sovereignty. Refusal to submit meant annihilation, the ultimate negative sanction.

Submission, on the other hand, brought not only survival but also the possibility for advancement. As loyal and active mansabdars, the Bārah *sayyids* could obtain far greater status than they could as local chieftains. They gained an imperial identity without sacrificing their regional influence and status as *sayyids*. In addition, the Tīmūrid dynasty had greater prestige than any other Muslim ruling family in Hindustan. Akbar built on that foundation, and, in doing so, won the loyalty of a heterogeneous ruling class. Satish Chandra writes:

> At first, the nobles had little sense of loyalty to the Timurid dynasty, and hardly any common traditions or sense of common purpose. Some of the more ambitious among them dreamt of displacing the Timurids, and rose in rebellion. Akbar's essential humanism and generosity, high sense of purpose and personal magnetism, coupled with his unfailing success in the field of battle gradually won the devotion and loyalty of the nobility, and created a definite tradition.

> But Akbar was not satisfied with this. By means of the *mansabdari* system he sought to weld the various heterogeneous elements into an organised and harmonious whole, so that the nobility could become an efficient and dependable instrument of the royal will. Akbar seems to have desired that the various ethnic, national and religious groups in the nobility should be so balanced that the king did not become dependent on any one section, and enjoyed the maximum freedom of action.[5]

Chandra correctly emphasizes the importance of Akbar's personality and military achievements in winning the loyalty of a diverse group of officers. His description of the balancing of the ethnic components of the nobility is misleading; it assumes that Chaghatays, Iranians, Indo-Muslims and Rajputs functioned as political factions. The discussions of the Uzbeg revolt and great revolt show that they did not.

Akbar did win the devotion of the members of the different groups, but his position did not depend on balancing ethnic factions against each other. He succeeded by making his sovereignty acceptable to Hindus as well as Muslims but did not alienate most Muslims in doing so. The rituals of the *darbār* reinforced the ties between the individual officers and the ruler, and helped to make mansabdars perceive themselves as Mughal servants. The prestige of the dynasty, focused by Abū al-Fażl's presentation of Akbar's reign as a central moment in world history, supplanted the standard justification of Muslim rulers as supporters of the Sharīʿah. Akbar's abandonment of public Islam, elimination of the *jizyah*, and projection of himself as an independent spiritual guide meant that he did not represent the rule of Muslims as Muslims over Hindus. Most Muslims continued to perceive themselves as the ruling class of the empire and Muslims still formed the great majority of mansabdars. But Akbar, perhaps because he turned away from the Muslim notables who furnished most of the ulema, granted a permanent place to Hindus which earlier Muslim rulers did not. He offered a secure and satisfactory place to men of a wide variety of ethnic and religious backgrounds and of political expectations.

[5] Satish Chandra, *Parties and Politics at the Mughal Court, 1707–1740*, 3rd. ed. (New Delhi: People's Publishing House, 1979), pp. xvii–lv.

To do so, Akbar compromised the principles of centralized government which he and his closest advisers shared. Political and fiscal realities made the jāgīr system necessary. Jāgīrs satisfied the desire of those mansabdars who were not bureaucrats for autonomous geographic bases. Jāgīrs also reduced the difficulty and expense of collecting and distributing revenue. The armed peasantry and zamindars prevented the extension of the hand of the central government to the individual peasant. The need to maintain organized contigents in the provinces, to use men with ties in specific regions for recruiting, and the desire of most mansabdars for their own military contingents, prevented the establishment of a large central army under the direct control of the central bureaucracy. The *dāgh* regulations, as they existed on paper, made the mansabdars subject to the central bureaucracy to a degree many of them could not accept, so Akbar allowed enforcement to become lax. The Mughal central bureaucracy closely resembled the Ottoman central bureaucracy, but the Mughal regime differed enormously from the Ottoman regime. The Mughal revenue records came from local officials, not cadastral surveys by agents of the central government. The Mughals considered individual households the theoretical unit of revenue assessment and collection, but in practice never dealt with them.[6] That difference represented the Akbarī compromise.

8.3 The Nature of the Mughal Polity

This understanding of the results of Akbar's political initiatives permits an effort to provide a description of the Mughal polity. The existing categorizations of Oriental despotism, bureaucratic empire, and gunpowder empire have only limited validity.

Karl Wittfogel presents Oriental despotism as the predecessor of modern totalitariansim, with a dominant bureaucracy.[7] In a chapter entitled 'Total Terror, Total Submission, Total Loneliness', he describes

[6] This paradox resolves the disagreement of Irfan Habib, *The Agrarian System of Mughal India* (Bombay: Asia, 1963), pp. 172–5, and S. Nurul Hasan, 'Zamindars under the Mughals', in Robert Eric Frykenberg, ed., *Land Control and Social Structure in Indian History* (Madison, Wi.: University of Wisconsin Press, 1969), p. 28.

[7] Karl A. Wittfogel, *Oriental Despotism*, with a new foreword (New York: Random House Vintage, 1981), pp. 5–6.

the fate of a Chinese historian and official, Ssu-ma Ch'ien, who was sentenced to castration for disagreeing with his emperor. By dynastic law, he could have avoided the penalty by paying a large fine, but none of his rich and influential friends would help him for fear of offending the emperor themselves. He suffered both physical mutilation and emotional isolation.[8] The case of Ssu-ma Ch'ien contrasts with that of Shīrāzī. Both men suffered because their fellow state servants would not support them in confrontation with the ruler. But Shīrāzī's fellow mansabdars did not refuse to stand as surety not out to fear, but out of hate. He confronted not a despot, but an imperial ruling class united by a threat to its interests, manipulating the sovereign. The mansabdars could not rid themselves of Shīrāzī by complaining of the effects of his practices. They could and did destroy him by subterfuge without suffering any penalty when their act became known. Akbar's policy of centralization threatened the ruling class in general. Resistance to it forced him to accept limits. Wittfogel's vision does not fit the reality of Mughal politics.[9]

Wittfogel and S. N. Eisenstadt both emphasize the role of bureaucracy.[10] Eisenstadt would classify Akbar with the founders of centralized polities, who seek 'to establish a more centralized, unified polity [so as to] monopolize political decisions and [set] political goals.' The opposition to Akbar's programme fits, in the most general terms, his description of resistance among existing holders of power to centralization.[11] The correspondence of Eisenstadt's general discussion of centralizing rulers with Akbar's behaviour does not, however, mean that his view of the results of centralization provides an adequate description of the Mughal polity. He argues that, in different societies, with different resources available to the rulers, they could obtain their goals to a greater or lesser degree.[12] One cannot question this statement because of its generality. But placing the range of societies in a single

[8] Ibid., p. 159.

[9] By criticizing Wittfogel's conception of Oriental despotism as an interpretation of Mughal politics, I am not supporting critics of other aspects of his work.

[10] S. N. Eisenstadt, *The Political Systems of Empires*, with a new foreword by the author (New York: Free Press, 1969), pp. 10–12.

[11] Ibid., p. 14. See also p. 21.

[12] Ibid., pp. 153–5.

category obscures their diversity. Describing the Mughal empire as a bureaucratic society reflects the self-perception of the officials, but obscures the reality of government in the provinces, where the imperial bureaucracy was distant, with little influence on daily life. In the Mughal empire, small wars could be fought between neighbouring potentates in the provinces without necessarily affecting the central government at all. Positioning the Mughal empire within Eisenstadt's framework, though not impossible, does not illuminate Mughal politics. Though the model of patrimonial-bureaucratic empire which Stephen Blake elucidates clearly fits Mughal realities better than the model of bureaucratic despotism, it places the relationship of the mansabdars with the emperor in a vacuum.

The gunpowder empires hypothesis seeks to explain the development of a bureaucratic empire as the result of technical innovation. In addition to the weaknesses of this explanation discussed in chapter 3, the Mughal polity does not fit the image of centralization which the hypothesis assumes.

Burton Stein's application of the concept of segmentary state to the subcontinent facilitates construction of a better capsule description of the Mughal empire. He emphasizes two aspects, pyramidal segmentation of political power and the division between ritual sovereignty and the distribution of political power. The Mughal empire had these characteristics. A single centre, the Mughal court, had ritual sovereignty. The emperor's control was complete at the centre, but belonged to his ritual subordinates in distant political segments. The hierarchy of political units began with individual villages, proceeded through the several levels of zamindaris, to imperial jāgīrs, *paraganahs, sarkars*, and provinces. One may classify some segments as indigenous, produced by the local population, with only recognition from the centre, and others as imperial, created by the centre. The distinction does not, however, coincide with the levels of segmentation. The *watan-jāgīrs* of Rajput lineages were indigenous, though often augmented with imperial jāgīrs, but fit in the same place in the hierarchy with imperial jāgīrs and *sarkars*. Provincial and sarkar governments and the establishments of individual mansabdars had military establishments, small bureaucracies and all the other characteristics of the subordinate foci in a segmentary hierarchy. The existence of imperial segments and the transferability of jāgīrs made the Mughal empire different from the segmentary states which Stein describes.

Stein asserts that the segments form part of the hierarchy, but simultaneously oppose one another for some purposes. In the Mughal empire, vertical opposition—i.e. clashes between zamindars and jagirdars—was quite common. Horizontal clashes were rarer. Provincial governors and *fawjdārs* did not fight each other; jagirdars rarely did. Only at zamindar level did horizontal clashes become more common. These circumstances show that the Mughal empire did not fit the definition of a segmentary state which Stein propounds for a different period and region of the subcontinent. The Mughal central government had far greater power in the provinces and could thus regulate the relationships among the imperial segments, and, to a degree, the indigenous segments as well. It could not eliminate the friction among them, but reduced and channelled it. Judged by the standards of imperial centralization in the Irano-Islamic tradition of government, the Mughals barely approached the norm. Judged in contrast to earlier segmentary polities in the subcontinent, Akbar and his successors had enormous central power.

One may envision the Mughal empire as a hybrid, Islamic—in the broadest sense—at the centre; Indian in the provinces. An Ottoman Sulṭān would have found the central bureaucracy familiar; a Chola Rājah would have understood the limited imperial role in the provinces. One may also describe the Mughal government as an imperial centre supported by a shifting structure of segments. It could manipulate the segments, but not fuse them, even in the heart of the empire, the Ganges-Jumna Duab. The instability in the provinces did not threaten the Mughals. It was a part of the dynamic *modus vivendi* of the empire.

Select Bibliography

Persian, Turkish, and Mongol Texts

N.B.: Abbreviations follow the text entries in bold face.

Abū al-Fażl 'Allamī ibn Shaykh Mubarak Nagawrī, Shaykh. *Akbar-nāma*. Edited by Abdur Rahim. 3 vols. Calcutta: Asiatic Society of Bengal, 1873–87. Translated by Henry Beveridge. Calcutta; Asiatic Society of Bengal, 1897–1921; reprint ed., New Delhi: Ess Ess Publications, 1979, **A.N.**

———. *A'in-i Akbarī*. Edited by H. Blochmann. Calcutta: Asiatic Society of Bengal, 1867–77. 3 vols. Translated by H. Blochmann, revised by D. C. Phillott (1), by H. S. Jarrett, revised by Sir Jadunath Sarkar (2 and 3). 2nd ed. Calcutta: Asiatic Society of Bengal, 1927–49; reprint ed., New Delhi: Oriental Books Reprint, 1977–78. **A.A.**

'Alī Muḥammad Khān. *Mir'at-i Ahmadī*. Edited Sayyid Nawab 'Ali. 3 vols. Gaekwad's Oriental Series nos. 3, 34, 50 Baroda: Oriental Institute, 1927–35. Translated by M. F. Lokhandawala. Gaekwad's Oriental Series 146. Baroda: Oriental Institute, 1935. **M.A.**

Bābur, Ẓahīr al-Dīn Muḥammad Pādishāh Ghazī. *Bābur-nāma*. Facsimile edited by Annette Susannah Beveridge. Gibb Memorial Series no. 1. London: E. J. W. Gibb Memorial Trust, 1905; reprint ed., London E. J. W. Gibb Memorial Trust, 1971. Translated by Annette Susannah Beveridge. 2 vols. London: By the Author, 1922; reprint ed., New Delhi: Oriental Books Reprint, 1979. **B.N.**

Bada'ūnī, 'Abd al-Qādir ibn Mulūk Shāh. *Muntakhab al-Tawārīkh*. Edited by Maulavi Ahmad 'Ali. 3 vols. Calcutta: Asiatic Society of Bengal, 1864–69. Translated by George S. A. Ranking (1), W. H. Lowe (2), T. W. Haig (3). Calcutta: Asiatic Society of Bengal, 1899–1925; reprint ed., Patna: Academica Asiatica, 1973. **M.T.**

Bayāzīd Biyāt. *Tadhkira-i Humāyūn wa Akbar*. Edited by M. Hidayat Hosain. Bibliotheca Indica, no. 264. Calcutta: Royal Asiatic Society of Bengal, 1941. **T.H.W.A.**

Bhakkarī, Shaykh Farid. *Dhakirat al-Khawānīn*. Edited By Dr Syed Moinul Haq. 3 vols. Karachi: Pakistan Historical Society, 1961–75. **Z.K.**

Dawānī, Jalāl al-Dīn Muḥammad ibn as 'ad. *Lawamī'al-Ishraq fī Makarim al-Akhlaq*. Lahore: Nawal Kishore, 1866–67. **L.I.**

Ghazālī, Abū Ḥamīd Muḥammad. *Naṣīhat al-Mulūk*. Edited by Sayyid Jalāl al-Dīn Humā'ī. Tehran: Silsilah-yi Intisharat-i Anjuman Asar Milli, 1972 (1351). Translated by F. R. C. Bagley as *Ghazali's Book of Rules for Kings*. London: Oxford University Press, 1964. **N.M.**

Gīlānī, Hakīm Abū al-Fath. *Ruq'at-i Hakīm Abū al-Fath*. Edited by Mohd. Bashir Ahmad. Lahore: Idarah-i Tahqiqat-i Pakistan, 1968. **R.H.**

Gulbadān Begum. *Humāyūn-Nāmah*. Facsimile Edited and Translated as *The History of Humayun* by Annette S. Beveridge. London: Royal Asiatic Society, 1902; reprint ed., New Delhi: Oriental Books Reprint, 1983 **H.N.**

Husaini, Khwajah Kamgar. *Ma'āsir-i Jahāngīrī*. Edited by Azra Alavi. Bombay: Asia Publishing House, 1978. **M.J.**

Jahāngīr, Nūr al-Dīn Muḥammad. *Tūzuk-i Jahāngīrī*. Edited by Muḥammad Hashim. Tehran: Bunyād-i Frahang-i Īrān, 1980 (1359). Translated by Alexander Rogers. Revised by Henry Beveridge. London: Royal Asiatic Society 1909–14; reprint ed., New Delhi: Munshiram Manoharlal, 1978. **T.J.**

Lahawrī, 'Abd al-Hamīd. *Bādshah-Nāmah*. Edited by Kabiruddin Ahmad and Abdur Rahim. Calcutta: Asiatic Society of Bengal, 1867. **B.N.L.**

Mirza Nathan. *Baharistan-i Ghaybi*. Edited and translated by M. I. Borah. 2 vols. Gauhati: Government of Assam, 1936. **B.G.**

Muḥammad Barārī 'Ummī ibn Muḥammad Jamshīd ibn Jabbārī Khān ibn Majnūn Khān Qāqshāl. *Ṭabaqat-i Tīmūrī.* Ousely MS 311. Oxford: Oxford University Press Microfilm, 1982. **T.T.**

Mu'tamad Khān. *Iqbal-nāmah-yi Jahāngīrī.* Edited by Maulavi 'Abd al-Hayy and Maulavi Ahmad 'Ali Sahun. Calcutta: Asiatic Society of Bengal, 1865. **I.J.**

Navā'ī, 'Abd al-Ḥusayn, ed. *Asnad u Maktūbāt-i Tarīkhi-yi Īrān az Tīmūr tā Shāh Ismā'īl.* Tehran: B.T.N.K., 1962 (1341). **A.M.**

Nihavandī, Mulla 'Abd al-Bāqī. *Ma'asir-i Rahīmī.* Edited by Shams ul-'Ulama' M. Hidayat Hosain. 3 vols. Calcutta: Asiatic Society of Bengal, 1924–31. **M.R.**

Niẓām al-Mulk, Abū 'Alī Ḥasan Ṭūsī. *Siyāsat-nāmah* or *Siyār al-Mulūk.* Edited by H. Darke. Tehran: B.T.N.K., 1962. Translated as *The Book of Government or Rules for Kings* by H. Darke. 2nd. ed. London: Routledge & Kegan Paul, 1978. **S.N.**

Niẓām al-Dīn Aḥmad, Khwājah. *Ṭabaqat-i Akbarī.* Edited B. De. 3 vols. Calcutta: Asiatic Society of Bengal, 1913–31. **T.A.**

Qandahārī, Hajjī Muḥammad 'Arif. *Tarīkh-i Akbarī,* better known as *Tārīkh-i Qandaharī.* Edited by Hajji Mu'in al-Din Azhar 'Ali Dihlawi and Imtiyaz 'Ali 'Arshi. Rampur: Raza Library, 1962. **T.Q.**

The Secret History of the Mongols. Translated by Francis Cleaves. Cambridge: Harvard University Press, 1982. **S.H.**

Shāh Nawāz Khān, Nawwāb Ṣamṣām al-Daula and 'Abdul Hayy. *Ma'asir al-Umarā.* 3 vols. Edited by M. Abdur Rahim, and M. 'Alī Ashraf. Calcutta: Astiatic Society of Bengal, 1887–96. Translated by H. Beveridge. Revised and Completed by Baini Prasad. 2nd ed. Calcutta: Asiatic Society of Bengal, 1941–52; reprint ed., Patna: Janaki Prakashan, 1979. **M.U.**

Sidi 'Alī Reis. *Mir'at al-Mamalik.* Istanbul: Kitab Khanahyi Aydin, 1895 (1313). Translated by A. Vambery as *The Travels of a Turkish Admiral.* London: Luzac, 1899; reprint ed., Lahore: Al-Biruni, 1975. **M.M.**

Tursun Bey. *History of Mehmed the Conqueror.* Facsimile edited and translated by Halil Inalcik and Rhoads Murphy. Chicago: Bibliotheca Islamica, 1978. **T.B.**

Yazdī, Mawlānā Sharaf al-Dīn 'Alī. *Ẓafar-nāmah.* Edited by Muhammad 'Abbasi. Tehran: Amir-i Kabir, 1957–58 (1366). **Z.N.**

Travellers' Accounts

Bernier, François. *Travels in the Mughal Empire*. Translated by Archibald Constable. Revised by Vincent Smith. London: Oxford University Press, 1934; reprint ed., New Delhi: Oriental Books Reprint, 1983.

[De Laet, Joannes.] *A Contemporary Dutch Chronicle of Mughal India*. Translated by Brij Narain and S. R. Sharma. Calcutta: Susil Gupta, 1957.

Du Jarric, Pierre. *Akbar and the Jesuits*. Translated by C. H. Payne. New York: Harper & Brothers, 1926.

Foster, William, ed. *Early Travels in India, 1583–1619*. London: Humphrey Milford, 1921; reprint ed., New York: AMS Press, 1975.

Manucci, Nicolao. *Storia Do Mogor or Mogul India*. Translated by William Irvine. 4 vols. Indian Text Series. London: Government of India, 1907–8; reprint ed., New Delhi: Oriental Books Reprint, 1981.

Mundy, Peter. *The Travels of Peter Mundy in Europe and Asia*. Edited by R. C. Temple. London: Hakluyt Society, 1914–24.

Roe, Sir Thomas. *The Embassy of Sir Thomas Roe to India, 1615–19*. Edited by Sir William Foster. London: Humphrey Milford, 1926.

Tavernier, Jean-Baptiste. *Travels in India*. Translated by W. Ball. Revised by William Crook. 2 vols. London: Humphrey Milford, 1925.

Tod, James. *Annals and Antiquities of Rajasthan*. Preface by Douglas Sladen. 2 vols. London: George Routlege and Sons, 1914; reprint ed., New Delhi: M.N. Publishers, 1978.

Secondary Works

Ahmad, Aziz. *Studies in Islamic Cultures in the Indian Environment*. Oxford: Clarendon Press, 1964.

Alam, Muzaffar. *The Crisis of Empire in Mughal North India: Awadh and the Punjab, 1707–1748*. Delhi: Oxford University Press, 1986.

Alavi, Azra. Introduction to *Ma'asir-i Jahāngīrī*, by Khwjah Kamgar Husaini. Bombay: Asia Publishing House, 1978.

Alavi, R.A. *Studies in the History of the Medieval Deccan*. New Delhi: Idarah-i Adabiyat-i Delli, 1977.

———. 'New Light on Mughal Cavalry'. *Medieval India: A Miscellany* 2 (1972):70–99.

Altekar, Anant Sashiv. *Rashtrakutas and their Times*. Poona: Oriental Book Agency, 1967.

Andreades, Andre. M. 'Public Finances: Currency, Public Expenditure, Public Revenue'. In *Byzantium*, pp. 71–85. Edited by Norman H. Baynes and H. St L. B. Moss. Oxford:Clarendon Press, 1948.

Athar Ali, M. *The Apparatus of Empire: Awards of Ranks, Offices and Titles to the Mughal Nobility, 1573–1658*. New Delhi: Oxford University Press, 1985.

———. *Mughal Nobility under Aurangzeb*. Bombay: Asia Publishing House, 1968.

Aubin, Jean. 'Comment Tamerlain Prennait les Villes'. *Studia Islamica* 19 (1963):83–122.

Aziz, Abul. *The Mansabdari System and the Mughal Army*. London: 1945, reprint ed., New Delhi: Idarah-i Adabiyat-i Delli, 1972.

———. 'Thrones, Chairs and Seats used by the Indian Mughals'. *Journal of Indian History* 16 (1937):181–228.

Babinger, Franz. *Mehmed the Conqueror and His Time*. Translated by Ralph Manheim. Edited by William Hickman. Princeton: Princeton University Press, 1978.

Bartol'd, Vasilii Vladimirovitch. *Sochineniya* (Collected Works). Edited by A. M. Belenitskii et al. Vol. 2: *Raboti po otd'el'nim probl'emam istorii Sredney Azii Ulugh Beg i yego vrem'ya*. Vol. 6: *Raboti po istorii islama i arabskovo khalifata*. Moscow: Izdatel' stvo nauka glavnaya redak siya vostochney literaturi, 1964, 1966.

———. *Mussulman Culture*. Translated by Shahib Suhrawardy. Calcutta: University of Calcutta Press, 1934; reprint ed., Philadelphia: Porcupine, 1977.

———. as Barthold, V. V. *Four Studies on the History of Central Asia*. Vol. 2: *Ulugh Beg*. Translated by V. and T. Minorsky. Leiden: E. J. Brill, 1958.

Bhargava, Visheshwar Sarup. *Marwar and the Mughal Emperors*. New Delhi: Munshiram Manoharlal, 1966.

Blake, Stephen P. 'The Patrimonial-Bureaucratic Empire of the Mughals'. *Journal of Asian Studies* 39 (1979):77–94.

Bosworth, C. E. 'The Political and Dynastic History of the Iranian

World (AD 1000–1217)'. In *The Cambridge History of Iran, Volume 5: the Saljuq and Mongol Periods*, pp. 1–184. Edited by J. A. Boyle. Cambridge: Cambridge University Press, 1968.

Braudel, Fernand. *The Mediterranean and the Mediterranean World in the Age of Phillip II*. Translated by Sian Reynolds. 2 vols. New York: Harper & Row, 1972–73.

Buckler, F. W. 'Th Oriental Despot'. *Anglican Theological Review*. 10 (1927–28):238–49.

———. 'A New Interpretation of Akbar's Infallibility Decree of 1579.' *Journal of the Royal Asiatic Society* (1924), pp. 590–608.

———. *Legitimacy and Symbols: The South Asian Writings of F. W. Buckler*. Edited by M. N. Pearson. Michigan Papers on South and Southeast Asia, no. 26. Ann Arbor: Center for South and Southeast Asian Studies, the University of Michigan, 1985.

Burn, Sir Richard, ed. *Cambridge History of India, Volume 4: the Mughal Period*. Cambridge: Cambridge University Press, 1937.

Cahen, Claude. 'L'Evolution de L'Iqta' du XI'e au XIII'e Siecle'. *Annales* 8 (1953):25–52.

Chandra, Satish. *Parties and Politics at the Mughal Court*. 3rd. ed. New Delhi: People's Publishing House, 1979.

Christensen, Arthur. *L'Iran Sous Les Sassanides*. Copenhagen: Ejner Munksgaard, 1944.

Clausewitz, Carl von. *On War*. Translated by Michael Howard and Peter Paret. Princeton: Princeton University Press, 1976.

Cohn, Bernard S. *India: The Social Anthropology of a Civilization*. Englewood Cliffs, N.J.: Prentice-Hall, 1971.

———. 'Political Systems in Eighteenth Century India'. *Journal of the American Oriental Society* 82 (1962):312–20.

———. 'Representing Authority in Victorian India'. In *The Invention of Tradition*, pp. 165–209. Edited by E. J. Hobsbawm and Terence Ranger. Cambridge: Cambridge University Press, 1983.

———. 'African Models and Indian Histories'. In *Realm and Region*, pp. 90–113. Edited by Richard G. Fox. Duke University Comparative Studies on Southern Asia Monograph and Occasional Papers series, no. 14. Durham N.C.: Duke University Press, 1977.

———. 'The Mughal, Court Rituals, and the Theory of Authority' in the sixteenth and seventeenth centuries (Unpublished).

Cook, M. A. *Population Pressure in Anatolia*. London: Oxford University Press, 1972.

Dennett, Daniel C. *Conversion and the Poll Tax in Early Islam*. Cambridge: Harvard University Press, 1950.

De Rachelwiltz, Igor. 'Some Remarks on the Ideological Foundations of Chingiz Khan's Empire'. *Papers in Far Eastern History* 7 (1973):20–36.

Dickson, Martin B. 'Uzbek Dynastic Theory in the Sixteenth Century'. In *Proceedings of the 25th International Congress of Orientalists*, 3:208–16. 4 vols. Moscow: n.p., 1963.

———. 'Shah Tahmasb and the Uzbeks'. Ph.D. Dissertation. Princeton University, 1958.

Digby, Simon. *War Horse and Elephant in the Delhi Sultanate*. Oxford: Oxford Monographs, 1971.

Duffy, Christopher. *Siege Warfare*. London: Routledge & Kegan Paul, 1979.

Eaton, Richard M. 'Approaches to the Study of Conversion to Islam in India'. In *Approaches to Islam in Religious Studies*, pp. 106–23. Edited by Richard C. Martin. Tucson: University of Arizona Press, 1985.

Eisenstadt, S. N. *The Political System of Empires*. New York: Free Press, 1969.

Encyclopedia of Islam, 2nd. ed. S.v. 'Djizyah, iii. India', by Peter Hardy.

Encyclopedia of Islam 2nd ed. S.v. 'Kanun: Financial and Public Administration', by Halil Inalcik.

Encyclopedia of Islam, 2nd ed. S. V. 'Hawala', by Halil Inalcik.

Encyclopedia of Islam, 2nd ed. S.v. 'Khalifa', by Dominique Sourdel.

Encyclopedia of Islam, 2nd ed. S.v. 'Kanunname', by Halil Inalcik.

Encyclopedia of Islam, 2nd ed. S.v. 'Bayram Khan', by A. S. Basmee Ansari.

Esper, Thomas. 'The Replacement of the Longbow by Firearms in the English Army'. *Technology and Culture* 61 (1965):382–93.

Friedmann, Yohanan. *Shaykh Ahmad Sirhindi: An Outline of His Thought and a Study of His Image in the Eyes of Posterity*. McGill Islamic Studies vol. 2. Montreal: McGill-Queen's University Press, 1971.

Gibb, Sir Hamilton. 'Some Considerations on the Sunni Theory of the

Caliphate'. In *Studies on the Civilization of Islam*, pp. 144–8. Edited by Stanford J. Shaw and William R. Polk. Boston: Beacon, 1962.

Gordon, Stewart. 'Legitimacy and Loyalty in Some Successor States in the Eighteenth Century'. In *Kingship and Authority in South Asia*, pp. 268–92. Edited by J. F. Richards. South Asian Studies, University of Wisconsin Madison, no. 3. Madison, Wi.: University of Wisconsin, Madison South Asian Studies, 1978.

Grabar, Oleg. 'The Architecture of Power: Palaces, Citadels, Fortifications'. In *Architecture of the Islamic World*, pp. 64–79. Edited by George Michell. New York: William Morrow, 1978.

Grewal, J. S. *Muslim Rule in India*. London: Oxford University Press, 1970.

———. *Medieval India: History and Historians*. Amritsar: Guru Nanak University, 1975.

Grousset, Rene. *The Empire of the Steppes*. Translated by Naomi Walford. New Brunswick, N.J.: Rutgers University Press, 1970.

Guilmartin, John Francis, Jr. *Gunpowder and Galleys*. Cambridge Studies in Early Modern History. Cambridge: Cambridge University Press, 1974.

Habib, Irfan. *The Agrarian System of Mughal India*. Bombay: Asia Publishing House, 1963.

———. *Atlas of the Mughal Empire*. New Delhi: Oxford University Press, 1982.

Habib, Mohammad. *Collected Works of Mohammad Habib*. Edited by K. A. Nizami. Vol. 2: *Politics and Society in the Medieval Period*. New Delhi: People's Publishing House, 1981.

Haig, Sir Wolseley. 'The Lodi Dynasty'. In *The Cambridge History of India, Volume 3: Turks and Afghans*, pp. 228–50. Cambridge: Cambridge University Press, 1928; reprint ed., New Delhi: S. Chand, 1958.

Hambly, Gavin. *The Cities of Mughal India*. New York: G. P. Putnam's Sons, 1968.

Hardy, Peter. *The Muslims of British India*. Cambridge South Asian Studies, no. 12. Cambridge: Cambridge University Press, 1972.

———. 'Commentary and Critique'. *Journal of Asian Studies* 35 (1976):257–63.

Hasan, Ibn. *The Central Structure of the Mughal Empire*. London:

1936; reprint ed., New Delhi: Munshiram Manoharlal, 1980.

Hasan, S. Nurul. 'Zamindars under the Mughals'. In *Land Control and Social Structure in Indian History*, pp. 17–28. Edited by Robert Eric Frykenberg. Madison: University of Wisconsin-Madison Press, 1969.

Hocart, A. M. *Kings and Councillors*. Edited by Rodney Needham. Introduction by E. E. Evans-Pritchard. Chicago: University of Chicago Press, 1970.

———. *Kingship*. London: Oxford University Press, 1927; reprint ed , 1969.

Hodgson, Marshall G. S. *The Venture of Islam*. 3 vols. Chicago: University of Chicago Press, 1974.

Holt, P. M. *Egypt and the Fertile Crescent*. Ithaca: Cornell University Press, 1966.

Horn, Paul. *Das Heer-und Kriegswesen der Grossmoghuls*. Leiden: E. J. Brill, 1894.

Humphreys, R. Stephen. *From Saladin to the Mongols: the Ayyubids of Damascus, 1193–1260*. Albany: State University of New York Press, 1977.

Husain, Afzal. 'Growth of Irani Element in Akbar's Nobility'. *Proceedings of the Indian Historical Congress* 36 (1975):166–79.

———. 'The Letters of Hakim Abul Fateh Gilani—An Unexplored Source for Akbar's Reign'. *Proceedings of the Indian Historical Congress* 44 (1983):189–93.

———. 'Emperor's Relations with the Nobility under Akbar and Jahangir'. Paper presented at the 1976 meeting of the Indian Historical Congress but not included in the *Proceedings*.

———. 'Liberty and Restraint—A Study of Shi'aism in the Mughal Nobility'. *Proceedings of the Indian Historical Congress* 41 (1980): 248–64.

———. 'Marriage among Mughal Nobles as an Index of Status and Aristocratic Integration'. *Proceedings of the Indian Historical Congress* 33 (1972):304–13.

Husain, Yusuf. *Indo-Muslim Polity: Turko-Afghan Period*. Simla: Indian Institute of Advanced Study, 1971.

———. 'Les Kayasthas ou 'scribes' castes hindous iranisee, et la culture musalmane dans Inde'. *Revue d'etudes Islamiques* 1 (1927):455–8.

Ikram, S. M. *Muslim Civilization in India*. Edited by Ainslie T. Embree. New York: Columbia University Press, 1964.

Inalcik, Halil. *The Ottoman Empire: the Classical Age, 1300–1600*. Translated by Norman Itzkowitz and Colin Imber. London: Weidenfeld and Nicolson, 1973.

———. 'Land Problems in Turkish History'. *Muslim World* 45 (1958): 221–8.

———. 'Capital Formation in the Ottoman Empire'. *Journal of Economic History* 29 (1969):97–108.

———. 'Ottoman Methods of Conquest'. *Studia Islamica* 2 (1954): 103–29.

———. 'The Problem of the Relationship between Byzantine and Ottoman Taxation'. *Akten des XL: Internationalen Byzantinisten Kongresses 1958*. Munich: C. H. Beck, 1966.

———. 'The Rise of the Ottoman Empire'. In *The Cambridge History of Islam*, 1:295–303. Edited by P. M. Holt, Anne K. S. Lambton, and Bernard Lewis. 2 vols. Cambridge: Cambridge University Press, 1970.

———. 'Mehmed the Conqueror (1432–81) and his Time'. *Speculum* 35 (1960):408–27.

———. 'Rice Cultivation and Celtukci-reaya System in the Ottoman Empire'. *Turcica* 14 (1982):69–141.

Inden, Ronald. 'Ritual, Authority and Cyclic Time in Hindu Kingship'. In *Kingship and Authority in South Asia*, pp. 28–73. Edited by J. F. Richards. South Asian Studies, University of Wisconsin Madison, no. 3 Madison, Wi.: University of Wisconsin, Madison South Asian Studies, 1978.

———. 'Cultural-Symbolic Constitutions in Ancient India'. (Unpublished).

———. 'Orientalist Constructions of India'. *Modern Asian Studies* 20 (1986): pp. 401–46.

Irvine, William. *The Army of the Indian Moghuls*. London: 1903; reprint ed., New Delhi: Eurasia, 1962.

Islam, Riazul. *Indo-Persian Relations*. Tehran: Iranian Culture Foundation, 1970.

Joshi, Rita. *The Afghan Nobility and the Mughals*. New Delhi: Vikas Publishing House, 1985.

Kane, P. V. 'The Kayastha'. *New Indian Antiquary* 1 (1929):116–89.

Kennedy, E. S. 'The Exact Sciences in Iran under the Saljuqs and Mongols'. In *The Cambridge History of Iran 5: the Saljuq and Mongol Periods*, pp. 659–79. Edited by J. A. Boyle. Cambridge: Cambridge University Press, 1968.

Khan, Ahsan Raza. *Chieftains in the Mughal Empire*. Simla: Indian Institute of Advanced Study, 1977.

Khan, Iqtidar Alam. *The Political Biography of a Mughal Noble: Mun'im Khan Khan-i Khanan, 1497–1575*. New Delhi: Orient Longman, 1973.

———. *Mirza Kamran*. New York: Asia Publishing House, 1964.

———. 'The Nobility under Akbar and the Development of His Religious Policy'. *Journal of the Royal Asiatic Society* (1968), pp. 29–36.

———. 'Mughal Court Politics during Bairam Khan's Regency'. *Medieval India: A Miscellany* 1 (1969):21–38.

Khan, Kunwar Refaqat Ali. *The Kachhwahas under Akbar and Jahangir*. New Delhi: Kitab Publishing House, 1976.

Kolff, Dirk Herbert Arnold. 'An Armed Peasantry and Its Enemies'. Ph.D. Dissertation, Rijksuniversiteit te Leiden, 1983.

Lambton, A. K. S. 'Islamic Political Thought'. In *The Legacy of Islam*, pp. 404–24. Edited by Joseph Schacht and C. E. Bosworth. Oxford: Clarendon Press, 1974.

Lambton, A. K. S. 'Quis Custodiet Custodes: Some Reflections on the Persian Theory of Kingship'. *Studia Islamica* 5, 6 (1956):125–48, 125–46.

———. 'Justice in the Medieval Persian Theory of Kingship'. *Studia Islamica* 17, pp. 91–119.

———. 'Reflections on the Iqta'. In *Arabic and Islamic Studies in Honor of H. A. R. Gibb*, pp. 358–76. Edited by G. Makdisi. Leiden: E. J. Brill, 1965.

———. *Theory and Practice in Medieval Persian Government*. London: Variorum Reprints, 1980.

———. *State and Government in Medieval Islam*. London Oriental Series vol. 36. Oxford: Oxford University Press, 1981.

Lannoy, Richard. *The Speaking Tree*. London: Oxford University Press, 1971.

Lattimore, Owen. *Inner Asia Frontiers of China*. New York: American Geographical Society, 1940.

Lewis, Bernard. *The Jews of Islam*. Princeton: Princeton University Press, 1984.

———. *The Muslim Discovery of Europe*. New York: W. W. Norton, 1982.

Leonard, Karen Isaksen. *Social History of an Indian Caste*. Berkeley: University of California Press, 1979.

———. 'The Great Firms Theory of Mughal Decline'. *Comparative Study in Society and History* 21 (1979):151–67.

McNeill, William H. *The Pursuit of Power*. Chicago: University of Chicago Press, 1982.

Majumdar, R. C., gen. ed. *The History and Culture of the Indian People*. 11 vols. Bombay: Bharatiya Vidya Bhavan, 1951–74. Vol. 11: *The Mughal Empire*.

Martin, Gary. 'Key Monuments of Islamic Architecture'. In *Architecture of the Islamic World*, pp. 264–74. Edited by George Michell. New York: William Morrow, 1978.

Moosvi, Shireen. 'Evolution of the Mansab System under Akbar'. *Journal of the Royal Asiatic Society* (1978), pp. 171–83.

Mukhia, Harbans. *Historians and Historiography During the Reign of Akbar*. New Delhi: Vikas Publishing House, 1976.

Naqvi, H. K. *Urbanization and Urban Centres under the Mughals*. Simla: Indian Institute of Advanced Study, 1971.

Nasr, Seyyed Hossein. *Three Muslim Sages*. Cambridge: Harvard University Press, 1964; reprint ed., Delmar, N.Y.: Caravan, 1976.

Nizami, Khaliq Ahmad. *On History and Historians in Medieval India*. New Delhi: Munshiram Manoharlal, 1983.

———. 'Naqshbandi Influence on Mughal Rulers and Politics'. *Islamic Culture* 39 (1965):41–52.

Pannikar, K. M. *A Survey of Indian History*. 4th. ed. New York: Asia Publishing House, 1964.

Pant, Chandra. *Nur Jahan and Her Family*. Allahabad: Dandewal Publishing House, 1979.

Parry, V. J. 'The Reigns of Bayazid II and Selim I, 1480–1520', and 'The Reign of Sulayman the Magnificent, 1520–66'. In *A History of the Ottoman Empire to 1730*, pp. 54–102. Edited by M. A.

Cook. Cambridge: Cambridge University Press, 1976.

Pearson, M. N., 'Political Participation in Mughal India'. *Indian Economic and Social History Review* 9 (1972):113–31.

———. 'Shivaji and the Decline of the Mughal Empire'. *Journal of Asian Studies* 35 (1976):221–35.

Perry, J. R. 'Justice for the Underprivileged: the Ombudsman Tradition of Iran'. *Journal of Near Eastern Studies* 37 (1978):203–15.

Phul, Raj Kumar. *Armies of the Great Mughals*. New Delhi: Oriental Publishers and Distributors, 1978.

Pipes, Daniel. *Slave Soldiers and Islam*. New Haven: Yale University Press, 1981.

Prasad, Baini. *History of Jahangir*. 5th ed. Allahabad: Indian Press, 1973.

Qaisar, A. J. 'Shahbaz Khan Kambu'. *Medieval India: A Miscellany* 1 (1962):48–60.

Qureshi, Ishtiaq Husain. *The Muslim Community of the Indian Subcontinent*. 2nd ed. Karachi: Ma'aref, 1971.

———. *The Administration of the Mughal Empire*. Patna: N.V. Publications, n.d.

———. *Akbar*. Karachi: Ma'aref, 1978.

———. 'India under the Mughals'. In *The Cambridge History of Islam*, 2:35–63. Edited by P. M. Holt, Anne K. S. Lambton, and Bernard Lewis. 2 vols. Cambridge: Cambridge University Press, 1970.

Rahman, Fazlur. *Islam*. New York: Doubleday, 1968.

Raychaudhuri, Tapan. *Bengal under Akbar and Jahangir*. 2nd imp. New Delhi: Munshiram Manoharlal, 1969.

Richards, J. F. *Mughal Administration in Golconda*. Oxford: Clarendon Press, 1975.

———. 'The Imperial Crisis in the Mughal Deccan'. *Journal of Asian Studies* 35 (1976):237–56.

———. 'The Formation of Imperial Authority under Akbar and Jahangir'. In *Kingship and Authority in South Asia*, pp. 252–89. Edited by J. F. Richards. South Asian Studies, University of Wisconsin Madison, no. 3. Madison, Wi.: University of Wisconsin, Madison South Asian Studies, 1978.

———. 'Norms of Comportment among Imperial Mughal Officers'.

In *Moral Conduct and Authority: the Place of Adab in South Asian Islam*, pp. 255–89. Edited by Barbara Daly Metcalf. Berkeley: University of California Press, 1984.

Rizvi, Saiyid Athar Abbas. *A History of Sufism in India.* 2 vols. New Delhi: Munshiram Manoharlal, 1975–83.

———. *Muslim Revivalist Movements in Northern India*. Agra: Agra University, 1965.

———. *Religious and Intellectual History of the Muslims in Akbar's Reign*. New Delhi: Munshiram Manoharlal, 1975.

———. 'The Mughal Elite in the Sixteenth and Seventeenth Century'. *Abr-nahrain* 11 (1971):69–104.

Rizvi, Saiyid Athar Abbas, and Flynn, Vincent John Adams. *Fathpur Sikri*. Bombay: Taraporevala, 1975.

Roemer, H. R. 'Timur in Iran', 'The Successors of Timur', 'The Turkmen Dynasties', and 'The Safavid Period'. In *The Cambridge History of Islam 6: the Timurid and Safavid Periods*, pp. 42–146, 147–74, 189–350. Edited by Peter Jackson and Lawrence Lockhart. Cambridge: Cambridge University Press, 1986.

Rohrborn, Klaus. *Untersuchungen zur Osmanischen Verwaltungsgeschichte*. Studien zur Sprache, Geschichte, und Kultur des Islamischen Orients n.s. 5. Berlin: Walter de Gruyter, 1973.

———. *Provinzen und Zentgralgewalt Persiens*. Studien zur Sprache, Geschichte, und Kultur des Islamischen Orients n.s. 2. Berlin: Walter de Gruyter, 1966.

Rosenthal, E. I. J. *Political Thought in Medieval Islam*. New York: Cambridge University Press, 1958.

Rowland, Benjamin. *The Art and Architecture of India*. Revised by J. C. Harle. Harmondsworth: Penguin, 1977.

Saksena, Banarasi Prasad. *History of Shahjahan of Dihli*. Allahabad: Central Book Depot, 1962.

Saran, Paramata. *The Provincial Government of the Mughals*. 2nd ed. Bombay: Asia Publishing House, 1973.

Sardesai, Govind Sakharam. *New History of the Marathas*. Rev. ed. Bombay: Phoenix, 1957.

Sarkar, Sir Jadunath. *History of Aurangzib*. 2nd ed. 5 vols. as 4. Calcutta: 1952; reprint ed., Bombay: Orient Longman, 1974.

———. *Military History of India*. Bombay: Orient Longman, 1960.

———. *Mughal Administration*. 3rd ed. 1935, reprint ed., Bombay: Orient Longman, 1972.

Savory, Roger, 'The Safavid Administrative System'. In *The Cambridge History of Islam 6: the Timurid and Safavid Periods*, pp. 351–72. Edited by Peter Jackson and Lawrence Lockhart. Cambridge: Cambridge University Press, 1986.

———. *Iran under the Safavis*. Cambridge: Cambridge University Press, 1980.

Schimmel, Annemarie. *Mystical Dimensions of Islam*. Chapel Hill, N.C.: University of North Carolina Press, 1975.

Sharma, Gopi Nath. *Mewar and the Mughal Emperors*. Foreword by A. L. Srivastava. Agra: Shiva Lal Agarwala, 1954.

Sharma, S. R. *The Religious Policy of Mughal Emperors*. 3rd ed. Agra: Shiva Lal Agarwala, 1972.

Shastri, K. A. Nikilantha. *The Cholas*. 2nd ed. Madras: University of Madras, 1955.

Shinder, Joel. 'Early Ottoman Administration in the Wilderness: Some Limits on Comparison'. *International Journal of Middle East Studies* 9 (1978):497–517.

Siddiqui, Iqtidar Husain. *Modern Writings on Islam in India*. Aligarh: International Book Traders, 1972.

———. *Mughal Relations with the Indian Ruling Elite*. New Delhi: Munshiram Manoharlal, 1983.

———. *History of Sher Shah Sur*. Aligarh: D. C. Swadash Sreni, 1971.

———. *Some Aspects of Afghan Despotism in India*. Aligarh: Three Men Publication, 1969.

Singh, M. P. 'Akbar's Resumption of *Jagir*, 1575'. *Proceedings of the Indian Historical Congress* 27 (1966):208–11.

Smail, R. C. *Crusading Warfare*. Cambridge: Cambridge University Press, 1956.

Smith, Wilfred Cantwell. *Islam in Modern History*. Princeton: Princeton University Press, 1957.

Smith, Vincent. A. *Akbar the Great Moghul*. 2nd rev. ed. New Delhi: S. Chand, 1962.

Srivastava, Ashirabadi Lal. *Akbar the Great*. 2nd ed. 3 vols. Agra: Shiva Lal Agarwala, 1972.

———. *The Mughul Empire, 1526–1803* AD 8th ed. Agra: Shiva Lal Agarwala, 1977.

Stein, Burton. *Peasant State and Society in Medieval South India.* New Delhi: Oxford University Press, 1980.

Tabataba'i, 'Allamah Sayyid Muhammad Husayn. *Shi'ite Islam.* Translated and edited by Seyyed Hossein Nasr. Albany: State University of New York Press, 1975.

Thapar, Romila. *A History of India, Volume 1.* Harmondsworth: Penguin, 1966.

Trimingham, J. Spencer. *The Sufi Orders in Islam.* New York: Oxford University Press, 1971.

Vladimirtsov. B. *Le Regime Social des Mongols.* Translated by Michel Carsow. Preface by Rene Grousset. Paris: Adrien-Maisonneuve, 1948.

Voegelin, Eric. 'The Mongol Orders of Submission to the European Powers'. *Byzantion* 15 (1940–41):378–413.

———. *The New Science of Politics.* Foreword by Dante Germino. Chicago: University of Chicago Press, 1987.

Watt, W. Montgomery. *The Formative Period of Islamic Thought.* Edinburgh: Edinburgh University Press, 1973.

Wheatley, Paul. *The Pivot of the Four Quarters.* Chicago: Aldine, 1971.

Wink, Andre. *Land and Sovereignty in India: Agrarian Society and Politics under the Eighteenth Century Maratha Svarajya.* Cambridge: Cambridge University Press, 1986.

Wittfogel, Karl August. *Oriental Despotism.* New Foreword by the author. New York: Free Press, 1969.

Wolpert, Stanley. *A New History of India.* New York: Oxford University Press, 1977.

Woods, John E. *The Aqquyunlu: Clan, Confederation Empire.* Chicago: Bibliotheca Islamica, 1976.

Ziegler, Norman. 'Action, Power, and Service in Rajasthani Culture: A Social History of the Rajputs of Middle Period Rajasthan'. Ph.D. Dissertation, University of Chicago, 1972.

Index

Personal names are indexed under the first element of the name as it appears in the text, e.g. Shaykh Mubarak Nagawri, even when the first element is actually a title not a personal name. This rule has two exceptions: the titles Rajah, Rana, Ray, and Rawal, which most readers will have no difficulty identifying as titles, and the word Sultan when used as the title of a Mughal prince, are omitted. Footnotes are included in the index only when a substantive point is discussed.